Photograph by: CJ Walker

A DESIGNS DIRECT PUBLISHING BOOK

Presented by

Sater Design
COLLECTION

The Sater Design Collection, Inc.
25241 Elementary Way, Suite 201, Bonita Springs, FL 34135

Dan F. Sater, II — CEO and Author

Amy Fullwiler — Editor-in-Chief

Laura Hurst Brown — Editor

Suzi Coker — Contributing Editor

Dave Jenkins — Illustrator

Diane J. Zwack — Art Director

Kim Campeau — Graphic Artist

Wayne Chambers — Graphic Artist

CONTRIBUTING PHOTOGRAPHERS

Tom Harper, Richard Leo Johnson, Joseph Lapeyra, Laurence Taylor, Doug Thompson and CJ Walker

Front Cover Photo: CJ Walker / Back Cover Photo: CJ Walker / Flap Photos: Tom Harper

A SPECIAL THANKS TO CONTRIBUTING BUILDERS

Oasis Property Development of Delaware,

RL Construction of Georgia and Sandcastle Construction of Florida.

Printed by: Toppan Printing Co., Hong Kong

First Printing, September 2004

10 9 8 7 6 5 4 3 2 1

All floor plans, renderings, text designs and illustrative material copyright © The Sater Design Collection, Inc.
Entire publication copyright © 2004 Verandah Publishing, Inc. and may not be reproduced by
any means without permission. No part of this publication may be reproduced in any form or by any means—electronic,
mechanical, photomechanical, recorded or otherwise —without the prior written permission of the publisher.
ISBN softcover: 1-932553-03-7

Photograph by: CJ Walker

Contents

Photograph by: Tom Harper, Doug Thompson

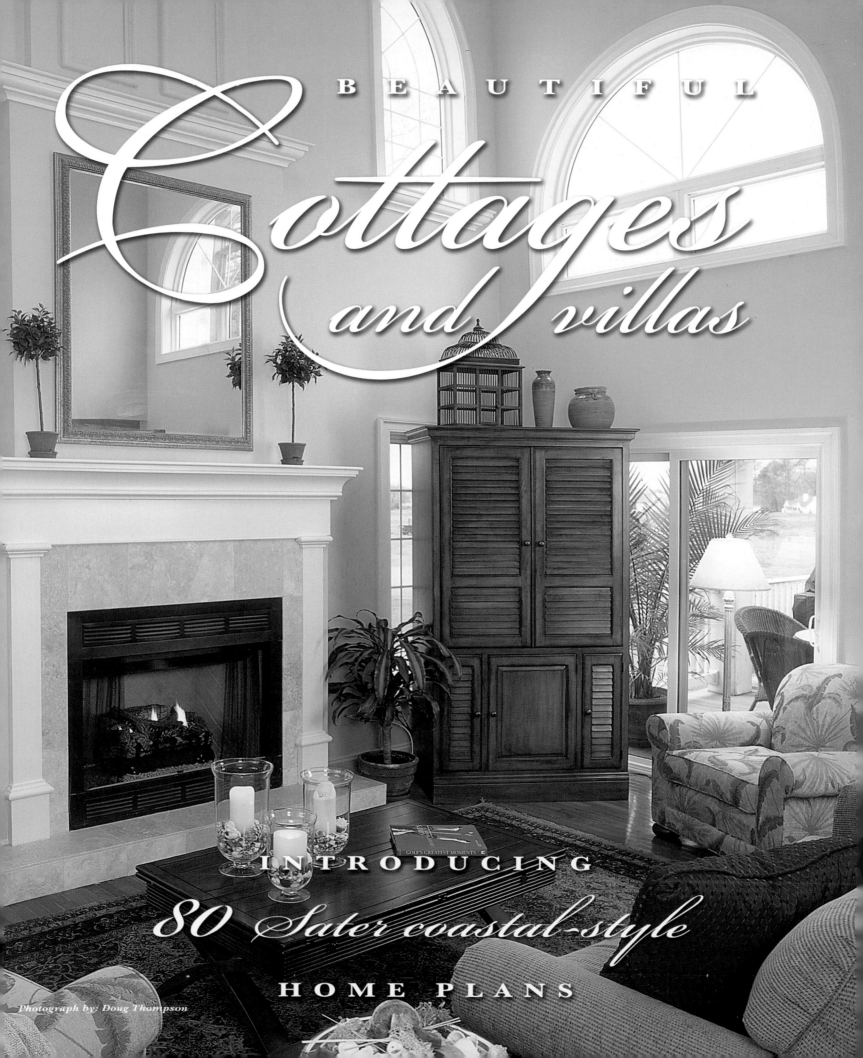

BEAUTIFUL
Cottages
and villas

INTRODUCING
80 Sater coastal-style
HOME PLANS

Photograph by: Doug Thompson

Photograph by: Tom Harper, Doug Thompson

Photograph by: Doug Thompson

Cottages that inspire

Houses by the sea inspire us as few other styles in modern architecture. In an artsy beach community or at the water's edge, retreats that hug the shore extract something of the untamed grandeur of an ever-changing frontier, with a backdrop of sky and water that stirs the soul and seeps into our dreams. Regions rife with beaches, lakes, wetlands and waterways present the kind of geography that inspires views and invigorates view-oriented elevations.

Clapboard siding, rough-hewn shingles, metal roofing and graceful arched windows prevalent in homes along the Northeastern seaboard call up the naïve characteristics of the freely crafted cottages of eras past. Charleston Row and Caribbean plantation styles in the South have yielded modern interpretations of the region's rich heritage.

Photograph by: CJ Walker

Splendid wraparound porches, spacious porticos and expansive decks extend interior boundaries that take advantage of views. Broad galleries and loggias permit fresh air to mingle with inside spaces, and provide shelter from the occasional extremes of a sun-country climate.

Here we open the doors to a portfolio of houses that effectively connect with nature and carefully embrace the traditional vernaculars. This is a diverse collection of plans, with open rooms and outer spaces that reach toward pristine views and rolling terrain. These are homes that breathe with a new-century spirit, with broad glimpses of lake, sound or sea and fluid boundaries that create unexpected relationships with the outside.

Photograph by: Laurence Taylor

Villa comfort

Cool Mediterranean villas stir the senses with inviting visions of placid, outside-in spaces and capacious rooms that open to courtyards and terraces. Bold and beautiful elevations layered with tactile surfaces surround smart living areas that own the capacity to flex and change according to the owners' preferences.

A romantic air flirts with the clean simple lines of these refined manors, with enchanting mixes of sleek fascia, rough-hewn rafter tails, classic columns and shapely balustrades. Hip roofs and varied gables call up an architectural past that is rich with history yet speaks to a style that's futuristic.

Cast-stone accenting, exposed brackets, arched transoms and well-articulated entries lend an authentic ambience to the homes, with finely detailed flourishes — decorative vents, keystones and fanlights — that create eye-pleasing streetscapes and savory curb appeal.

These villas present a comfortable mix of Euro-style manors, hardworking coastal villas and relaxed retreats, in varied shapes and sizes. Some plans are cozy with lots of intimate sunlit spaces, while others flow into decks and verandahs with views to infinity. Glass walls retreat, rows of French doors open and wide windows stretch to ceiling heights, encouraging an artful merger of landscape and décor. Flexible interiors tame even voluminous spaces and capture panoramas of scenery, while outdoor arenas extend the livability of highly functional rooms.

Photograph by: Laurence Taylor

SAVANNAH, GEORGIA

Photographs by: Richard Leo Johnson

Please note: Photography may differ from working drawings.

Photo above: Ample windows allow the outside in as sunlight blankets the interior of this Caribbean villa. The Spanish tile roof and stucco exterior evoke memories of vacations past and make this charming villa a relaxing everyday retreat.

▶ *Photo right: The interior is rich in detail yet perfectly balanced to create a very pleasing coastal retreat. The archway beckons guests to the French doors which lead to a magnificent wrap-around porch.*

▲

Top photo: *Relaxed in feel and exquisite in detail, the gourmet kitchen employs columns to outline the hall and frame the view. The bar connects the two spaces allowing casual dining for two and terrific views through spans of glass facing the veranda.*

▲

Bottom photo: *The scenery creates a portrait through the three French doors and curved wall of glass in the master suite. The layout also allows for a sitting arrangement — perfect for reading a novel or simply enjoying the lovely views.*

▲

Photo above: With a taste of Southern Plantation-style, the rear of this home is a spectacular display with its wrap-around verandah and rows of windows and shutters. The balmy summer breeze mingles through the columns as the sunset filters through the windows.

▲
Photo above: Classic interior trim seamlessly
frames the wall of windows in the great room.
This stunning room features built-in cabinets
and a fireplace perfect for special evenings
spent indoors.

PLAN | *6688*

▲

Photo above: Overlooking the pool, rows of columns and archways add symmetry and graceful elegance.

◀ *Photo left: Guests feel at home in their own private suite with a walk-in closet, full bath and morning kitchen. Ingenious design provides this space with both front and rear views.*

FOR PLAN DETAILS
SEE PAGES 196-197

Photographs by: Tom Harper

Please note: Photography may differ from working drawings.

▲

Photo above: A walkway canopied with greenery leads the way to the wrap-around front porch, while multiple windows and transoms provide a glimpse of the interior beauty.

▶ *Photo far right: The gourmet kitchen plays host to a sprawling center island and a sea of white-washed cabinets. The design, while elegant, presents a perfect match of Southern grace and country charm throughout.*

PLAN | *6667*

Photo left page: The great room's focal point, multi-paned transom windows, which span two stories, top the sliding glass doors that open to the pool.

▲

Photo above: Allowing the morning sun to peek through the shutters, the bay windows add dimension to this spacious bedroom.

◀ *Photo left: Columns and arches wind around the parlor, painting a picture reminiscent of days gone by when time moved a bit slower and life seemed simpler.*

▲

Photo above: Soaring columns and numerous panes of glass set a grand stage for outdoor entertaining. Cheery yellow clapboard siding adorns the idyllic cottage, creating a quaint country ambience without sacrificing luxury.

PLAN | *6667*

▼ *Photo below: A built-in hutch and pass-thru between the kitchen and the dining area is appreciated by the chef and family alike.*

▲

Photo above: Family gatherings seem second nature with a casual bar allowing conversation through both spaces. Rich hardwood floors seamlessly join all the rooms, while pleasant vistas filter in through an abundance of windows.

FOR PLAN DETAILS
SEE PAGES 138-139

Photographs by: Doug Thompson

Please note: Photography may differ from working drawings.

▲

Photo above: This precious cottage seems to smile on its own. Full of seaside charm, this comfortable home hosts a wrap-around porch and second-story balcony.

▲
Photo above: The great room has it all.
Built-in cabinets and art niches frame the
fireplace, while the front porch peeks
through French doors.

PLAN | *6701*

Photo left page: Life seems to slow down and yield more enjoyment on this front porch. Serve up a helping of Southern hospitality when neighbors drop by to sip tea and sit a spell.

Photo above: Preparing large dinners is a pleasure with double ovens and a sea of cabinets. An L-shaped island and cook's pantry add to the kitchen's functional luxury.

Photo left: Morning sun streams in the dining room, casting a glow on the pinewood floors. The staircase leads to the upstairs bedrooms and study.

Photo above: A quiet getaway, the master suite has French doors with sunlit transoms above that lead out to its wrap-around deck — perfect for relaxing and enjoying your morning coffee.

PLAN | *6701*

▲
Photo above: True to its Southern style,
this cottage graciously welcomes
backdoor friends and intimate gatherings.

◀ *Photo left: An archway and columns*
wrap around the large soaking tub
in the master bath. A rectangular
transom above the double vanity
maintains privacy, while allowing
sunlight to brighten the room.

FOR PLAN DETAILS
SEE PAGES 84-85

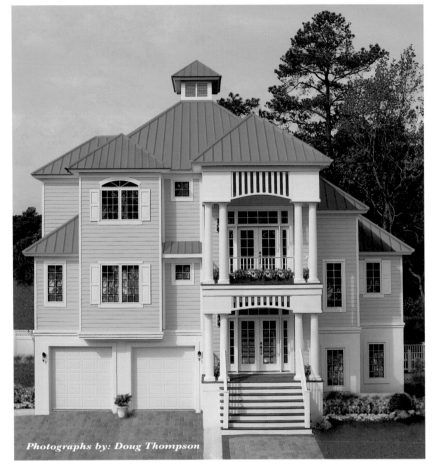

Photographs by: Doug Thompson

Please note: Photography may differ from working drawings.

▲

Photo above: Double columns frame the glass door entry and balcony above. Clapboard siding and a metal roof complete the coastal charm.

▲
Photo above: Grand open spaces are strengthened with pillars and panes of glass. The bar separates the kitchen from the great room, providing more room for entertaining. Artful decoration blends the spaces seamlessly.

▲

Photo above: This glamorous kitchen, complete with double ovens, pantry and rows of cherry cabinets, will make even a novice cook feel like a chef.

PLAN | *6808*

Photo right: A graceful curve spans the overlook and breaks the vaulted space between the main living area and the master suite above. ▶

◀ *Photo left: With its many patios and balconies, this beachside cottage has plenty of space to kick off your shoes and enjoy the view.*

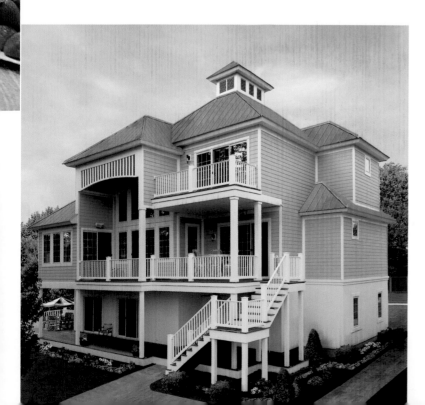

PLAN | *6808*

Photo left page: Vivid colors complement the architecture and a wall of glass provides uninterrupted views, creating a splendid work-of-art.

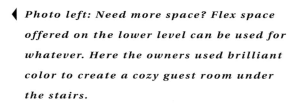

Photo above: The open floor plan still allows for comfortable places to gather. The dining room seats eight comfortably and shares the view of the sitting room beyond.

Photo left: Need more space? Flex space offered on the lower level can be used for whatever. Here the owners used brilliant color to create a cozy guest room under the stairs.

FOR PLAN DETAILS
SEE PAGES 80-81

Photographs by: Doug Thompson

Please note: Photography may differ from working drawings.

▲

Photo above: This best selling cottage commands attention in a not-so-humble way. Stairs climb to an elevated entry, topped by clever roof lines and a widow's walk.

▲

Photo above: Just inside the foyer, the fireplace warms the great room, while windows from above shower it with sunlight.

Photo above: With a curved island,
stainless appliances and a corner pantry,
the kitchen design makes cooking a joy, and
allows friends and family to gather while
preparing meals and dining.

PLAN | *6840*

▲

Photo above: Be the envy of the neighborhood with your own billiard room by making use of the lower-level bonus space. With a full wet-bar, pool table and lots of elbow room, it's the perfect place for fun and spirits.

◀ *Photo left: Just a few steps away from the kitchen, the dining room features pine floors and a picture window and is a cozy place to enjoy a quiet dinner.*

Photo above: The master suite offers decorative features, such as a tray ceiling and art niche, as well as a private balcony to enjoy coastal evening breezes.

PLAN | *6840*

▲

Photo above: The rear elevation is a lovely display of spaces for gathering together and enjoying all the views that beckon you outdoors.

◀ *Photo left: Soak the day's troubles away in a calming garden tub, where relaxation is the resounding theme in this pampering master bath.*

FOR PLAN DETAILS
SEE PAGES 76-77

SANIBEL, FLORIDA

Photographs by: Tom Harper

Please note: Photography may differ from working drawings.

Photo above: Come home to paradise. Gentle sunburst transoms and narrow shutters adorn this tropical villa. With a Spanish tile roof and stucco walls, this home is timeless in style.

▶ **Photo far right: Sunset adds a glow to the soothing fountain and charming stepping stones in the lap pool, which skirts an expansive section of the wrap-around porch.**

▲

Photo above: Evening breezes flow through the double set of French doors, exposing a spacious verandah which holds center stage and extends the drama of the master suite. A rich mix of textured fabrics puddles opulently on hardwood floors, a testament to the home's relaxed atmosphere.

PLAN | *6688*

▼ *Photo below: Company will want to stay longer in the second-story guest suite. Along with picturesque views from both front and rear of the villa, this suite features a walk-in closet and morning kitchen.*

▲
Photo above: A tapestry of palms peaks through the French doors in the great room. Easy access from the porch, as well as the kitchen or dining room, makes this an ideal space for casual entertaining.

Photo above: The back porch provides ample space to enjoy pleasant summer afternoons, while earthy tones and textures create a warmth of their own, year-round.

▲

Photo above: A tray ceiling and generous lighting look down on the gourmet kitchen's center island and breakfast table. Stained glass windows add a hint of color to the natural hues that permeate the kitchen.

◀ *Photo left: The master bath is full of charm and luxury. The soaking tub nestled among bay windows is a tranquil getaway, while his and her vanities and a walk-in shower make early mornings a pleasure.*

FOR PLAN DETAILS
SEE PAGES 196-197

Photographs by: Doug Thompson

Please note: Photography may differ from working drawings.

▲

Photo above: No matter what season, this seaside beauty will always feel warm and inviting. Dormers and clapboard siding add a homey feel to this distinguished cottage. The corner verandah is a pleasant spot to relax amidst salty sea breezes.

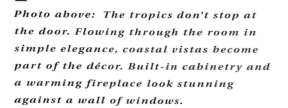

▲

Photo above: The tropics don't stop at the door. Flowing through the room in simple elegance, coastal vistas become part of the décor. Built-in cabinetry and a warming fireplace look stunning against a wall of windows.

▲

Photo above: Luxurious cherry floors offset by an impressive staircase with white railings create a magnificent backdrop to this open floor plan.

PLAN | *6800*

▲
Photo above: The kitchen is a cook's paradise
with tropical flair. Sparing nothing, this
area boasts a spacious center island, a corner
pantry and an abundance of cabinets.

◀ *Photo left: Sit barefoot poolside and*
enjoy the breezes that flow through
the lengthy verandah or welcome in
the day from the balcony off the
master suite. Luxury is redefined
with plenty of outdoor spaces.

FOR PLAN DETAILS
SEE PAGES 130-131

Photographs by: Doug Thompson

Please note: Photography may differ from working drawings.

▲

Photo above: An impressive façade gives this cottage a stately presence, while splashes of light seep through panes of glass.

▶ *Photo to right: The rear is decked-out with fancy fretwork and tranquil outdoor places.*

Photo above: Shaker cabinets topped with moss green granite countertops are an ideal backdrop in this high-function kitchen. A breakfast nook nestled in the corner offers a cozy place to get together.

PLAN | *6808*

◀ *Photo left page: Sprawling ceilings and a tiered mantle create a sense of grandeur, while hardwood floors and the glow from the fire create a cozy ambience.*

▲

Photo above: Creamy yellow walls compliment the brillant blue sky framed by several windows in the dining room.

◀ *Photo left: The tray ceiling with subtle lighting makes this room the perfect place to settle in with a book or to watch your favorite movie. This is another great use of flex space on the lower level.*

FOR PLAN DETAILS
SEE PAGES 80-81

Photograph by: Tom Harper

Cottages

Somewhere between rustic charm and urbane comfort lies the pure simplicity of a seaside cottage. Deep covered porches and open decks permit breezes to flow into spacious rooms designed to capture views. Outdoor havens take on the attitude of the surrounding terrain, and compete with panoramas of sky, sea and endless stretches of sand. Clapboard siding and arched windows establish an authentic presence at the streetscape and introduce highly functional interiors with flexible rooms. French doors and retreating glass walls create fluid boundaries with breezy solanas and sundecks, and call up the outside-in Caribbean and Gulf Coast houses of eras past. Enhanced with 21st-century amenities, these plans harbor computer lofts, libraries and living spaces that easily convert to guest quarters, craft rooms and home offices.

Cottage | 1288 SQ. FT.

© THE SATER DESIGN COLLECTION, INC.

Mallory Square

Welcome home to casual, unstuffy living with this comfortable tidewater design. Asymmetrical lines celebrate the turn of the new century and blend a current Gulf Coast style with vintage elements brought forward from its regional past.

The inside foyer overlooks a decorative half-wall to wide views offered through French doors. The heart of this home is the great room, where a put-up-your-feet atmosphere prevails, and the dusky hues of sunset can mingle with the sounds of ocean breakers. A galley-style kitchen serves an eating bar, while a convenient pass-through offers magnificent views to the cook.

French doors open the master suite to a private area of the covered porch, where sunlight and sea breezes mingle with a spirit of bon vivant.

PLAN | 6691

Bedroom: 2   Width: 32'4"
Bath: 2   Depth: 60'0"
Foundation: Crawlspace
Exterior Walls: 2x6

Main Level: 1,288 sq ft
Living Area: 1,288 sq ft
Price Code: **A4**

1-800-718-PLAN

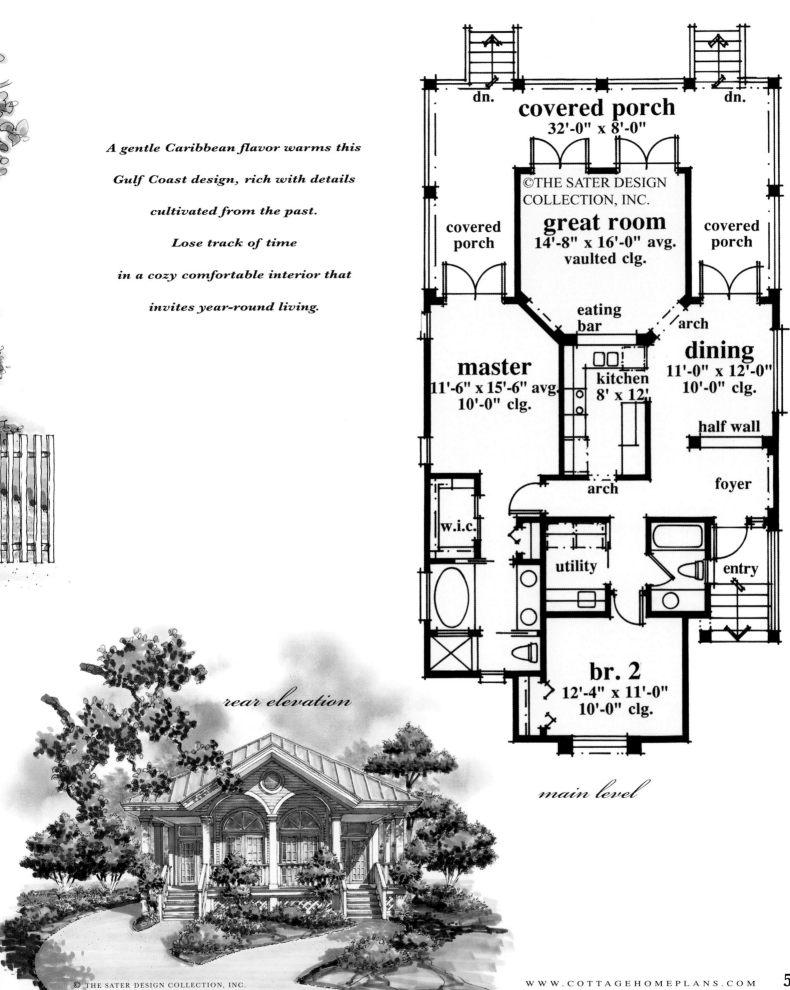

A gentle Caribbean flavor warms this

Gulf Coast design, rich with details

cultivated from the past.

Lose track of time

in a cozy comfortable interior that

invites year-round living.

covered porch
32'-0" x 8'-0"

©THE SATER DESIGN COLLECTION, INC.

great room
14'-8" x 16'-0" avg.
vaulted clg.

covered porch

covered porch

eating bar

arch

master
11'-6" x 15'-6" avg.
10'-0" clg.

dining
11'-0" x 12'-0"
10'-0" clg.

kitchen
8' x 12'

half wall

foyer

w.i.c.

arch

utility

entry

br. 2
12'-4" x 11'-0"
10'-0" clg.

rear elevation

main level

© THE SATER DESIGN COLLECTION, INC.

© THE SATER DESIGN COLLECTION, INC.

Church Street

The modest detailing of Greek Revival style gave rise to this grand cottage, rich with architectural character. A mid-level foyer eases the trip from ground level to the raised living area, while an arched vestibule announces the great room. French doors flank the heart of the home, adding views as well as a sense of whimsy.

The formal dining room opens through a dropped arch soffit ceiling, and French doors lead to the covered porch. Fixed glass windows above the built-in cabinetry allow natural light to fill the great room. A well-appointed kitchen enjoys generous views from beyond.

Upstairs, each of two private suites has French doors to a sundeck. The upper gallery hall leads to a computer loft with built-ins and a balcony overlook.

PLAN | 6687

Bedroom: 2   Width: 32'0"
Bath: 2-1/2   Depth: 40'6"
Foundation: Post/Pier
Exterior Walls: 2x6

Main Level: 908 sq ft
Upper Level: 562 sq ft
Living Area: 1,470 sq ft

Price Code: **A4**

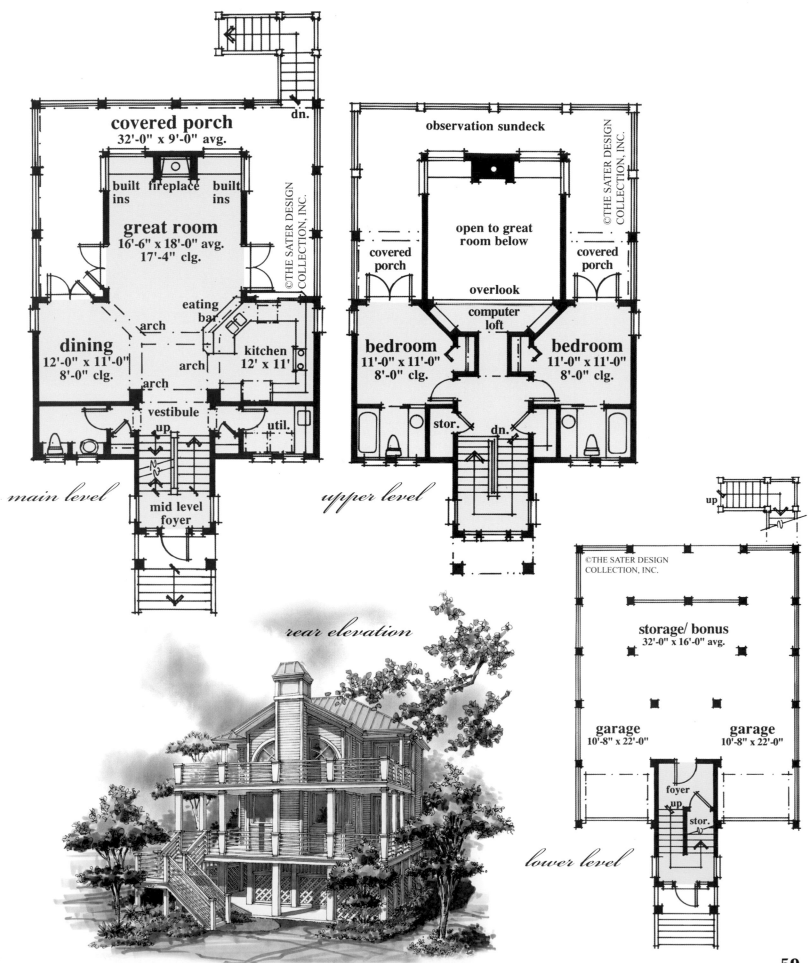

main level

covered porch
32'-0" x 9'-0" avg.

built ins   fireplace   built ins

great room
16'-6" x 18'-0" avg.
17'-4" clg.

eating bar

dining
12'-0" x 11'-0"
8'-0" clg.

arch

arch

arch

kitchen
12' x 11'

vestibule
up

util.

mid level foyer

dn.

©THE SATER DESIGN COLLECTION, INC.

upper level

observation sundeck

open to great room below

covered porch

covered porch

overlook

computer loft

bedroom
11'-0" x 11'-0"
8'-0" clg.

bedroom
11'-0" x 11'-0"
8'-0" clg.

stor.

dn.

©THE SATER DESIGN COLLECTION, INC.

rear elevation

up

©THE SATER DESIGN COLLECTION, INC.

storage/ bonus
32'-0" x 16'-0" avg.

garage
10'-8" x 22'-0"

garage
10'-8" x 22'-0"

foyer
up

stor.

lower level

Cottage | 1690 SQ. FT.

© THE SATER DESIGN COLLECTION, INC.

Runaway Bay

Here's a seaside retreat with an easygoing style. This Floridian home is built for the coastal climate, with a raised living area that invites the balmy ocean breezes and allows distant views.

The entry leads through a well-lit foyer to an expansive great room, warmed by a fireplace. Lovely French doors lead out to a screened verandah, also accessed from a well-appointed gourmet kitchen and dining area. A roomy sundeck hosts casual meals and morning coffee.

Split sleeping quarters offer a secondary bedroom and study on the main level. The upper level is dedicated to a luxurious master suite that features a spacious private bath with a knee-space vanity and a dressing area. Storage and bonus space surround an ample carport on the lower level.

PLAN | *6616*

Bedroom: 3   Width: 39'9"
Bath: 2   Depth: 45'0"
Foundation: Post/Pier
Exterior Walls: 2x6

Main Level: 1,134 sq ft
Upper Level: 556 sq ft
Living Area: 1,690 sq ft
Price Code: **C1**

1-800-718-PLAN

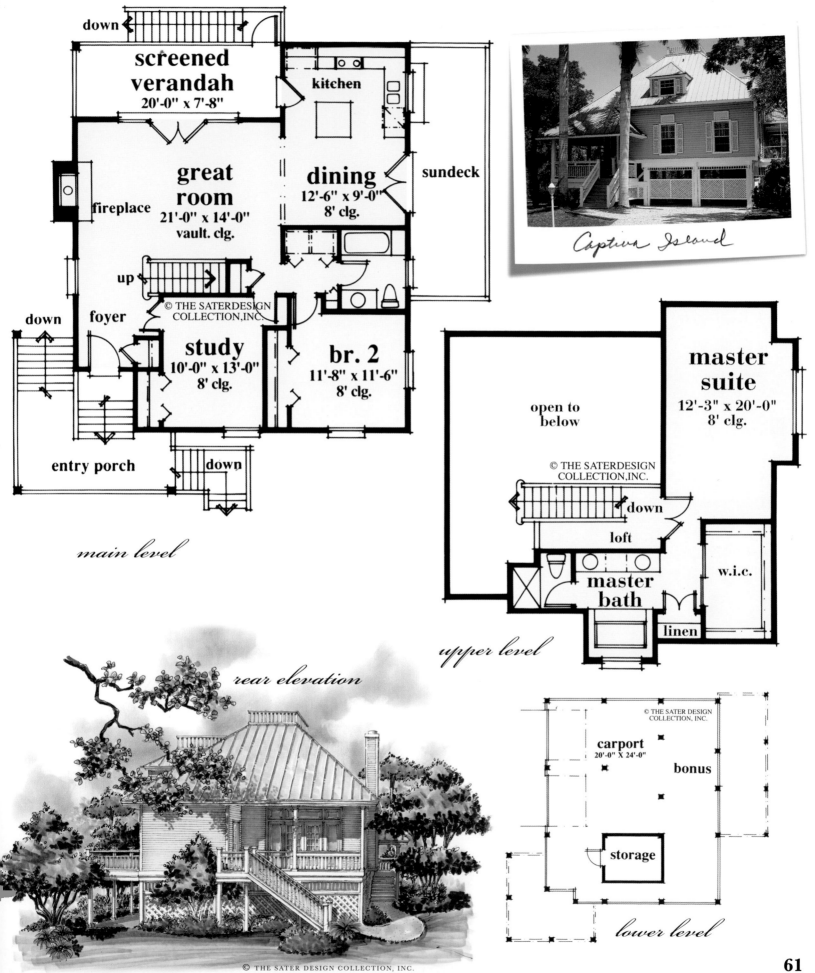

screened verandah
20'-0" x 7'-8"

down

kitchen

great room
21'-0" x 14'-0"
vault. clg.

fireplace

dining
12'-6" x 9'-0"
8' clg.

sundeck

up

foyer

© THE SATER DESIGN COLLECTION, INC.

down

study
10'-0" x 13'-0"
8' clg.

br. 2
11'-8" x 11'-6"
8' clg.

entry porch

down

main level

open to below

© THE SATER DESIGN COLLECTION, INC.

master suite
12'-3" x 20'-0"
8' clg.

down

loft

w.i.c.

master bath

linen

upper level

rear elevation

Captiva Island

carport
20'-0" X 24'-0"

© THE SATER DESIGN COLLECTION, INC.

bonus

storage

lower level

© THE SATER DESIGN COLLECTION, INC.

61

Cottage | 1706 SQ. FT.

© THE SATER DESIGN COLLECTION, INC.

Saddle River

Lattice fretwork and symmetrical gables create a pure geometry on this easy-living river cottage, while a stair tower adds a sense of grandeur. A host of French doors on the main level invites the outside in, where an air of comfortable elegance prevails.

The formal dining room, gallery and great room open through sets of lovely French doors to the columned verandah. Traditional events, such as holidays, will enjoy an unstuffy atmosphere in joyful rooms that lead outdoors and invite a sense of nature. Wrapping counters in the gourmet kitchen surround an island counter large enough for two cooks.

Sleeping quarters upstairs include the spacious master suite, which opens to a private balcony where gentle sea breezes can invigorate the senses.

PLAN | *6681*

Bedroom: 2   Width: 40'0"
Bath: 2-1/2   Depth: 37'0"
Foundation: Post/Pier
Exterior Walls: 2x6

Main Level: 906 sq ft
Upper Level: 714 sq ft
Tower Loft: 86 sq ft

Living Area: 1,706 sq ft

Price Code: **C1**

1-800-718-PLAN

covered porch
40'-0" x 8'-0"

© THE SATER DESIGN
COLLECTION, INC.

© THE SATER DESIGN
COLLECTION, INC.

arch

great room
15'-6" x 15'-6"
vaulted clg.

dining
15'-0" x 12'-0"
8' flat clg.

gallery

storage

garage
13'-0" x 24'-0"

garage
13'-0" x 24'-0"

arch

up

mid level
entry

up

kitchen
14' x 10'

down   up

**pwdr.
bath**   **utility**

covered porch

lower level

main level

observation deck

tower loft
11'-4" x 6'-6"

down

© THE SATER DESIGN
COLLECTION, INC.

tower loft

master
12'-6" x 14'-0"
vaulted clg.

bath

am
kitchen

built
ins

rear elevation

w.i.c.

bath

down   up

br. 2
10'-4" x 10'-0"
vaulted clg.
wdw
seat

upper level

© THE SATER DESIGN COLLECTION, INC.

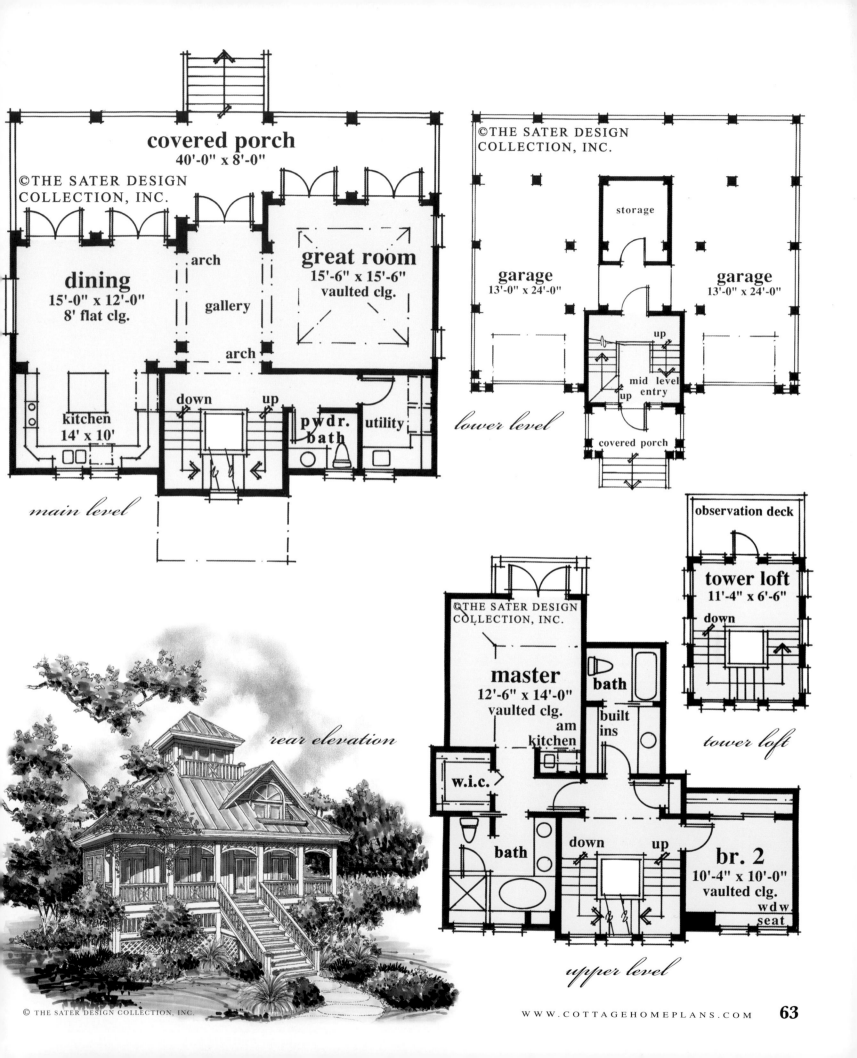

Cottage | 1764 SQ. FT.

© THE SATER DESIGN COLLECTION, INC.

Tradewind Court

This charming two-story cottage is suited for a myriad of building situations, with carefree and comfortable outdoor areas that encourage year-round living.

Deep overhangs above the entry and forward windows shield the interior from harsh sunlight. Two sets of French doors to the back of the plan open the great room and dining room to sea breezes and prime views, complemented by a cozy fireplace. A windowed double sink opens the kitchen to views and sunlight, while a convenient laundry keeps the living area tidy.

The homeowner's private bath features two lavatories, a separate shower and a door to a secluded area of the screened verandah. Upstairs, a secondary bedroom with a dormer window shares a full bath with a cozy loft or third bedroom.

PLAN | 6617

Bedroom: 3	Width: 46'0"
Bath: 2-1/2	Depth: 45'0"
Foundation: Piling	
Exterior Walls: 2x6	

Main Level:	1,124 sq ft
Upper Level:	640 sq ft
Living Area:	1,764 sq ft
Price Code:	**C 2**

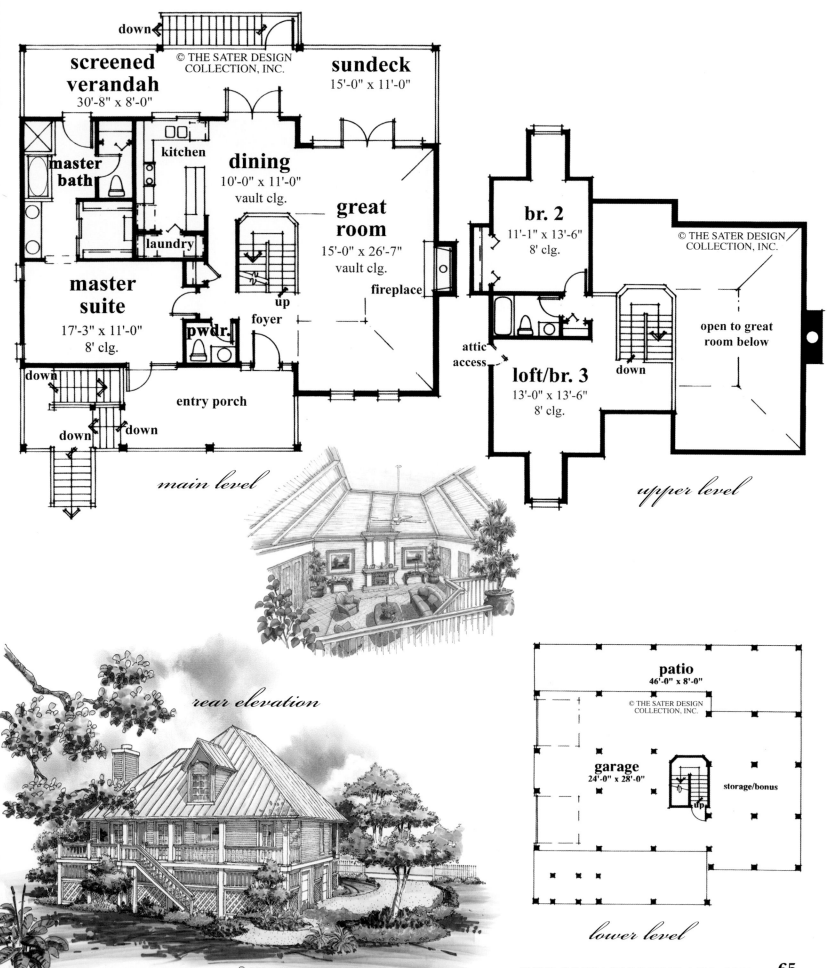

screened verandah
30'-8" x 8'-0"

down

© THE SATER DESIGN COLLECTION, INC.

sundeck
15'-0" x 11'-0"

kitchen

dining
10'-0" x 11'-0"
vault clg.

great room
15'-0" x 26'-7"
vault clg.

master bath

laundry

master suite
17'-3" x 11'-0"
8' clg.

up

foyer

fireplace

pwdr.

down

down   down

entry porch

main level

br. 2
11'-1" x 13'-6"
8' clg.

© THE SATER DESIGN COLLECTION, INC.

down

open to great room below

attic access

loft/br. 3
13'-0" x 13'-6"
8' clg.

upper level

rear elevation

patio
46'-0" x 8'-0"

© THE SATER DESIGN COLLECTION, INC.

garage
24'-0" x 28'-0"

up

storage/bonus

lower level

© THE SATER DESIGN COLLECTION, INC.

Cottage | 1792 SQ. FT.

© THE SATER DESIGN COLLECTION, INC.

Cayman Court

A charming porte-cochere sets off a perfect blend of Southern Cracker comfort and Gulf Coast style with this seaside retreat. Exposed rafters, lattice panels and a deep covered porch make a strong architectural statement that's tuned to a 1940's personality.

Inside, decorative arches and columns make a grand entrance to the living and dining areas. The gourmet kitchen provides a pass-through to the formal dining room, while the focal-point fireplace warms the great room.

A secluded master suite nestles to the back of the plan, with private access to a sundeck and French doors to the covered porch. The bayed sitting area offers space for reading and sunlight to the homeowner's retreat. This plan includes pier and crawlspace foundation options.

PLAN | *6694*

Bedroom: 2   Width: 33'0"

Bath: 2   Depth: 82'0"

Foundation: Post/Pier or Crawlspace

Exterior Walls: 2x6

Main Level: 1,792 sq ft

Living Area: 1,792 sq ft

Price Code: **C1**

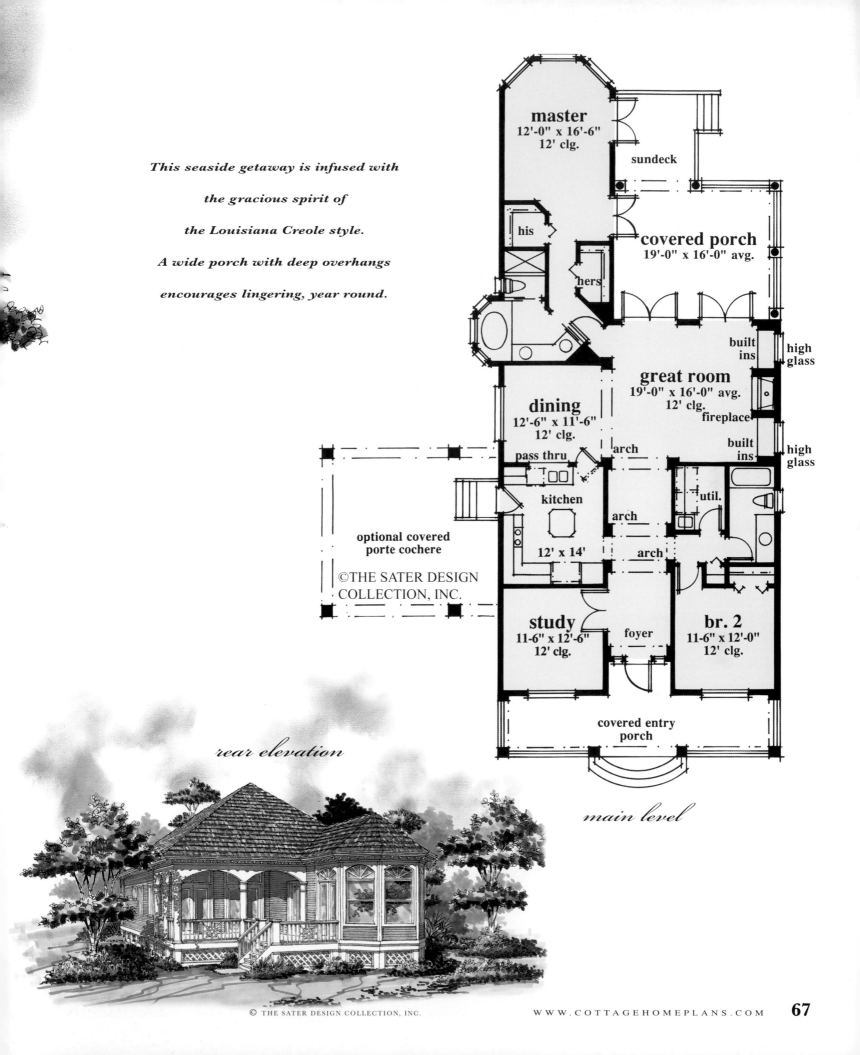

This seaside getaway is infused with the gracious spirit of the Louisiana Creole style. A wide porch with deep overhangs encourages lingering, year round.

master
12'-0" x 16'-6"
12' clg.

sundeck

covered porch
19'-0" x 16'-0" avg.

his

hers

built ins

high glass

great room
19'-0" x 16'-0" avg.
12' clg.

fireplace

built ins

high glass

dining
12'-6" x 11'-6"
12' clg.

pass thru

arch

util.

kitchen

12' x 14'

arch

arch

optional covered
porte cochere

©THE SATER DESIGN
COLLECTION, INC.

study
11-6" x 12'-6"
12' clg.

foyer

br. 2
11-6" x 12'-0"
12' clg.

covered entry
porch

main level

rear elevation

© THE SATER DESIGN COLLECTION, INC.

© THE SATER DESIGN COLLECTION, INC.

Plymouth Bay

This seaside cottage is the perfect get-away retreat. Spiral columns, custom arches, and unique windows render a subtle Gothic design. Revealing the impressive interior, the foyer opens to expansive rear views through a wall of glass and a wrap-around deck. The main room boasts a beautiful fireplace, built-in cabinetry and visions of the blue sky. Through columns, the dining room adjoins the spacious kitchen, where a pantry and pass-though serve the porch. The main floor also hosts a powder room, laundry room, guest bedroom and bath.

Upstairs is home to the intimate master suite and private bath. An open loft oversees the great room below and French doors spring open to a viewing deck. If needed, the basement-level bonus room easily converts to additional living space.

PLAN | *6852*

Bedroom: 2   Width: 32'0"
Bath: 2-1/2   Depth: 57'0"
Foundation: Island basement
Exterior Walls: 2x6

Main Level: 1,143 sq ft
Upper Level: 651 sq ft
Living Area: 1,794 sq ft
Price Code: **C1**

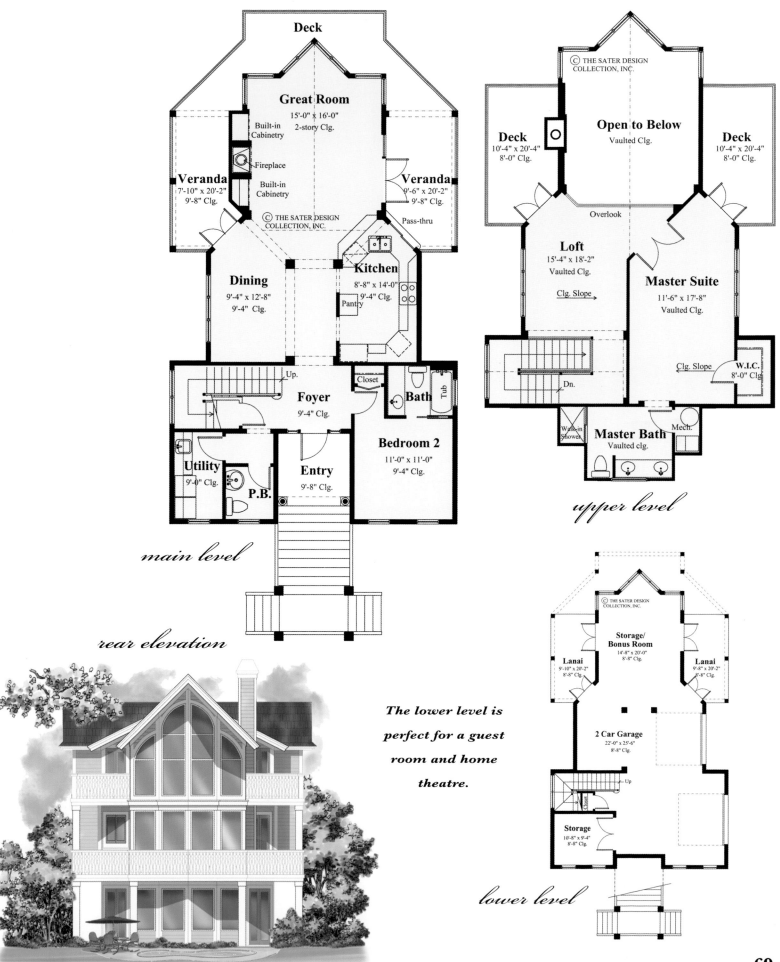

Deck

Great Room
15'-0" x 16'-0"
2-story Clg.

Built-in Cabinetry

Fireplace

Built-in Cabinetry

Veranda
7'-10" x 20'-2"
9'-8" Clg.

© THE SATER DESIGN COLLECTION, INC.

Veranda
9'-6" x 20'-2"
9'-8" Clg.

Pass-thru

Dining
9'-4" x 12'-8"
9'-4" Clg.

Kitchen
8'-8" x 14'-0"
9'-4" Clg.

Pantry

Up.

Foyer
9'-4" Clg.

Closet

Bath

Tub

Utility
9'-0" Clg.

P.B.

Entry
9'-8" Clg.

Bedroom 2
11'-0" x 11'-0"
9'-4" Clg.

main level

rear elevation

© THE SATER DESIGN COLLECTION, INC.

Open to Below
Vaulted Clg.

Deck
10'-4" x 20'-4"
8'-0" Clg.

Deck
10'-4" x 20'-4"
8'-0" Clg.

Overlook

Loft
15'-4" x 18'-2"
Vaulted Clg.

Clg. Slope →

Master Suite
11'-6" x 17'-8"
Vaulted Clg.

← Clg. Slope

W.I.C.
8'-0" Clg

Dn.

Walk-in Shower

Master Bath
Vaulted clg.

Mech.

upper level

---

*The lower level is
perfect for a guest
room and home
theatre.*

© THE SATER DESIGN COLLECTION, INC.

**Storage/
Bonus Room**
14'-8" x 20'-0"
8'-8" Clg.

Lanai
9'-10" x 20'-2"
8'-8" Clg.

Lanai
9'-8" x 20'-2"
8'-8" Clg.

2 Car Garage
22'-0" x 25'-6"
8'-8" Clg.

Up

Closet

Storage
10'-8" x 9'-4"
8'-8" Clg.

lower level

© THE SATER DESIGN COLLECTION, INC.

Cottage | 1838 SQ. FT.

© THE SATER DESIGN COLLECTION, INC.

Periwinkle Way

A romantic air flirts with the clean, simple lines of this seaside getaway, set off by stunning shingle accents and a sunburst transom. Horizontal siding complements an insulated metal roof to create a charming look that calls up a sense of 19th-century style. Inside, an unrestrained floor plan harbors cozy interior spaces and offers great outdoor views through wide windows and French doors.

At the heart of the home, the two-story great room features a corner fireplace and an angled entertainment center. Columns and sweeping archways define the formal dining room, while French doors open to the verandah, inviting dreamy ocean breezes inside. Upstairs, an expansive deck captures panoramic views from one of the secondary bedrooms.

PLAN | 6683

Bedroom: 3
Width: 38'0"
Bath: 2-1/2
Depth: 51'0"
Foundation: Crawlspace or basement
Exterior Walls: 2x6

Main Level: 1,290 sq ft
Upper Level: 548 sq ft
Living Area: 1,838 sq ft
Price Code: **C1**

1-800-718-PLAN

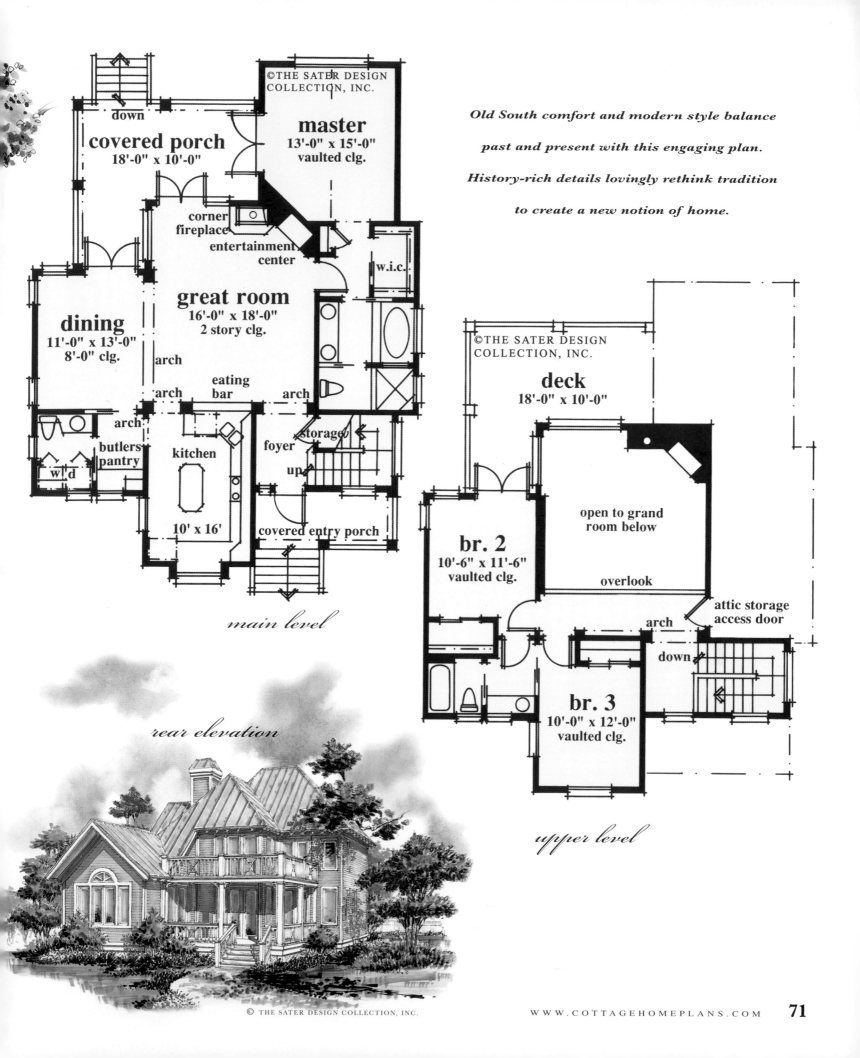

©THE SATER DESIGN COLLECTION, INC.

covered porch
18'-0" x 10'-0"

down

master
13'-0" x 15'-0"
vaulted clg.

corner fireplace

entertainment center

w.i.c.

great room
16'-0" x 18'-0"
2 story clg.

dining
11'-0" x 13'-0"
8'-0" clg.

arch

arch

arch

eating bar

arch

storage

foyer

up

butlers pantry

w d

kitchen
10' x 16'

covered entry porch

main level

Old South comfort and modern style balance past and present with this engaging plan. History-rich details lovingly rethink tradition to create a new notion of home.

©THE SATER DESIGN COLLECTION, INC.

deck
18'-0" x 10'-0"

open to grand room below

overlook

br. 2
10'-6" x 11'-6"
vaulted clg.

attic storage access door

arch

down

br. 3
10'-0" x 12'-0"
vaulted clg.

upper level

rear elevation

© THE SATER DESIGN COLLECTION, INC.

Nassau Cove

Classic clapboard siding sets off a metal roof and latticework fret detail on this island cottage. True to its tropical roots, this design features a raised living area and a balustered porch.

Double French doors lead to the rear deck from the grand room, which has a cozy fireplace. Both sides of the formal dining room open to decks, positioned to capture prevailing gentle breezes. The well-appointed kitchen overlooks the living area, splashed with the warmth of natural light.

Upstairs, a hall with balcony overlook leads to French doors, which announce the homeowner's retreat. A morning kitchen conveniently prepares juice and coffee, while a private observation deck invites sunning and stargazing. The master bath boasts a windowed, whirlpool tub, an oversized shower and a U-shaped walk-in closet.

PLAN | *6654*

Bedroom: 3   Width: 44'0"
Bath: 2   Depth: 40'0"
Foundation: Post/Pier
Exterior Walls: 2x6

Main Level: 1,342 sq ft
Upper Level: 511 sq ft
Living Area: 1,853 sq ft
Price Code: **C1**

1-800-718-PLAN

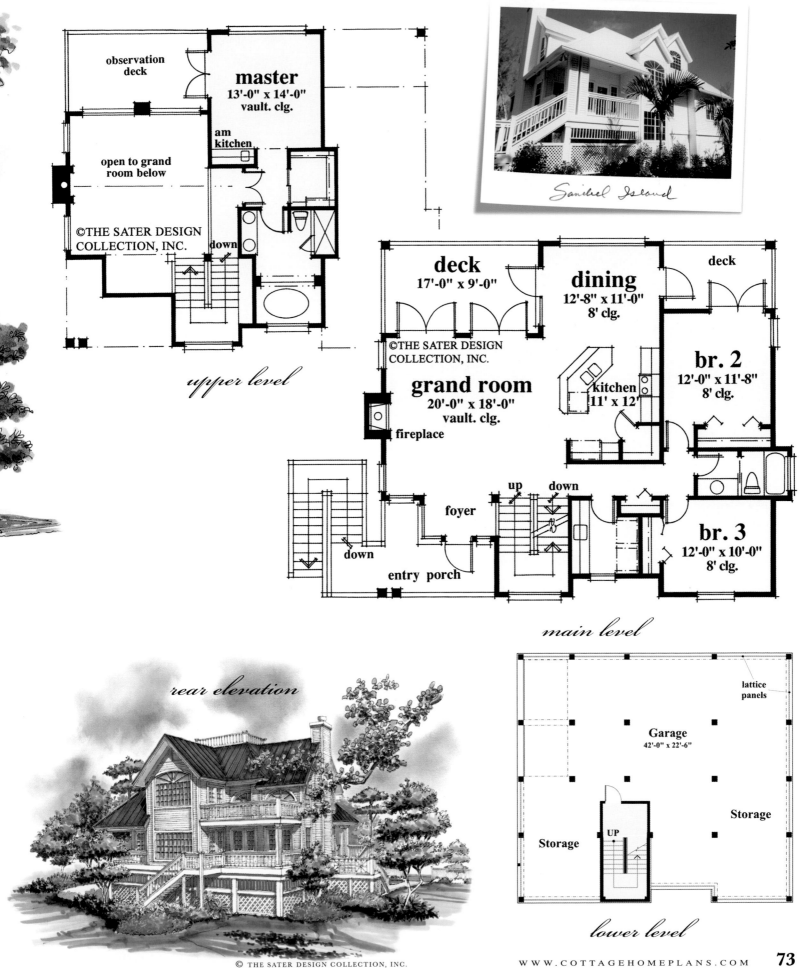

observation deck

master
13'-0" x 14'-0"
vault. clg.

am kitchen

open to grand room below

©THE SATER DESIGN
COLLECTION, INC.

down

upper level

Sanibel Island

deck
17'-0" x 9'-0"

dining
12'-8" x 11'-0"
8' clg.

deck

©THE SATER DESIGN
COLLECTION, INC.

grand room
20'-0" x 18'-0"
vault. clg.

kitchen
11' x 12'

br. 2
12'-0" x 11'-8"
8' clg.

fireplace

up   down

foyer

down

entry porch

br. 3
12'-0" x 10'-0"
8' clg.

main level

rear elevation

lattice panels

Garage
42'-0" x 22'-6"

Storage

UP

Storage

lower level

© THE SATER DESIGN COLLECTION, INC.

© THE SATER DESIGN COLLECTION, INC.

Jasmine Lane

An enchanting center gable announces a graceful, honest architecture that's at home with the easygoing nature of this coastal design. A columned porch and romantic fretwork lend balance and proportion outside, while gentle arches add pleasing definition to an open interior that enjoys a modern sense of space.

The well-appointed kitchen features a corner walk-in pantry, an eating bar for easy meals and an angled double sink. A box bay fills the dining room with light and allows space for a china hutch or buffet. French doors in the main-level secondary bedroom lead to a covered balcony with views of the front property.

Enjoy lofty views from the comfort of a chaise lounger in the quiet sitting area of the stair tower. This plan includes pier and crawlspace foundation options.

PLAN | *6680*

Bedroom: 3   Width: 43'8"
Bath: 3   Depth: 53'6"
Foundation: Pier or Crawlspace
Exterior Walls: 2x6

Main Level: 1,007 sq ft
Upper Level: 869 sq ft
Living Area: 1,876 sq ft

Price Code: **C1**

covered porch
32'-0" x 8'-0"

down

entertainment
center

corner
fireplace

dining
12'-0" x 12'-6"
8'-0" clg.

arch

great room
19'-0" x 16'-0"
2 story clg.

up

hutch
niche

eating
bar

arch

arch

foyer

storage

d

w

kitchen
12' x 12'

br. 2
11'-6" x 15'-0"
8'-0" clg.

covered
entry porch

©THE SATER DESIGN
COLLECTION, INC.

stair tower

down

covered balcony
12'-6" x 9'-0"

main level

great room

©THE SATER DESIGN
COLLECTION, INC.

open to grand
room below

br. 3
11'-0" x 10'-6"
8'-0" clg.

up

overlook

down

w.i.c.

master
11'-6" x 14'-6"
8'-0" clg.

rear elevation

covered balcony

upper level

© THE SATER DESIGN COLLECTION, INC.

© THE SATER DESIGN COLLECTION, INC.

Aruba Bay

"Alluring" is the word to describe this tropical cottage with clapboard façade and arch-top transom. A welcoming entry embellishes an unrestricted floor plan, with a ceiling that rises to the sky, above the foyer and great room. French doors open the great room, inviting unrestrained breezes and views from the porch.

The open kitchen displays function and style, extending service to the dining room, and allows for culinary arts and conversation. A genuine retreat, the master suite is lavished with a generous bath, making provisions for his and her comforts, with access to its own airy outdoor porch. The second floor provides two sizable guest suites, with outdoor vistas through high windows and a deck.

PLAN | 6840

Bedroom: 3   Width: 44'0"
Bath: 2-1/2   Depth: 40'0"
Foundation: Island basement
Exterior Walls: 2x6

Main Level: 1,342 sq ft
Upper Level: 511 sq ft
Tower Level Entry: 33 sq ft

Living Area: 1,886 sq ft

Price Code: **C1**

FOR PHOTOGRAPHY
SEE PAGES 34-39

1-800-718-PLAN

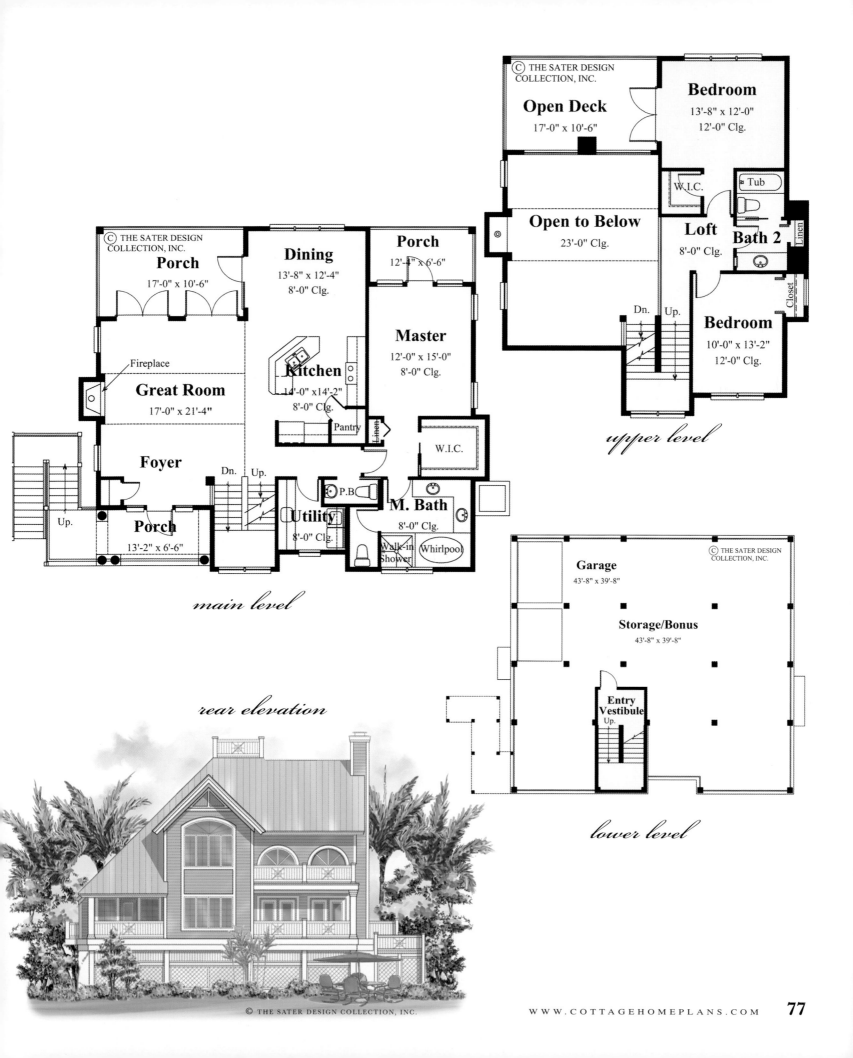

© THE SATER DESIGN COLLECTION, INC.

upper level

Open Deck
17'-0" x 10'-6"

Bedroom
13'-8" x 12'-0"
12'-0" Clg.

W.I.C.

Open to Below
23'-0" Clg.

Loft
8'-0" Clg.

Tub

Bath 2

Linen

Closet

Dn. Up.

Bedroom
10'-0" x 13'-2"
12'-0" Clg.

© THE SATER DESIGN COLLECTION, INC.

main level

Porch
17'-0" x 10'-6"

Dining
13'-8" x 12'-4"
8'-0" Clg.

Porch
12'-4" x 6'-6"

Fireplace

Great Room
17'-0" x 21'-4"

Kitchen
14'-0" x14'-2"
8'-0" Clg.

Master
12'-0" x 15'-0"
8'-0" Clg.

Pantry

Linen

W.I.C.

Foyer

Dn. Up.

P.B

Up.

Porch
13'-2" x 6'-6"

Utility
8'-0" Clg.

M. Bath
8'-0" Clg.

Walk-in
Shower

Whirlpool

rear elevation

© THE SATER DESIGN COLLECTION, INC.

lower level

Garage
43'-8" x 39'-8"

Storage/Bonus
43'-8" x 39'-8"

Entry
Vestibule
Up.

© THE SATER DESIGN COLLECTION, INC.

© THE SATER DESIGN COLLECTION, INC.

Georgetown Cove

PLAN | *6690*

The captivating charm of this popular cottage calls up a sense of gentler times, with a quaint front balcony, horizontal siding and fishscale shingles. A contemporary, high-pitched roof harmonizes with sunbursts and double porticos, while a glass-paneled entry opens the foyer, where a straightforward staircase leads to a bright vestibule.

In the great room, lovely French doors bring the outside in, and a fireplace framed by built-in cabinetry adds coziness and warmth. A gourmet kitchen sports an island counter with prep sink, and a peninsular counter with a casual eating bar. The formal dining room opens to a private area of the covered porch — an elegant invitation to dining outdoors.

Double French doors and circlehead windows fill the upper-level master suite with sunlight and open to a private sundeck.

Bedroom: 3	Width: 27'6"
Bath: 2-1/2	Depth: 64'0"
Foundation: Piling/Garage on Slab	
Exterior Walls: 2x6	

Main Level:	873 sq ft
Upper Level:	1,037 sq ft
Living Area:	1,910 sq ft
Price Code:	**C1**

1-800-718-PLAN

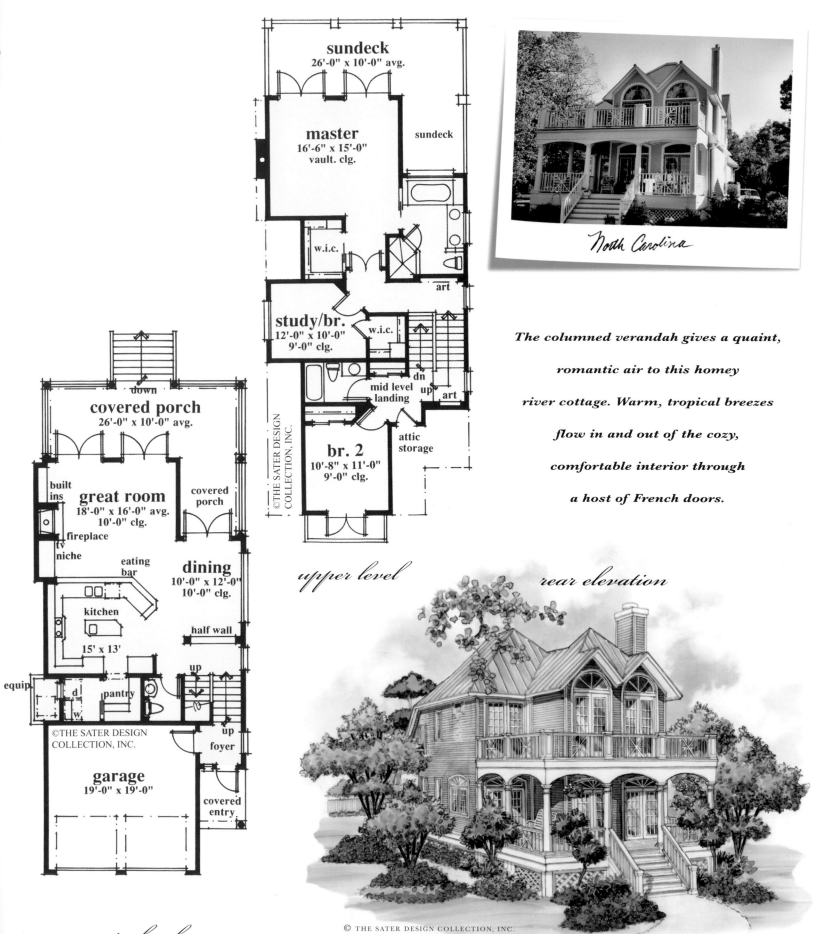

sundeck
26'-0" x 10'-0" avg.

master
16'-6" x 15'-0"
vault. clg.

sundeck

w.i.c.

art

study/br.
12'-0" x 10'-0"
9'-0" clg.

w.i.c.

dn
up

mid level
landing

art

attic
storage

br. 2
10'-8" x 11'-0"
9'-0" clg.

©THE SATER DESIGN COLLECTION, INC.

upper level

North Carolina

The columned verandah gives a quaint,

romantic air to this homey

river cottage. Warm, tropical breezes

flow in and out of the cozy,

comfortable interior through

a host of French doors.

down

covered porch
26'-0" x 10'-0" avg.

built
ins

great room
18'-0" x 16'-0" avg.
10'-0" clg.

fireplace

tv
niche

covered
porch

eating
bar

dining
10'-0" x 12'-0"
10'-0" clg.

kitchen

15' x 13'

half wall

up

equip

pantry

d
w

up

up
foyer

covered
entry

©THE SATER DESIGN
COLLECTION, INC.

garage
19'-0" x 19'-0"

main level

rear elevation

© THE SATER DESIGN COLLECTION, INC.

© THE SATER DESIGN COLLECTION, INC.

Santa Rosa

This beautiful variation of Key West Conch-style clearly emphasizes the benefits of living in a sunny climate. An abundance of windows invites warmth and light into this comfortable interior, while a dramatic rear offers a deck view from virtually every room in the house.

The two-story great room boasts a vaulted ceiling and French doors that open to the covered porch. Graceful arches and decorative columns define an open arrangement of the formal dining room and gourmet kitchen. The main-level bedrooms share a bath and have individual porch access. Upstairs is dedicated to the master suite. The lavish bath has a magnificent garden tub and a wrapping vanity.

PLAN | *6808*

Bedroom: 3   Width: 48'0"
Bath: 2   Depth: 42'0"
Foundation: Island basement
Exterior Walls: 2x6

Main Level: 1,383 sq ft
Upper Level: 595 sq ft
Living Area: 1,978 sq ft
Price Code: **C1**

FOR PHOTOGRAPHY
SEE PAGES
28-33, 50-53

1-800-718-PLAN

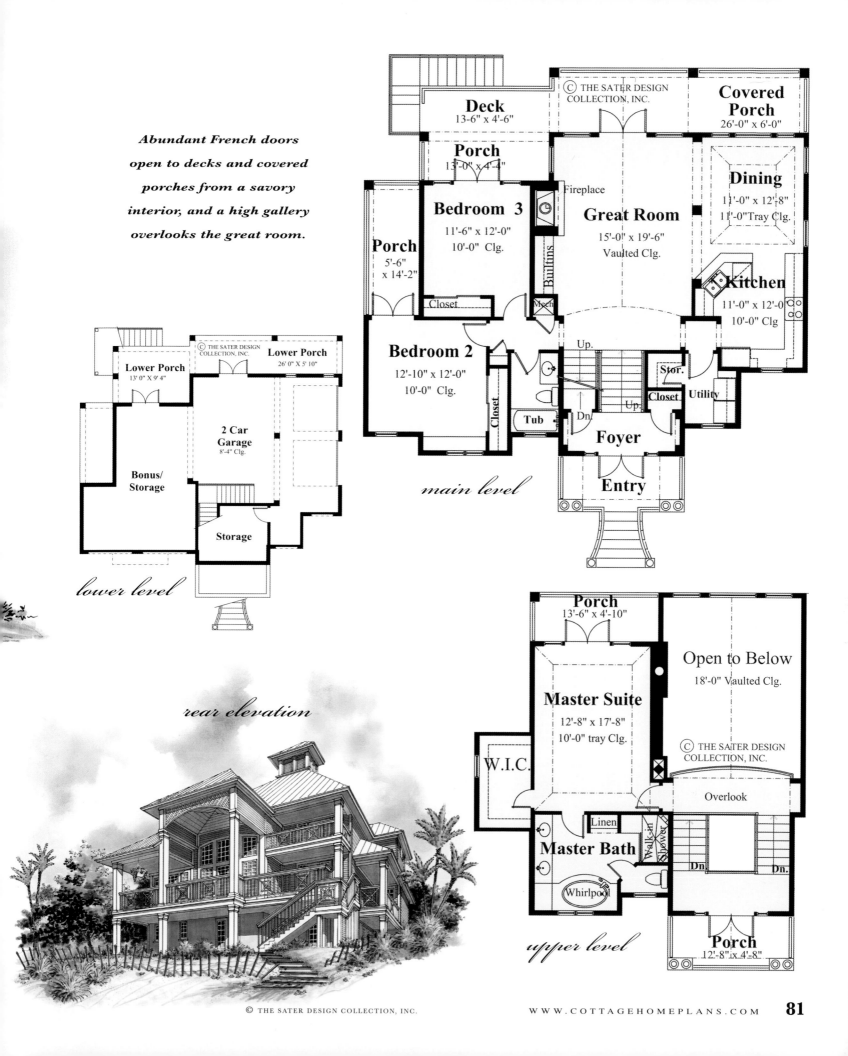

Abundant French doors open to decks and covered porches from a savory interior, and a high gallery overlooks the great room.

Deck
13-6" x 4'-6"

© THE SATER DESIGN COLLECTION, INC.

Covered Porch
26'-0" x 6'-0"

Porch
13'-0" x 4'-4"

Fireplace

Dining
11'-0" x 12'-8"
11'-0" Tray Clg.

Bedroom 3
11'-6" x 12'-0"
10'-0" Clg.

Porch
5'-6"
x 14'-2"

Great Room
15'-0" x 19'-6"
Vaulted Clg.

Builtins

Kitchen
11'-0" x 12'-0"
10'-0" Clg

Closet

Mech

Bedroom 2
12'-10" x 12'-0"
10'-0" Clg.

Closet

Up.

Stor.

Closet

Utility

Tub

Dn.

Up.

Foyer

Lower Porch
13' 0" X 9' 4"

Lower Porch
26' 0" X 5' 10"

© THE SATER DESIGN COLLECTION, INC.

2 Car Garage
8'-4" Clg.

Bonus/ Storage

Storage

lower level

main level

Entry

rear elevation

Porch
13'-6" x 4'-10"

Open to Below
18'-0" Vaulted Clg.

Master Suite
12'-8" x 17'-8"
10'-0" tray Clg.

© THE SATER DESIGN COLLECTION, INC.

W.I.C.

Overlook

Linen

Dn.

Dn.

Walk-in Shower

Master Bath

Whirlpool

upper level

Porch
12'-8" x 4'-8"

© THE SATER DESIGN COLLECTION, INC.

Charleston Hill

With charming curbside appeal, this Southern cottage calls up the past with its welcoming porch entry. A relaxed interior makes everyday life simple. An array of French doors open to the verandah, letting in breezes that reflect the freedom of movement between its living spaces.

The spacious kitchen, equipped with a stand-alone island, adjoins the dining area and nearby powder room. Upstairs, the main hall separates the guest bedrooms that share a bath. The master suite pampers the owners with a walk-in closet, lush bath and deck access. The ground level hosts the entry porch, foyer, oversized garage and a back lanai.

PLAN | *6855*

Bedroom: 3   Width: 34'0"
Bath: 2-1/2   Depth: 43'0"
Foundation: Island basement
Exterior Walls: 2x6

Main Level: 874 sq ft
Upper Level: 880 sq ft
Lower Foyer: 242 sq ft

Living Area: 1,996 sq ft

Price Code: **C 1**

1-800-718-PLAN

© THE SATER DESIGN COLLECTION, INC.

Porch
39' 0" x 7' 6"
10' 6" Clg.

Window Seat

Built-in Cabinetry

Great Room
18' 0" x 20' 0"
10' 0" Clg.

Fireplace

Built-in Cabinetry

Window Seat

Dining
10' 0" x 13' 0"
10' 0" Clg.

Kitchen
15' 0" x 15' 0"
10' 0" Clg.

Dn.

Up

Utility

P.B.

main level

© THE SATER DESIGN COLLECTION, INC.

Porch
39' 0" x 7' 6"
9' 0" Clg.

Walk-in Shower

Bedroom 3
10' 0" x 13'
9'-4" Clg.

Master Bath

Master Suite
13' 0" x 13' 0"
10'-4" Clg.

W.I.C.

W.I.C.

Linen

Dn.

Open to Below

Walk-in Shower

Bath 2

Bedroom 2
12' 8" x 11' 0"
9'-4" Clg.

upper level

rear elevation

© THE SATER DESIGN COLLECTION, INC.

Porch
39' 0" x 7' 6"
9' 4" Clg.

2 1/2 Car Garage
20' 0" x 29' 0"
10' 0" Clg.

Optional Utility

Mech.

W.I.C.

Foyer

Up

Entry Porch

lower level

© THE SATER DESIGN COLLECTION, INC.

Cottage | 2123 SQ. FT.

© THE SATER DESIGN COLLECTION, INC.

Duvall Street

Key West Conch-style blends Old World charm with up-to-date comfort in this picturesque design. A glass-paneled entry lends a warm welcome and complements a captivating front balcony.

Two sets of French doors open the great room to wide views and extend the living areas to the back covered porch. A gourmet kitchen is prepared for any occasion with a prep sink, plenty of counter space, an ample pantry and an eating bar. The mid-level landing leads to two additional bedrooms, a full bath and a windowed art niche.

Double French doors open the upper level master suite to a sundeck and offer powerful views from the bedroom, where sunsets may be viewed from the privacy of the deck.

PLAN | *6701*

Bedroom: 3   Width: 27'6"
Bath: 2-1/2   Depth: 64'0"
Foundation: Post/Pier
Exterior Walls: 2x6

Main Level: 878 sq ft
Upper Level: 1,245 sq ft
Living Area: 2,123 sq ft
Price Code: **C2**

FOR PHOTOGRAPHY
SEE PAGES 22-27
1-800-718-PLAN

upper level

sundeck
26'-0" x 10'-0" avg.

master
16'-6" x 15'-0"
vault. clg.

sundeck

©THE Sater DESIGN
COLLECTION, INC.

w.i.c.

art

study/br.
12'-0" x 10'-0"
9'-0" clg.

w.i.c.

dn.
up

landing

art

br. 2
9'-8" x 11'-0"
9'-0" clg.

br. 3
9'-8" x 11'-0"
9'-0" clg.

upper level

main level

down

covered porch
26'-0" x 10'-0" avg.

built ins

great room
18'-0" x 16'-0" avg.
10'-0" clg.

covered porch

fireplace

tv niche

eating bar

dining
10'-0" x 12'-0"
10'-0" clg.

kitchen

15' x 13'

half wall

up

equip

d
w

pantry

up

©THE Sater DESIGN
COLLECTION, INC.

foyer

garage
19'-0" x 19'-0"

covered entry

main level

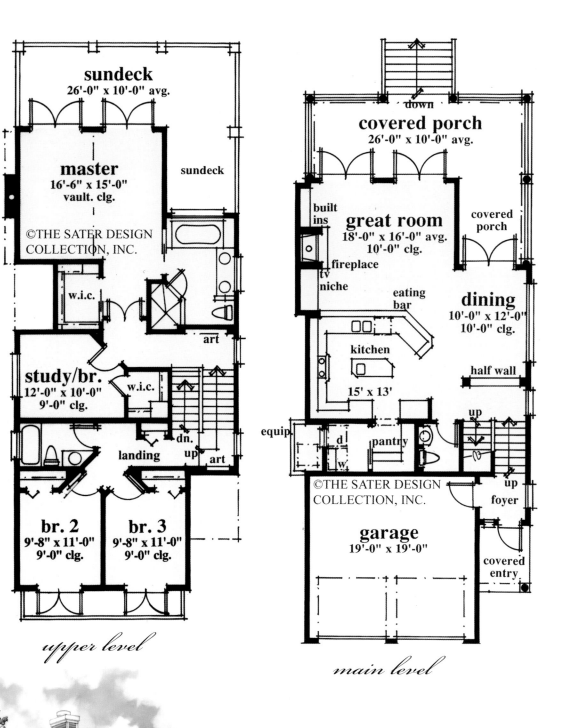

rear elevation

*Double porticos and sunburst
transoms dress up this
Key West Conch plan.
Round columns define the
covered porch,
while crafted details unify the
living levels with room for
growth and guests.*

© THE SATER DESIGN COLLECTION, INC.

Cottage | 2136 SQ. FT.

© THE SATER DESIGN COLLECTION, INC.

Newport Cove

This raised Tidewater design, featuring a steep metal roof, horizontal siding and arched-top windows, combines a sense of the past, while a redefined interior provides today's modern conveniences. At the heart of the home, a hip vaulted ceiling, a cozy fireplace, and wall of built-in cabinetry enhance the great room. French doors open, letting in fresh air and sunshine from the porch. For more formal events, radiant dining room windows highlight an outdoor view of the sunset.

Secondary bedrooms decorated with beautiful windows and ample wardrobes share a Jack and Jill bath. The lower level has a two-car garage and additional storage, which could easily convert to a game room or home theater.

PLAN | *6843*

Bedroom: 3   Width: 44'0"

Bath: 2   Depth: 63'0"

Foundation: Island basement

Exterior Walls: 2x6

Main Level: 2,136 sq ft

Living Area: 2,136 sq ft

Price Code: **C2**

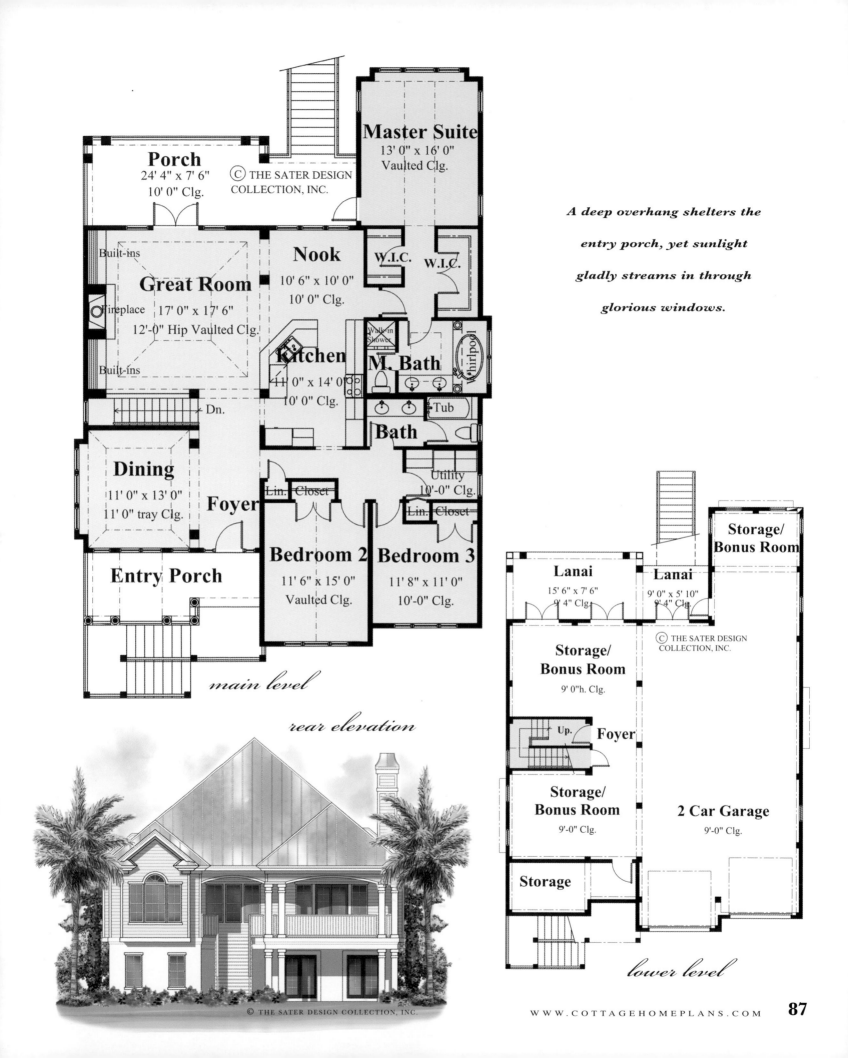

Porch
24' 4" x 7' 6"
10' 0" Clg.

Master Suite
13' 0" x 16' 0"
Vaulted Clg.

© THE SATER DESIGN
COLLECTION, INC.

*A deep overhang shelters the
entry porch, yet sunlight
gladly streams in through
glorious windows.*

Built-ins

Nook
10' 6" x 10' 0"
10' 0" Clg.

W.I.C.

W.I.C.

Great Room
17' 0" x 17' 6"
12'-0" Hip Vaulted Clg.

Fireplace

Built-ins

Kitchen
11' 0" x 14' 0"
10' 0" Clg.

Walk-in Shower

M. Bath

Whirlpool

Dn.

Bath

Tub

Dining
11' 0" x 13' 0"
11' 0" tray Clg.

Foyer

Lin. Closet

Utility
10'-0" Clg.

Lin. Closet

Entry Porch

Bedroom 2
11' 6" x 15' 0"
Vaulted Clg.

Bedroom 3
11' 8" x 11' 0"
10'-0" Clg.

main level

Lanai
15' 6" x 7' 6"
9' 4" Clg.

Lanai
9' 0" x 5' 10"
9' 4" Clg.

**Storage/
Bonus Room**

**Storage/
Bonus Room**
9' 0"h. Clg.

© THE SATER DESIGN
COLLECTION, INC.

Up.

Foyer

**Storage/
Bonus Room**
9'-0" Clg.

2 Car Garage
9'-0" Clg.

Storage

lower level

rear elevation

© THE SATER DESIGN COLLECTION, INC.

Captiva Island

© THE SATER DESIGN COLLECTION, INC.

Abaco Bay

Lattice walls and horizontal siding complement a relaxed island-style design. Sunburst transoms lend a romantic spirit to this seaside destination, perfect for waterfront properties. Inside, an elegant interior doesn't miss a step, with an open foyer that leads to an expansive great room, made cozy by a warming hearth.

The upper level is dedicated to the master suite — a perfect, and private, homeowner's retreat. French doors reveal a vestibule open to both bedroom and bath. A sizeable walk-in closet and a morning kitchen complement lavish amenities in the bath: a vanity with an arched soffit ceiling above, a dormered spa-style tub and an oversized shower with a seat. Enclosed storage plus bonus space is tucked away on the lower level.

PLAN | 6655

Bedroom: 3	Width: 50'0"
Bath: 2	Depth: 44'0"
Foundation: Post/Pier	
Exterior Walls: 2x6	

Main Level:	1,586 sq ft
Upper Level:	601 sq ft
Living Area:	2,187 sq ft
Price Code:	**C2**

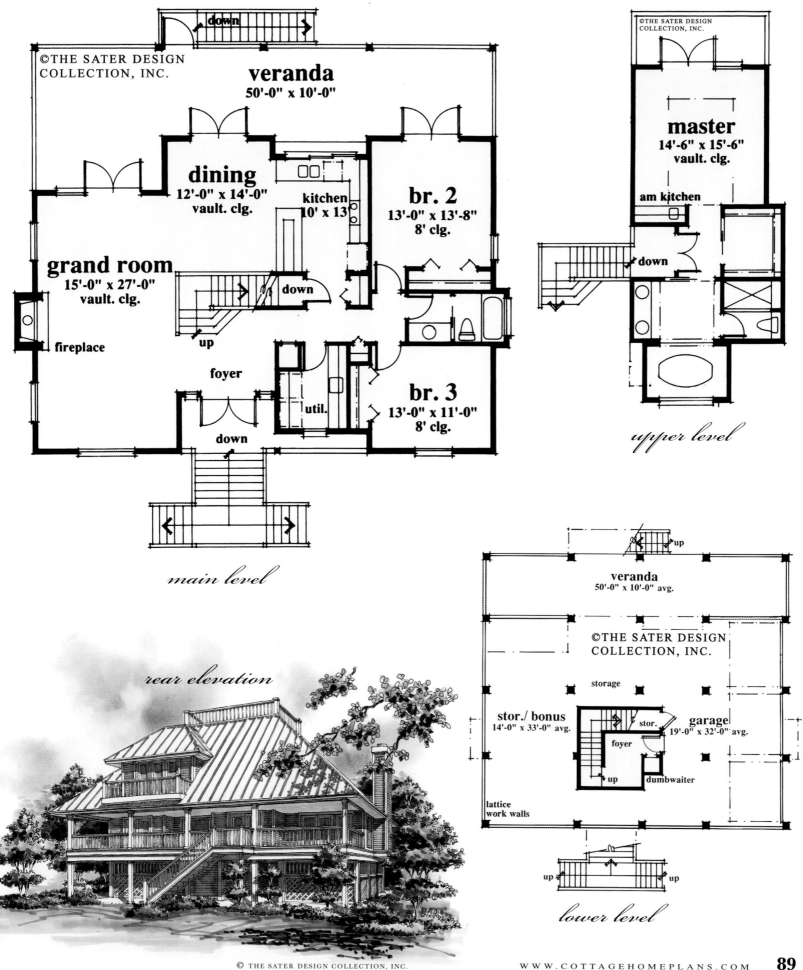

©THE SATER DESIGN
COLLECTION, INC.

veranda
50'-0" x 10'-0"

dining
12'-0" x 14'-0"
vault. clg.

kitchen
10' x 13

br. 2
13'-0" x 13'-8"
8' clg.

grand room
15'-0" x 27'-0"
vault. clg.

down

fireplace

up

foyer

util.

br. 3
13'-0" x 11'-0"
8' clg.

down

main level

rear elevation

©THE SATER DESIGN
COLLECTION, INC.

master
14'-6" x 15'-6"
vault. clg.

am kitchen

down

upper level

veranda
50'-0" x 10'-0" avg.

©THE SATER DESIGN
COLLECTION, INC.

storage

stor./ bonus
14'-0" x 33'-0" avg.

stor.

foyer

up

dumbwaiter

garage
19'-0" x 32'-0" avg.

lattice
work walls

up

up

lower level

© THE SATER DESIGN COLLECTION, INC.

Cottage | 2190 SQ. FT.

© THE SATER DESIGN COLLECTION, INC.

Admiralty Point

A true Southern cottage, this seashore design boasts a great, livable floor plan with room to grow. An expansive great room offers a warming fireplace, built-in shelves and a perfect place for an aquarium. Ready for planned occasions and cozy gatherings, the dining room offers multifunctional space for active lifestyles. A corner walk-in pantry, an eating bar open to the grand room and a windowed morning nook brighten the kitchen.

A secluded master wing opens to the lanai through double French doors. Two walk-in closets surround a vestibule that leads from the bedroom to a luxurious bath. Double doors open from the foyer to a quiet study with wide views of the front property. Lower-level recreation space may be developed into a home theater, game room or hobby area.

PLAN | *6622*

Bedroom: 3   Width: 58'0"

Bath: 2   Depth: 54'0"

Foundation: Slab

Exterior Walls: 2x6

Main Level: 2,190 sq ft

Living Area: 2,190 sq ft

Price Code: **C 2**

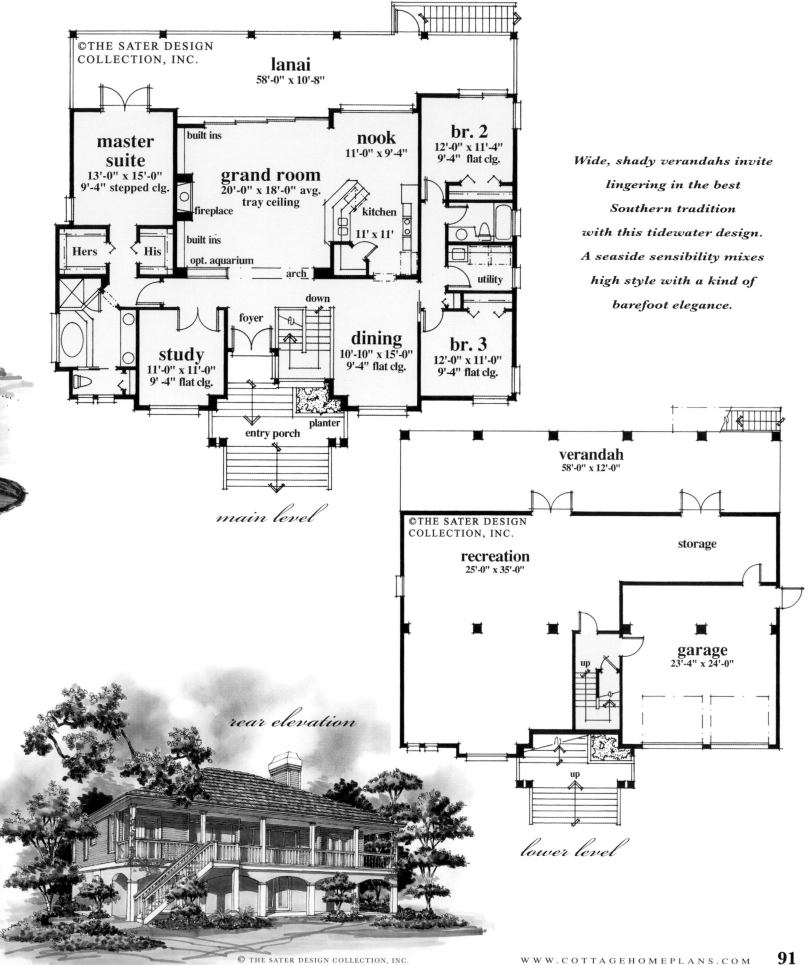

©THE Sater DESIGN
COLLECTION, INC.

lanai
58'-0" x 10'-8"

master
suite
13'-0" x 15'-0"
9'-4" stepped clg.

built ins

nook
11'-0" x 9'-4"

br. 2
12'-0" x 11'-4"
9'-4" flat clg.

grand room
20'-0" x 18'-0" avg.
tray ceiling

fireplace

kitchen
11' x 11'

built ins

Hers   His

opt. aquarium

arch

utility

down

foyer

dining
10'-10" x 15'-0"
9'-4" flat clg.

br. 3
12'-0" x 11'-0"
9'-4" flat clg.

study
11'-0" x 11'-0"
9' -4" flat clg.

planter

entry porch

main level

Wide, shady verandahs invite
lingering in the best
Southern tradition
with this tidewater design.
A seaside sensibility mixes
high style with a kind of
barefoot elegance.

verandah
58'-0" x 12'-0"

©The Sater DESIGN
COLLECTION, INC.

storage

recreation
25'-0" x 35'-0"

garage
23'-4" x 24'-0"

up

up

rear elevation

lower level

© THE Sater DESIGN COLLECTION, INC.

WWW.COTTAGEHOMEPLANS.COM **91**

© THE SATER DESIGN COLLECTION, INC.

Tuckertown Way

The dramatic arched entry of this Southampton-style cottage borrows freely from its Southern coastal past. The foyer and central hall open to the grand room, where a crackling fire is an elegant complement to wild breezes that waft through the spacious interior.

A well-crafted kitchen with hard-working amenities serves the heart of the home. Wrapping counter space, a casual eating bar and a corner walk-in pantry please the cook.

On the opposite side, a secluded master suite offers access to the lanai through French doors. The bedroom leads to an opulent private bath through a dressing area flanked by his and her walk-in closets. A step-up soaking tub, twin lavatories and a glass-enclosed shower highlight the master bath.

PLAN | *6692*

Bedroom: 3	Width: 59'8"
Bath: 2	Depth: 54'0"
Foundation: Slab	
Exterior Walls: 2x6	

Main Level: 2,190 sq ft

Living Area: 2,190 sq ft

Price Code: **C 2**

©THE SATER DESIGN
COLLECTION, INC.

lanai
58'-0" x 10'-8"

down

built ins

**master
suite**
13'-0" x 15'-0"
9'-4" stepped clg.

grand room
20'-0" x 18'-0" avg.
tray ceiling

fireplace

built ins

nook
11'-0" x 9'-4"

br. 2
12'-0" x 11'-4"
9'-4" flat clg.

kitchen
11' x 11'

eating
bar

arch

hers

his

arch

arch

utility

foyer

down

study
11'-0" x 11'-0"
9'-4" flat clg.

dn.

up

dining
10'-10" x 15'-0"
9'-4" flat clg.

arch

br. 3
12'-0" x 11'-0"
9'-4" flat clg.

entry porch

planter

main level

Myrtle Beach, S. Carolina

*Triple gables add vintage Atlantic
character to the modern presence
of this coastal plan.
Galleries open the interior spaces
to gentle breezes, while recreation
space adds room to grow.*

up

verandah
58'-0" x 12'-0"

recreation
25'-0" x 35'-0"

storage

garage
23'-4" x 24'-0"

up

©THE SATER DESIGN
COLLECTION, INC.

up

lower level

rear elevation

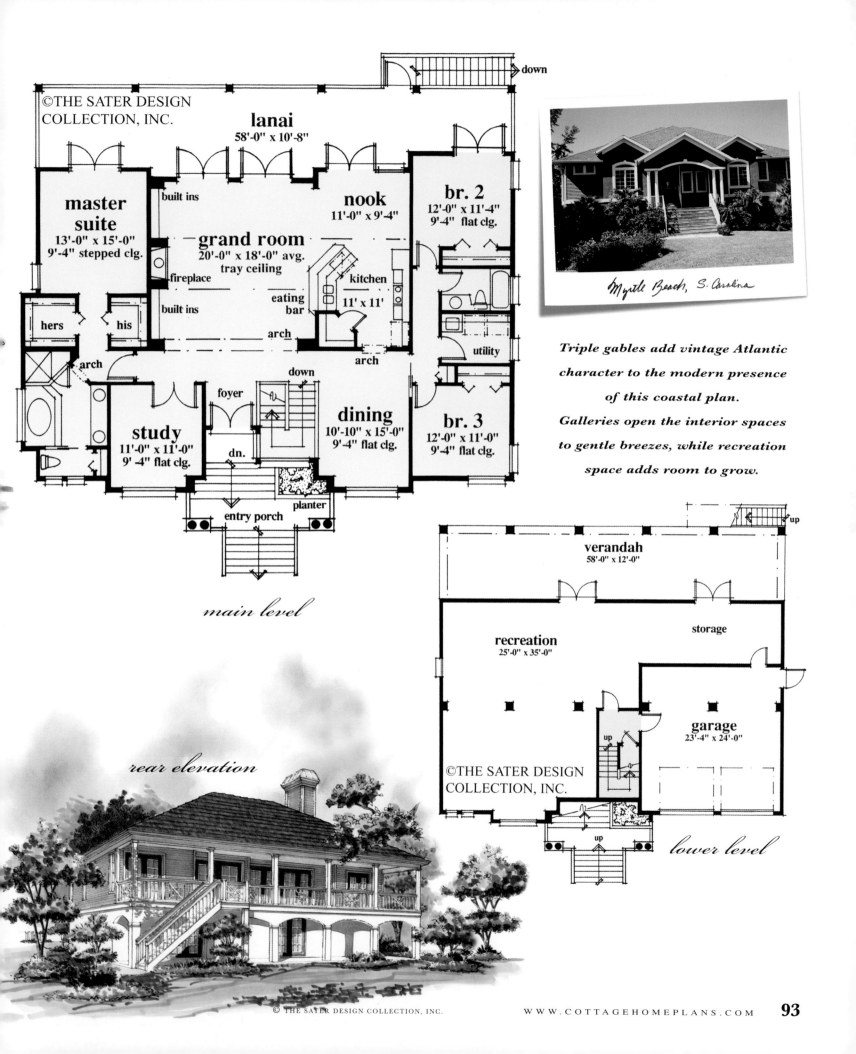

© THE SATER DESIGN COLLECTION, INC.

Papillon

Dramatic rooflines, a wide variety of windows, stucco and horizontal siding adorn this creative Caribbean façade. A mid-level entry opens into a stunning great room, which entertains a warming fireplace and captures views of the great outdoors.

Taking center stage and opening to the great room and dining area, the free-flowing kitchen welcomes any chef. Secluded, the master suite soars with a vaulted ceiling and pampers with a garden tub, walk-in shower and dual vanities. Intimate conversation and midnight air can be enjoyed from the private patio.

PLAN | *6813*

Bedroom: 3	Width: 45'4"
Bath: 2-1/2	Depth: 50'0"
Foundation: Island basement	
Exterior Walls: 2x6	

Main Level:	1,537 sq ft
Upper Level:	812 sq ft
Living Area:	2,349 sq ft
Price Code:	**C 2**

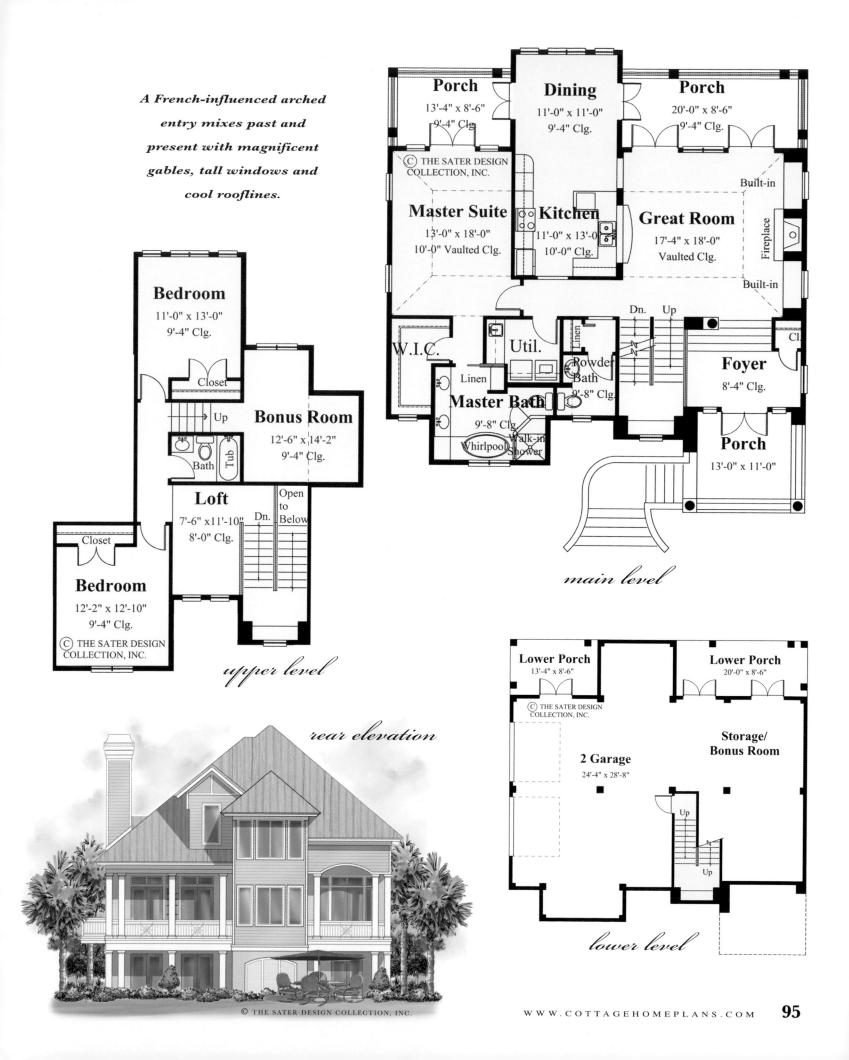

A French-influenced arched entry mixes past and present with magnificent gables, tall windows and cool rooflines.

Porch
13'-4" x 8'-6"
9'-4" Clg.

Dining
11'-0" x 11'-0"
9'-4" Clg.

Porch
20'-0" x 8'-6"
9'-4" Clg.

© THE SATER DESIGN COLLECTION, INC.

Master Suite
13'-0" x 18'-0"
10'-0" Vaulted Clg.

Kitchen
11'-0" x 13'-0"
10'-0" Clg.

Built-in

Great Room
17'-4" x 18'-0"
Vaulted Clg.

Fireplace

Built-in

W.I.C.

Util.

Linen

Dn.   Up

Cl.

Foyer
8'-4" Clg.

Linen

Master Bath
9'-8" Clg.

Powder Bath
9'-8" Clg.

Whirlpool

walk-in Shower

Porch
13'-0" x 11'-0"

main level

Bedroom
11'-0" x 13'-0"
9'-4" Clg.

Closet

Up

Bath

Tub

Bonus Room
12'-6" x 14'-2"
9'-4" Clg.

Closet

Bedroom
12'-2" x 12'-10"
9'-4" Clg.

Loft
7'-6" x 11'-10"
8'-0" Clg.

Dn.

Open to Below

© THE SATER DESIGN COLLECTION, INC.

upper level

Lower Porch
13'-4" x 8'-6"

Lower Porch
20'-0" x 8'-6"

© THE SATER DESIGN COLLECTION, INC.

2 Garage
24'-4" x 28'-8"

Storage/ Bonus Room

Up

Up

lower level

rear elevation

© THE SATER DESIGN COLLECTION, INC.

© THE SATER DESIGN COLLECTION, INC.

Linden Place

This delightful cottage with its array of windows and doors invites in the sights and sounds of nature. A porch adorns the front entryway and opens into the main foyer, which sports an art niche. The great room, with its high ceiling, features a natural fireplace and built-in cabinets and opens onto the back porch by pairs of French doors. Large windows set off the formal dining room and bring in tranquil views.

The kitchen is conveniently located near the main living areas, making entertaining easy. The master suite is enriched with a tray ceiling, tall windows and a pampering bath. On the upper level, the loft is situated between two guest rooms — both equipped with private baths and covered porches and connected by an open viewing deck.

PLAN | 6805

Bedroom: 3   Width: 44'0"
Bath: 3-1/2   Depth: 49'0"
Foundation: Island basement
Exterior Walls: 2x6

Main Level: 1,510 sq ft
Upper Level: 864 sq ft

Living Area: 2,374 sq ft

Price Code: **C2**

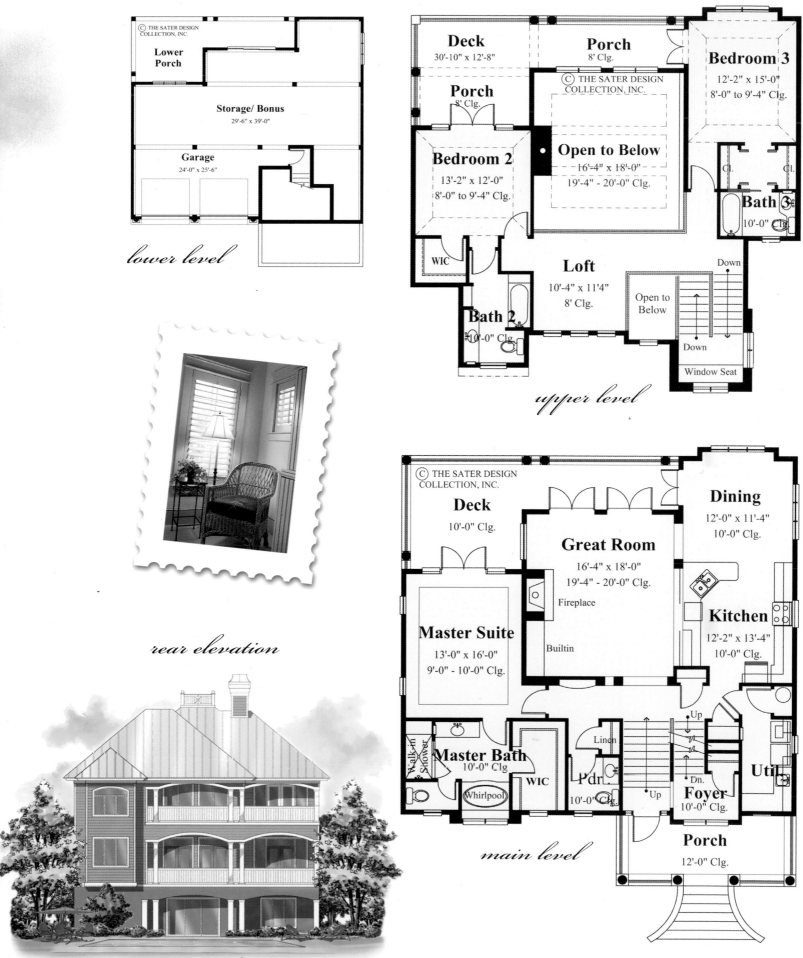

© THE SATER DESIGN COLLECTION, INC.

Lower Porch

Storage/ Bonus
29'-6" x 39'-0"

Garage
24'-0" x 25'-6"

lower level

Deck
30'-10" x 12'-8"

Porch
8' Clg.

© THE SATER DESIGN COLLECTION, INC.

Porch
8' Clg.

Bedroom 3
12'-2" x 15'-0"
8'-0" to 9'-4" Clg.

Bedroom 2
13'-2" x 12'-0"
8'-0" to 9'-4" Clg.

Open to Below
16'-4" x 18'-0"
19'-4" - 20'-0" Clg.

Cl.   Cl.

Bath 3
10'-0" Clg.

WIC

Loft
10'-4" x 11'4"
8' Clg.

Open to Below

Down

Bath 2
10'-0" Clg.

Down

Window Seat

upper level

rear elevation

© THE SATER DESIGN COLLECTION, INC.

Deck
10'-0" Clg.

Great Room
16'-4" x 18'-0"
19'-4" - 20'-0" Clg.

Fireplace

Dining
12'-0" x 11'-4"
10'-0" Clg.

Kitchen
12'-2" x 13'-4"
10'-0" Clg.

Master Suite
13'-0" x 16'-0"
9'-0" - 10'-0" Clg.

Builtin

Walk-in Shower

Master Bath
10'-0" Clg.

Whirlpool

WIC

Linen

Up

Pdr.
10'-0" Clg.

Up

Dn.

Foyer
10'-0" Clg.

Util.

Porch
12'-0" Clg.

main level

© THE SATER DESIGN COLLECTION, INC.

97

Cottage | 2376 SQ. FT.

© THE SATER DESIGN COLLECTION, INC.

Spyglass Hill

Lattice panels, shutters and a steeply pitched metal roof speak softly of early Caribbean plantation style and add character to this island cottage.

Lovely French doors infuse the interior space with a sense of the outdoors, and invite gracious entertaining on the verandah. An elegant dining room shares the glow of the great room's fireplace and captures views of the rear grounds through a picture window. The open stairway wall nearby offers space for a buffet or a china hutch.

Upstairs in the sumptuous master suite, two walk-in closets introduce a grand bath that offers a windowed whirlpool tub, a double bowl vanity and a separate shower.

PLAN | *6615*

Bedroom: 3	Width: 54'0"
Bath: 2	Depth: 44'0"
Foundation: Slab/Piling	
Exterior Walls: 2x6	

Main Level:	1,736 sq ft
Upper Level:	640 sq ft
Living Area:	2,376 sq ft
Price Code:	**C 2**

1-800-718-PLAN

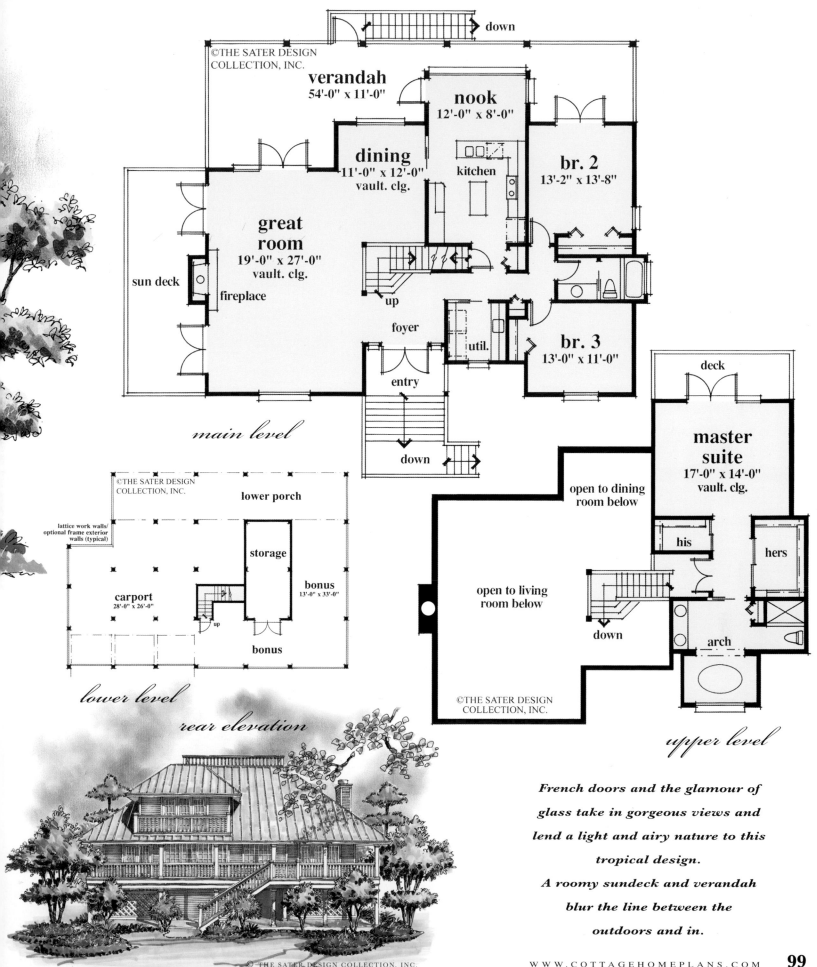

©THE SATER DESIGN
COLLECTION, INC.

verandah
54'-0" x 11'-0"

nook
12'-0" x 8'-0"

dining
11'-0" x 12'-0"
vault. clg.

kitchen

br. 2
13'-2" x 13'-8"

**great
room**
19'-0" x 27'-0"
vault. clg.

sun deck

fireplace

up

foyer

util.

br. 3
13'-0" x 11'-0"

entry

down

main level

©THE SATER DESIGN
COLLECTION, INC.

lower porch

lattice work walls/
optional frame exterior
walls (typical)

storage

carport
28'-0" x 26'-0"

bonus
13'-0" x 33'-0"

up

bonus

lower level

rear elevation

deck

**master
suite**
17'-0" x 14'-0"
vault. clg.

open to dining
room below

his

hers

open to living
room below

down

arch

©THE SATER DESIGN
COLLECTION, INC.

upper level

*French doors and the glamour of
glass take in gorgeous views and
lend a light and airy nature to this
tropical design.
A roomy sundeck and verandah
blur the line between the
outdoors and in.*

© THE SATER DESIGN COLLECTION, INC.

© THE SATER DESIGN COLLECTION, INC.

Cottage | 2494 SQ. FT.

Saint Martin

PLAN | *6846*

Cottage style revisits this quaint Caribbean design, promising warmth, comfort and charm. Anchored with a steep metal roof, flat board siding and arched details and enhanced by paned glass doors and windows, this design is truly an island classic. Inside, the foyer steps lead to the main living areas, where front balconies surround a study and multi-faceted utility room. Vaulted ceilings add a spacious feeling to the home, especially in the great room, which overlooks the rear deck.

The island kitchen is open to an adjacent dining nook and has an open serving counter. The master suite is secluded on the left for privacy and has walk-in closets and a pampering bath. Downstairs, alongside the two-car garage, are several storage rooms that offer future development.

Bedroom: 3   Width: 60'0"
Bath: 3   Depth: 52'0"
Foundation: Island basement
Exterior Walls: 2x6

Main Level: 2,385 sq ft
Lower Level Entry: 109 sq ft

Living Area: 2,494 sq ft

Price Code: **C 2**

1 - 8 0 0 - 7 1 8 - P L A N

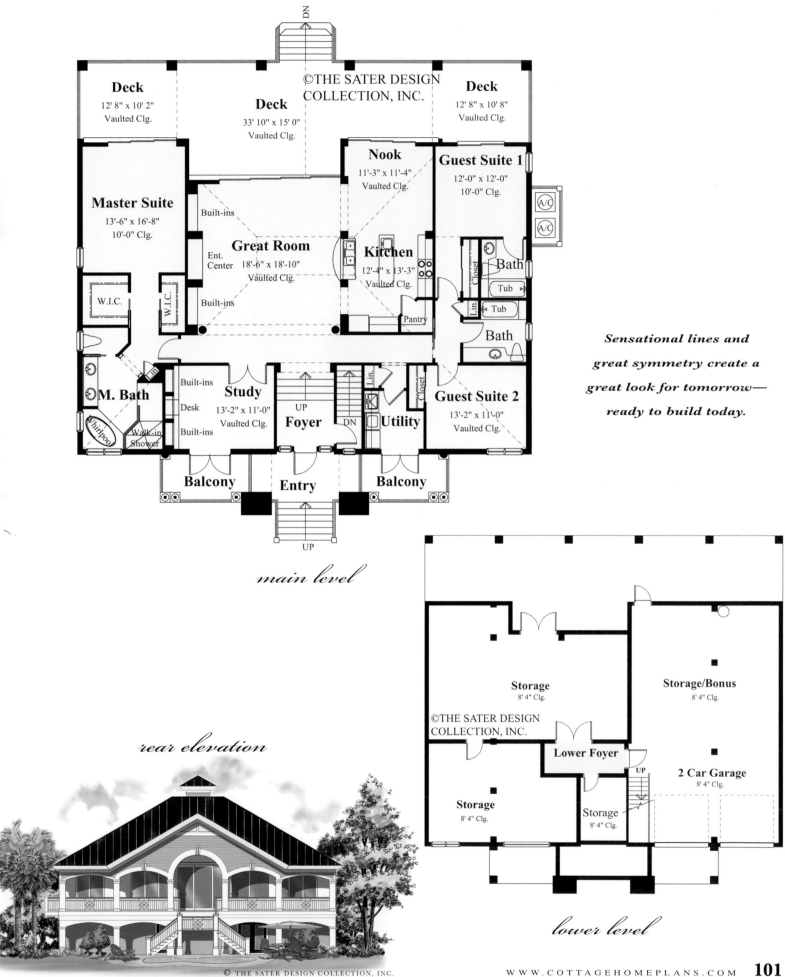

Deck
12' 8" x 10' 2"
Vaulted Clg.

Deck
33' 10" x 15' 0"
Vaulted Clg.

©THE SATER DESIGN
COLLECTION, INC.

Deck
12' 8" x 10' 8"
Vaulted Clg.

Nook
11'-3" x 11'-4"
Vaulted Clg.

Guest Suite 1
12'-0" x 12'-0"
10'-0" Clg.

Master Suite
13'-6" x 16'-8"
10'-0" Clg.

Built-ins

Great Room
18'-6" x 18'-10"
Vaulted Clg.

Kitchen
12'-4" x 13'-3"
Vaulted Clg.

Ent.
Center

Built-ins

W.I.C.

W.I.C.

Closet

Bath

Tub

Lin.

Tub

Pantry

Bath

*Sensational lines and
great symmetry create a
great look for tomorrow—
ready to build today.*

M. Bath

Built-ins

Study
13'-2" x 11'-0"
Vaulted Clg.

Desk

Built-ins

UP

Foyer

DN

Lin.

Closet

Utility

Guest Suite 2
13'-2" x 11'-0"
Vaulted Clg.

Whirlpool

Walk-in
Shower

Balcony

Entry

Balcony

UP

main level

Storage
8' 4" Clg.

Storage/Bonus
8' 4" Clg.

©THE SATER DESIGN
COLLECTION, INC.

rear elevation

Lower Foyer

UP

2 Car Garage
8' 4" Clg.

Storage
8' 4" Clg.

Storage
8' 4" Clg.

lower level

© THE SATER DESIGN COLLECTION, INC.

© THE SATER DESIGN COLLECTION, INC.

Carmel Bay

A high-pitched hip roof tops a Key West style that's light and airy. Sun-drenched porches invite lingering and lazy days. A welcoming foyer exposes a charming arrangement of casual rooms. French doors lead to a quiet study, which features a wall of built-in shelves and panoramic views from the arched window. The moonlight echoes throughout the great room from a wall of glass that also holds remarkable views.

Upstairs, a balcony hall showcases the living area below. The owners' retreat has a cozy alcove, perfect for a chaise lounger and relaxation. The pampering bath has a walk-in shower, garden tub, dual vanities and a large closet.

PLAN | *6810*

Bedroom: 4	Width: 46'0"
Bath: 3	Depth: 51'0"
Foundation: Island basement	
Exterior Walls: 2x6	

Main Level:	1,542 sq ft
Upper Level:	971 sq ft
Living Area:	2,513 sq ft
Price Code:	**C3**

Comfortable outdoor spaces define this perfect-for-entertaining cottage. Sun-kissed decks and covered porches invite sweet lingering and splendid parties.

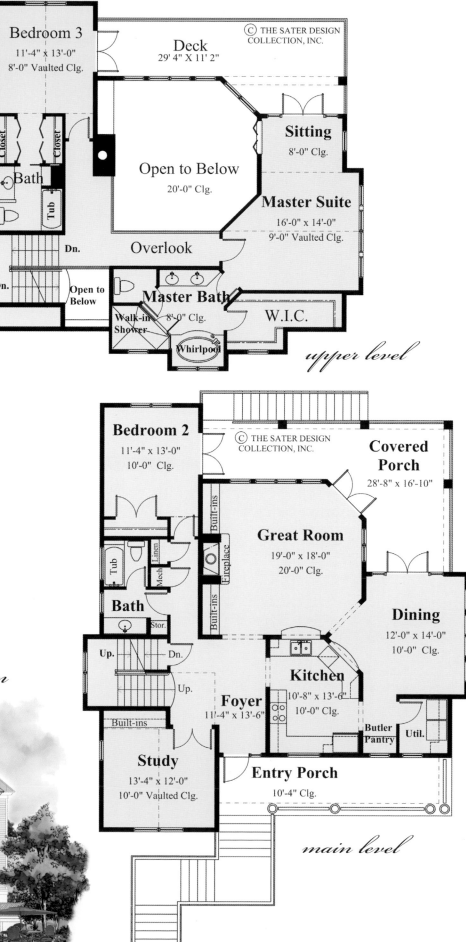

upper level

Bedroom 3
11'-4" x 13'-0"
8'-0" Vaulted Clg.

Deck
29' 4" X 11' 2"

© THE SATER DESIGN COLLECTION, INC.

Sitting
8'-0" Clg.

Closet
Closet

Bath

Tub

Open to Below
20'-0" Clg.

Master Suite
16'-0" x 14'-0"
9'-0" Vaulted Clg.

Dn.

Overlook

Dn.

Open to Below

Master Bath
8'-0" Clg.

Walk-in Shower

Whirlpool

W.I.C.

lower level

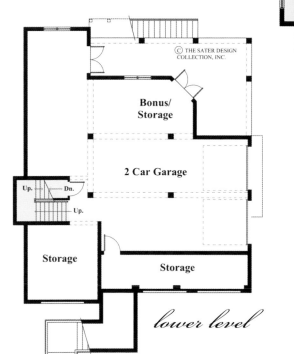

© THE SATER DESIGN COLLECTION, INC.

Bonus/Storage

2 Car Garage

Up. Dn.

Up.

Storage

Storage

rear elevation

main level

Bedroom 2
11'-4" x 13'-0"
10'-0" Clg.

© THE SATER DESIGN COLLECTION, INC.

Covered Porch
28'-8" x 16'-10"

Built-ins

Tub
Linen
Mech

Built-ins
Fireplace

Great Room
19'-0" x 18'-0"
20'-0" Clg.

Built-ins

Bath

Stor.

Up. Dn.

Up.

Foyer
11'-4" x 13'-6"

Kitchen
10'-8" x 13'-6"
10'-0" Clg.

Dining
12'-0" x 14'-0"
10'-0" Clg.

Butler Pantry

Util.

Built-ins

Study
13'-4" x 12'-0"
10'-0" Vaulted Clg.

Entry Porch
10'-4" Clg.

© THE SATER DESIGN COLLECTION, INC.

Cottage | 2520 SQ. FT.

© THE SATER DESIGN COLLECTION, INC.

Bridgeport Harbor

Jamaican plantation houses inspired this cottage design, lovingly revived by the old Charleston Row homes.

Wrap-around porticos on two levels offer seaside views to the living areas. Four sets of French doors bring the outside in to the great room. Fling them wide open and let the crackle of the fireplace play harmony to the soft sounds of the sea.

The upper level master suite features a spacious bath designed for two. Three sets of doors open to the observation deck with a special place for sunning. A guest bedroom on this level leads to a gallery hall with its own access to the deck. Generous bonus space awaits development on the lower level, which true to its Old Charleston roots opens gloriously to a garden courtyard.

PLAN | 6685

Bedroom: 3	Width: 30'6"
Bath: 2-1/2	Depth: 77'6"
Foundation: Slab/Island basement	
Exterior Walls: 2x6	

Main Level:	1,305 sq ft
Upper Level:	1,215 sq ft
Living Area:	2,520 sq ft
Price Code:	**C3**

1-800-718-PLAN

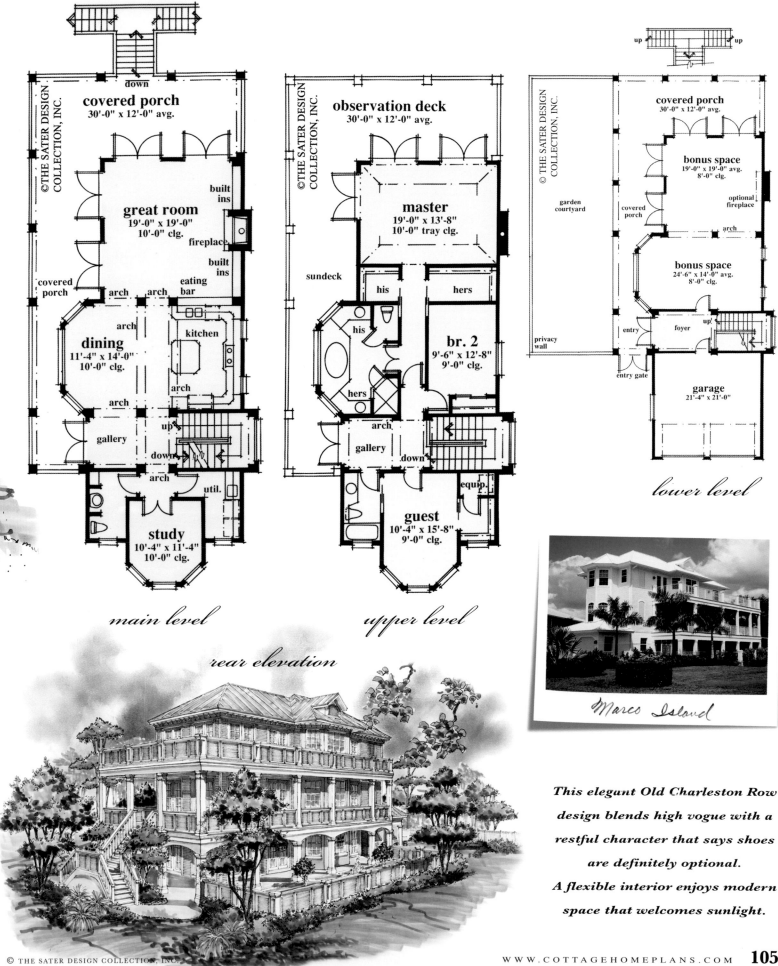

covered porch
30'-0" x 12'-0" avg.

©THE SATER DESIGN COLLECTION, INC.

great room
19'-0" x 19'-0"
10'-0" clg.

built ins

fireplace

built ins

covered porch

arch   arch

eating bar

dining
11'-4" x 14'-0"
10'-0" clg.

arch

kitchen

arch

arch

gallery

up

down

arch

util.

study
10'-4" x 11'-4"
10'-0" clg.

main level

---

observation deck
30'-0" x 12'-0" avg.

©THE SATER DESIGN COLLECTION, INC.

master
19'-0" x 13'-8"
10'-0" tray clg.

sundeck

his   hers

his

br. 2
9'-6" x 12'-8"
9'-0" clg.

hers

arch

gallery

down

equip.

guest
10'-4" x 15'-8"
9'-0" clg.

upper level

---

up   up

©THE SATER DESIGN COLLECTION, INC.

covered porch
30'-0" x 12'-0" avg.

garden courtyard

bonus space
19'-0" x 19'-0" avg.
8'-0" clg.

optional fireplace

covered porch

arch

bonus space
24'-6" x 14'-0" avg.
8'-0" clg.

privacy wall

entry

foyer

up

entry gate

garage
21'-4" x 21'-0"

lower level

---

rear elevation

Marco Island

This elegant Old Charleston Row design blends high vogue with a restful character that says shoes are definitely optional.
A flexible interior enjoys modern space that welcomes sunlight.

© THE SATER DESIGN COLLECTION, INC.

© THE SATER DESIGN COLLECTION, INC.

Laguna Beach

This engaging and comfortable cottage-style home is packed with personality — not to mention great views. Perfection abounds in decorative details without forfeiting convenience.

A formal dining room opens through a colonnade from the central gallery hall and shares the comfort of the fireplace in the great room. Indoor spaces transcend to outdoors, providing a peaceful place to unwind or create additional space for get-togethers. A food-preparation island and walk-in pantry highlight a well-planned kitchen, which provides a pass-thru to the dining room. Serving formal events is easy, with an open arrangement that allows guests to linger outside on the porches.

The home has two full guest suites and features an exceptional master bedroom with bath, views and access to a private porch.

PLAN | *6834*

Bedroom: 3   Width: 70'2"
Bath: 3   Depth: 53'0"
Foundation: Island basement
Exterior Walls: 2x6

Main Level: 2,430 sq ft
Lower Level: 125 sq ft
Living Area: 2,555 sq ft

Price Code: **C3**

1-800-718-PLAN

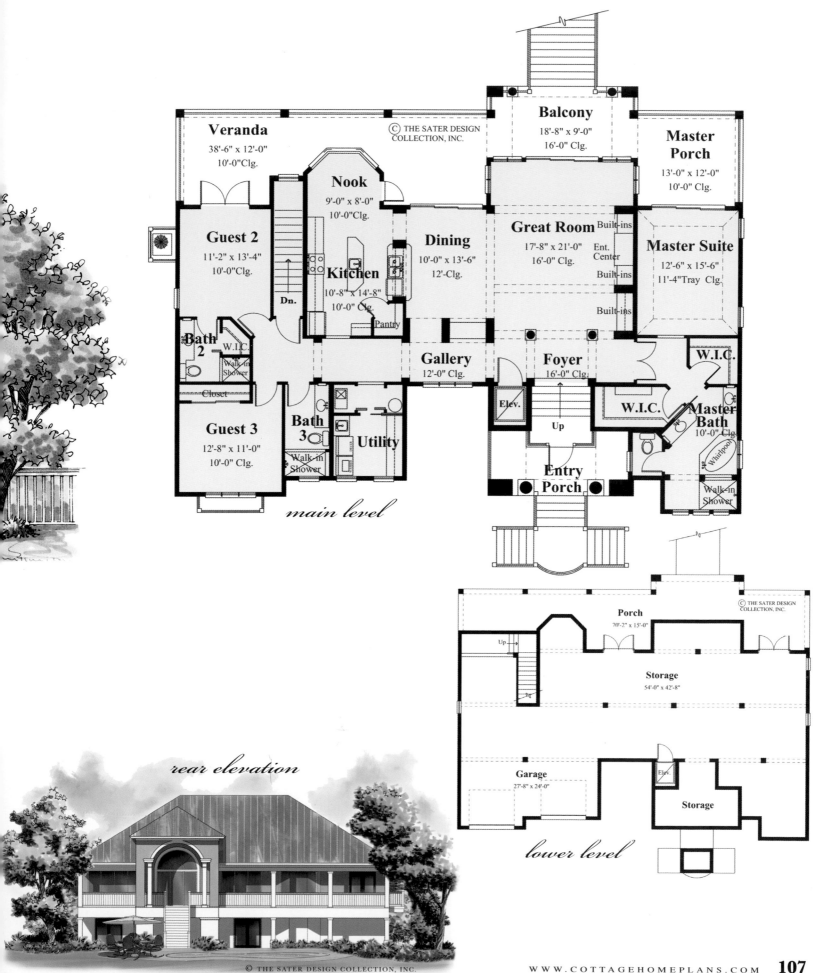

Veranda
38'-6" x 12'-0"
10'-0"Clg.

© THE SATER DESIGN
COLLECTION, INC.

Balcony
18'-8" x 9'-0"
16'-0" Clg.

Master Porch
13'-0" x 12'-0"
10'-0" Clg.

Nook
9'-0" x 8'-0"
10'-0"Clg.

Guest 2
11'-2" x 13'-4"
10'-0"Clg.

Kitchen
10'-8" x 14'-8"
10'-0" Clg.

Dining
10'-0" x 13'-6"
12'-Clg.

Great Room
17'-8" x 21'-0"
16'-0" Clg.

Built-ins
Ent. Center
Built-ins
Built-ins

Master Suite
12'-6" x 15'-6"
11'-4"Tray Clg.

Dn.

Pantry

Bath 2

W.I.C.

Walk-in Shower

Closet

Gallery
12'-0" Clg.

Foyer
16'-0" Clg.

Elev.

W.I.C.

W.I.C.

Master Bath
10'-0" Clg.

Up

Whirlpool

Guest 3
12'-8" x 11'-0"
10'-0" Clg.

Bath 3

Utility

Walk-in Shower

Entry Porch

Walk-in Shower

main level

rear elevation

© THE SATER DESIGN
COLLECTION, INC.

Porch
70'-2" x 15'-0"

Up

Storage
54'-0" x 42'-8"

Elev.

Garage
27'-8" x 24'-0"

Storage

lower level

Cottage | 2569 SQ. FT.

© THE SATER DESIGN COLLECTION, INC.

Walker Way

Lovely balconies and a magnificent circle-head window set off a three-story turret on this Gulf Coast design, perfect for a waterfront property.

A columned archway announces the elegant formal dining room, well lit by the bay windows. Nearby, French doors open to a front balcony where gentle breezes can mingle with the glow and warmth of the interior. The gourmet kitchen is open to the morning nook, which boasts its own bay windows and seaside views. A single French door leads out to the verandah.

The upper level is dedicated to a spacious master suite and a private bayed study. A corner fireplace warms both bedroom and bath in the homeowner's retreat. The soaking tub and glass-enclosed shower have views of the back property.

PLAN | *6697*

Bedroom: 3   Width: 60'0"
Bath: 2-1/2   Depth: 44'6"
Foundation: Slab with pilings
Exterior Walls: 2x6

Main Level: 1,642 sq ft
Upper Level: 927 sq ft
Living Area: 2,569 sq ft
Price Code: **C3**

1-800-718-PLAN

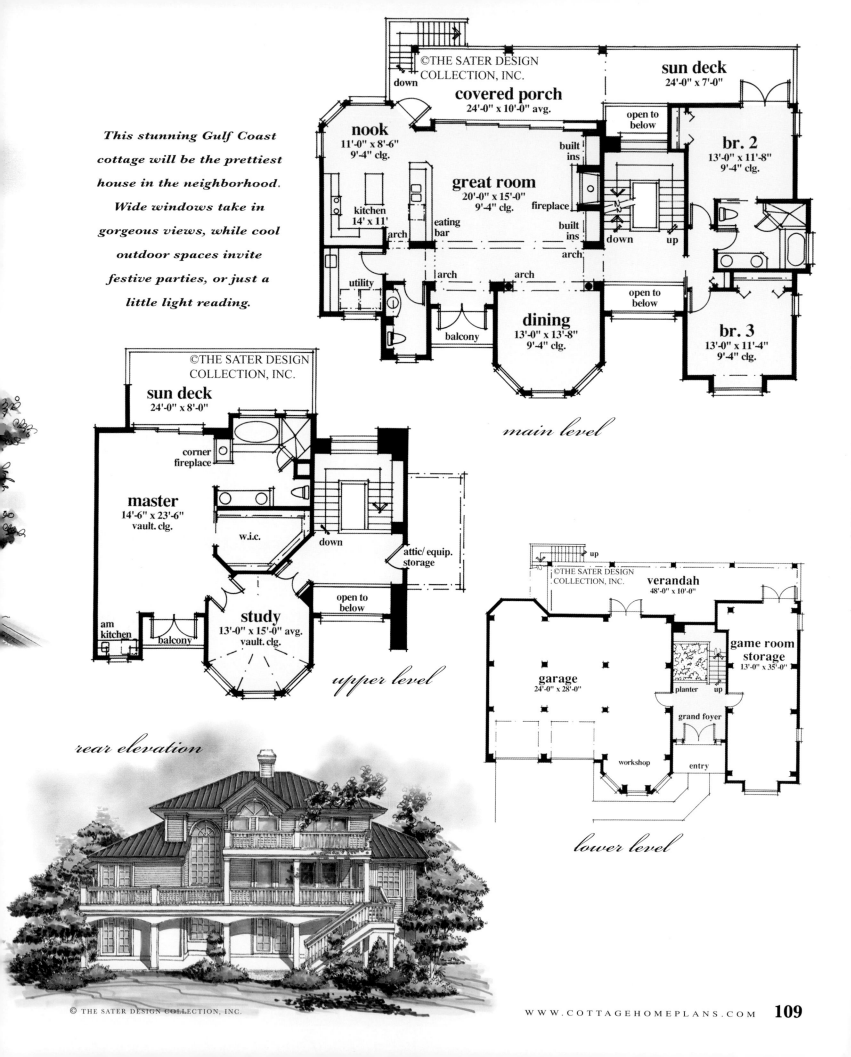

This stunning Gulf Coast cottage will be the prettiest house in the neighborhood. Wide windows take in gorgeous views, while cool outdoor spaces invite festive parties, or just a little light reading.

©THE Sater DESIGN COLLECTION, INC.

covered porch
24'-0" x 10'-0" avg.

sun deck
24'-0" x 7'-0"

down

nook
11'-0" x 8'-6"
9'-4" clg.

br. 2
13'-0" x 11'-8"
9'-4" clg.

open to below

built ins

great room
20'-0" x 15'-0"
9'-4" clg.

kitchen
14' x 11'

fireplace

built ins

eating bar

down

up

arch

arch

arch

arch

utility

balcony

open to below

dining
13'-0" x 13'-8"
9'-4" clg.

br. 3
13'-0" x 11'-4"
9'-4" clg.

main level

©THE Sater DESIGN COLLECTION, INC.

sun deck
24'-0" x 8'-0"

corner fireplace

master
14'-6" x 23'-6"
vault. clg.

w.i.c.

down

attic/ equip. storage

am kitchen

balcony

study
13'-0" x 15'-0" avg.
vault. clg.

open to below

upper level

up

©THE Sater DESIGN COLLECTION, INC.

verandah
48'-0" x 10'-0"

planter

up

game room storage
13'-0" x 35'-0"

garage
24'-0" x 28'-0"

grand foyer

workshop

entry

lower level

rear elevation

© THE Sater DESIGN COLLECTION, INC.

© THE SATER DESIGN COLLECTION, INC.

Key Largo

Welcoming wrap-around porches grace the front of this two-story, narrow cottage design. French doors open the great room and formal dining areas to the outdoors, blending the beauty of nature with the indoors. The island kitchen is thoughtfully designed with a cheerful breakfast nook.

The upstairs wing is home to the master bedroom, two guest suites that share an adjoining bath, and a quiet study. A delightful surprise — each room has doors that open onto the upper deck, offering a pleasant place to enjoy the tranquility of the countryside. At the top of the staircase, the luxurious master suite and octagon sitting area face a two-sided fireplace, the perfect spot to curl up with a book.

PLAN | *6828*

Bedroom: 3	Width: 34'0"
Bath: 2-1/2	Depth: 63'2"
Foundation: Crawlspace	
Exterior Walls: 2x6	

Main Level: 1,296 sq ft
Upper Level: 1,354 sq ft
Living Area: 2,650 sq ft
Price Code: **C3**

1-800-718-PLAN

Master Bath

Whirlpool

Walk-in Shower

W.I.C.

W.I.C.

Optional Vent-Free Fireplace

Sitting Area
13'-0" Octagon
Vaulted Clg

Master Suite
12'-5" x 22'-4"
10'-0" Clg.

Dn.

Bedroom 3
13'-2" x 12'-0"
10'-0" Clg.

W.I.C.

Bath 2

Tub

Loft

Bedroom 2
15'-6" x 12'-0"
10'-0" Clg.

Deck
8'-2" x 42'-4"

Mech.

Study
9'-0" x 14'-6"
11'-4" Clg.

Deck
26'-4" x 10'-0"

© THE SATER DESIGN COLLECTION, INC.

upper level

Rehoboth Beach, Delaware

rear elevation

Utility
10'-8" Clg.

Nook
13'-0" x 9'-0"
10'-8" Clg.

Dn.

Kitchen
12'-0" x 13'-6"
10'-8" Stepped Clg.

Pantry

P.B.

Dining
15' 6" x 12'0"
10'-8" Clg.

Great Room
15' 6" x 17' 8"
10' 8" Coffered Clg.

8' 2" x 42' 4"

Up.

Foyer
10'-0" x 29'-4"

Built-in Cabinetry

Entry Porch

Veranda
25' 6" x 9' 4"

© THE SATER DESIGN COLLECTION, INC.

main level

© THE SATER DESIGN COLLECTION, INC.

© THE SATER DESIGN COLLECTION, INC.

Bridgehampton

Tapered round columns grace the shaded porch area, while a hipped dormer punctuates the roofline above. Attractive corbels adorn the eves and bring character to this sunny cottage.

Elevated ceilings add depth to the open design while the verandahs create lovely outdoor living spaces. When entertaining a house full of guests, the open and functional great room, nook and kitchen create an inviting flow that allows visitors to mingle, even out to the patio. For more formal events, round columns and views of the outdoors define the front dining room.

The main floor also offers two guest rooms that share an adjoining bathroom and nearby laundry. The upstairs is dedicated to the expansive master suite, featuring a cozy sitting area, spacious bath and private veranda.

PLAN | *6837*

Bedroom: 3   Width: 44'0"

Bath: 2   Depth: 55'0"

Foundation: Island basement

Exterior Walls: 2x6

Main Level: 1,671 sq ft

Upper Level: 846 sq ft

Lower Level Entry: 140 sq ft

Living Area: 2,657 sq ft

Price Code: **C3**

1-800-718-PLAN

©THE SATER DESIGN COLLECTION, INC.

Veranda
25' 4" x 12' 0"

Nook
11' 0" x 8' 0"
9' 4"h. Clg.

Window Seat

Bedroom 3
11' 8" x 12' 4"
9' 4" Clg.

Built-in Cabinetry

Great Room
19' 6" x 19' 0"
2-story Clg.

Kitchen
9'-4" Clg.

Closet

Bath

Fireplace

Linen

Tub

Utility

Study
11' 0" x 13' 6"
14' 0" Clg.

Up

Up

Foyer

Dining
11' 0" x 13' 6"
14' 0" Clg.

Linen

Closet

Bedroom 2
11' 8" x 10' 6"
9' 4" Clg.

Entry Porch
32' 0" x 8' 6"
14' 0" Clg.

Dn.

main level

©THE SATER DESIGN COLLECTION, INC.

Lanai
40'-6" x 12'-0"

Storage/ Bonus Room
8'-8"Clg.

Vestibule
Up

3 Car Garage
22'-8" x 33'-8" avg.
9'-0" Clg.

lower level

rear elevation

©THE SATER DESIGN COLLECTION, INC.

Veranda
14' 6" x 7' 6"

Sitting
9' 4" Clg.

Open to Below
Vaulted Clg.

Master Suite
17' 0" x 17' 0"
10' 4" tray Clg.

W.I.C.

Overlook

Dn.

Mech.

Master Bath
9'-4" Clg.

Linen

Walk-in Shower

Whirlpool

upper level

© THE SATER DESIGN COLLECTION, INC.

Cottage | 2659 SQ. FT.

© THE SATER DESIGN COLLECTION, INC.

Seagrove Beach

Bright colors set off this historic but perfectly contemporary façade, enhanced by romantic bay windows, rich with sunburst transoms. Key West island classics inspired a high-pitched metal roof and rear porticos decked with balusters and columns.

A light and airy interior opens to the covered verandah through sliding glass and French doors. The great room brings in spectacular views and features a corner fireplace and an island entertainment center.

A main-level gallery hall leads to a secluded study, which enjoys its own access to the covered verandah. Upstairs, the master suite features a private balcony and sundeck, a well-lit bath and a separate room for computers and books. A gallery loft with a balcony overlook leads to a guest suite.

PLAN | 6682

Bedroom: 3
Bath: 3-1/2
Foundation: Piling
Exterior Walls: 2x6

Width: 50'0"
Depth: 54'0"

Main Level: 1,637 sq ft
Upper Level: 1,022 sq ft
Living Area: 2,659 sq ft
Price Code: **C3**

1-800-718-PLAN

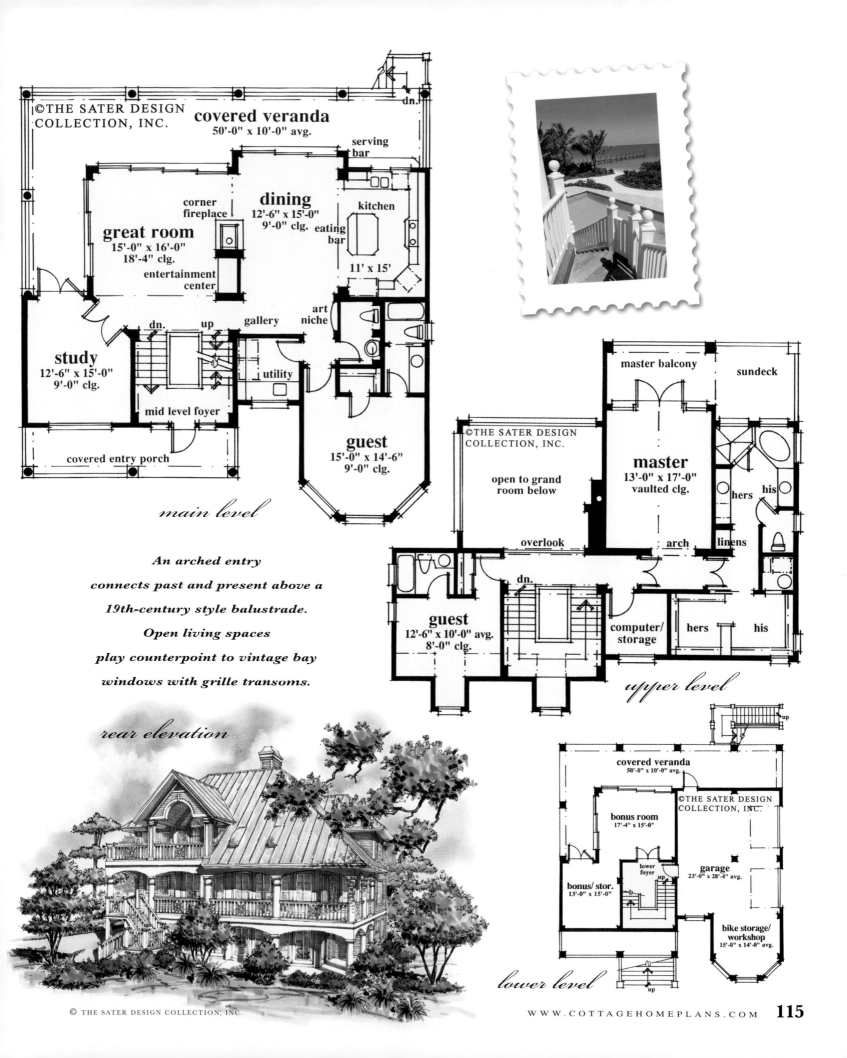

© THE SATER DESIGN COLLECTION, INC.

covered veranda
50'-0" x 10'-0" avg.

serving bar

corner fireplace

dining
12'-6" x 15'-0"
9'-0" clg.

kitchen

great room
15'-0" x 16'-0"
18'-4" clg.

eating bar

11' x 15'

entertainment center

art niche

study
12'-6" x 15'-0"
9'-0" clg.

dn.   up

gallery

utility

mid level foyer

covered entry porch

guest
15'-0" x 14'-6"
9'-0" clg.

main level

An arched entry
connects past and present above a
19th-century style balustrade.
Open living spaces
play counterpoint to vintage bay
windows with grille transoms.

©THE SATER DESIGN COLLECTION, INC.

master balcony

sundeck

open to grand room below

master
13'-0" x 17'-0"
vaulted clg.

hers   his

overlook   arch   linens

guest
12'-6" x 10'-0" avg.
8'-0" clg.

dn.

computer/ storage

hers   his

upper level

rear elevation

covered veranda
50'-0" x 10'-0" avg.

©THE SATER DESIGN COLLECTION, INC.

bonus room
17'-4" x 15'-0"

lower foyer

garage
23'-0" x 28'-4" avg.

bonus/ stor.
13'-0" x 15'-0"

bike storage/ workshop
15'-0" x 14'-0" avg.

lower level

Cottage | 2684 SQ. FT.

© THE SATER DESIGN COLLECTION, INC.

Palma Rios

Clapboard siding and a standing-seam roof set off this cottage elevation —
a comfortable seaside retreat with an easygoing style. A central turret
anchors a series of varied gables and rooflines, evoking the charm of
Caribbean style. Square columns and a spare balustrade define the
perimeter of a spacious entry porch, which leads to a gallery-style foyer.

Pocket doors seclude a forward study featuring a step ceiling and views
of the front property. An open arrangement of the formal rooms progresses
into the plan without restrictions, bounded only by wide views of the
outdoors. Retreating glass doors permit the living and dining spaces to
extend to the veranda. Upstairs, the master suite adjoins a spare room that
could serve as a study, and leads out to a rear deck.

PLAN | 6863

Bedroom: 4   Width: 40'0"
Bath: 2-1/2   Depth: 67'0"
Foundation: Slab
Exterior Walls: 2x6

Main Level: 1,554 sq ft
Upper Level: 1,130 sq ft

Living Area: 2,684 sq ft

Price Code: **C3**

1-800-718-PLAN

Leisure Room
15'-0" x 17'-2"
10'-0" to 11'-0"
Step Clg.

© THE SATER DESIGN
COLLECTION, INC.

Kitchen
14'-8" x 16'-6"
10'-0".

Dining
17'-0" x 12'-6"
10'-0" Clg.

Veranda
10'-10" x 11'-8"
9'-4" Clg.

Pantry

Storage

Desk

P.B.

Living Room
15'-6" x 18'-8"
10'-0"

Fireplace

Utility

Up

Garage
21'-0" x 21'-6"
10'-4" Clg.

Foyer
5'-6" x 10'-6"
10'-0"

Study
11'-8" x 11'-2"
10'-0" to 11'-0"
Step Clg.

Entry/Porch

main level

©THE SATER DESIGN
COLLECTION, INC.

Tub

Walk-in Shower

**Master
Bath**

Master Bedroom
17'-2" x 12'-6"
8'-0" to 9'-0" Tray Clg.

**Master
Porch**
10'-10" x 11'-8"
8'-0" Clg.

W.I.C.

**Open to
Below**
18'-0" Beamed Clg.

Dn.

Closet

Overlook

Bedroom 1
10'-2" x 12'-0"
8'-0" Clg.

Bath

Linen

Tub

Overlook

Closet

**Open
to
Below**

Closet

Bedroom 3
11'-8" x 10'-6"
8'-0" Clg.

Bedroom 2
10'-6" x 11'-8"
8'-0" Clg.

upper level

rear elevation

© THE SATER DESIGN COLLECTION, INC.

© THE SATER DESIGN COLLECTION, INC.

Monterrey Cove

Handsome symmetry defines the visual appeal of this congenial coastal cottage. The inviting entry porch is supported by pairs of columns and a standing-seam metal roof with dormers.

The great room, the gathering area of the home, hosts a two-story ceiling, an open fireplace shared by the dining room, and French doors that open to the verandah, bringing in glorious views. The kitchen stirs the excitement of any chef with a food-preparation island, convenient wrapping counters and a window facing out to the front porch.

A relaxed feeling is felt throughout this spacious home. The wrap-around porches remind us of days gone by, where rocking chairs are optional, of course.

PLAN | *6831*

Bedroom: 3   Width: 54'0"
Bath: 3-1/2   Depth: 57'0"
Foundation: Crawlspace
Exterior Walls: 2x6

Main Level: 1,798 sq ft
Upper Level: 900 sq ft
Living Area: 2,698 sq ft
Price Code: **C3**

1-800-718-PLAN

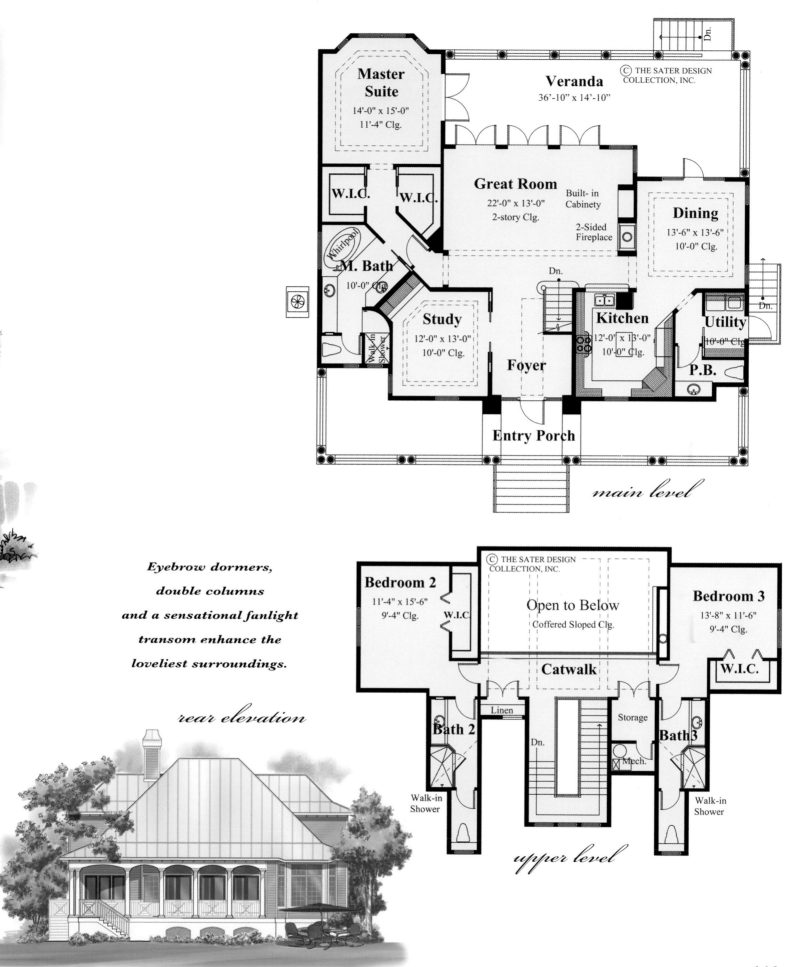

main level

Master Suite
14'-0" x 15'-0"
11'-4" Clg.

Veranda
36'-10" x 14'-10"

© THE SATER DESIGN COLLECTION, INC.

W.I.C.

W.I.C.

Great Room
22'-0" x 13'-0"
2-story Clg.

Built-in Cabinetry

2-Sided Fireplace

Dining
13'-6" x 13'-6"
10'-0" Clg.

Whirlpool

M. Bath
10'-0" Clg.

Walk-in Shower

Study
12'-0" x 13'-0"
10'-0" Clg.

Dn.

Foyer

Kitchen
12'-0" x 13'-0"
10'-0" Clg.

Utility
10'-0" Clg.

Dn.

P.B.

Entry Porch

Eyebrow dormers,
double columns
and a sensational fanlight
transom enhance the
loveliest surroundings.

rear elevation

upper level

Bedroom 2
11'-4" x 15'-6"
9'-4" Clg.

W.I.C.

© THE SATER DESIGN COLLECTION, INC.

Open to Below
Coffered Sloped Clg.

Catwalk

Bedroom 3
13'-8" x 11'-6"
9'-4" Clg.

W.I.C.

Bath 2

Linen

Storage

Bath 3

Walk-in Shower

Dn.

Mech.

Walk-in Shower

© THE SATER DESIGN COLLECTION, INC.

© THE SATER DESIGN COLLECTION, INC.

Monserrat

A truly romantic design, this Southern cottage provides a pleasant retreat to enjoy casual living at its best. The charming exterior adorns well-proportioned features that make the façade stunning. An abundance of glass doors in the octagonal great room invite the best views and plenty of sunlight and breezes to open the mind and soothe the spirit.

The open staircase rises to a lofty second floor that overlooks the main living spaces where two dormered bedrooms have their own baths. In the central hall, a kitchen alcove and computer center open to glorious views. The lower level houses the garage, storage and a bonus room for future growth. An attached patio is multi-functional for cookouts, access to water views or just hanging-out.

PLAN | *6858*

Bedroom: 3   Width: 66'0"
Bath: 3-1/2   Depth: 50'0"
Foundation: Island Basement
Exterior Walls: 2x6

Main Level: 1,855 sq ft
Upper Level: 901 sq ft
Living Area: 2,756 sq ft
Price Code: **C3**

1-800-718-PLAN

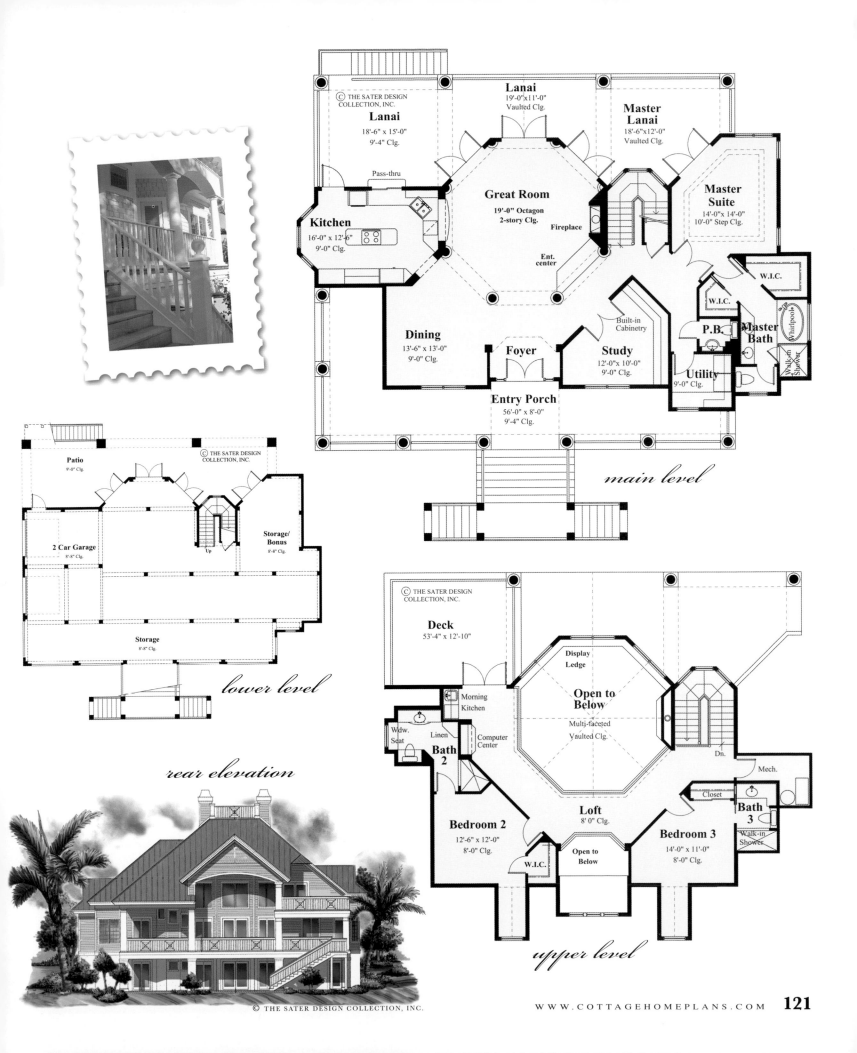

© THE SATER DESIGN COLLECTION, INC.

Lanai
18'-6" x 15'-0"
9'-4" Clg.

Lanai
19'-0"x11'-0"
Vaulted Clg.

Master Lanai
18'-6"x12'-0"
Vaulted Clg.

Pass-thru

Great Room
19'-0" Octagon
2-story Clg.

Fireplace

Master Suite
14'-0"x 14'-0"
10'-0" Step Clg.

Kitchen
16'-0" x 12'-6"
9'-0" Clg.

Ent. center

W.I.C.

W.I.C.

Built-in Cabinetry

P.B.

Master Bath

Whirlpool

Walk-in Shower

Dining
13'-6" x 13'-0"
9'-0" Clg.

Foyer

Study
12'-0"x 10'-0"
9'-0" Clg.

Utility
9'-0" Clg.

Entry Porch
56'-0" x 8'-0"
9'-4" Clg.

main level

© THE SATER DESIGN COLLECTION, INC.

Patio
9'-0" Clg.

2 Car Garage
8'-8" Clg.

Storage/Bonus
8'-8" Clg.

Up

Storage
8'-8" Clg.

lower level

rear elevation

© THE SATER DESIGN COLLECTION, INC.

Deck
53'-4" x 12'-10"

Display Ledge

Open to Below

Multi-faceted Vaulted Clg.

Morning Kitchen

Wdw. Seat

Linen

Computer Center

Bath 2

Loft
8' 0" Clg.

Dn.

Mech.

Closet

Bath 3

Walk-in Shower

Bedroom 2
12'-6" x 12'-0"
8'-0" Clg.

W.I.C.

Open to Below

Bedroom 3
14'-0" x 11'-0"
8'-0" Clg.

upper level

© THE SATER DESIGN COLLECTION, INC.

© THE SATER DESIGN COLLECTION, INC.

Galleon Bay

An array of elegant details creates a wonderful welcome to this contemporary home. A unique and dramatic double-stepped entry staircase and a curved balcony complement the high arched entryway.

With a large, open floor plan and an array of amenities, every gathering will be a success. The foyer embraces the living areas accented by a glass three-sided fireplace and a wet bar. Sliding glass doors bring in a feeling of nature and provide access to a screened-in porch that spans the rear of the home.

The gourmet kitchen delights with its openness to the rest of the house. Here, a nook adds convenience for the family. The kitchen easily interacts with the verandah for outdoor cooking and visiting.

PLAN | *6620*

Bedroom: 3	Width: 64'0"
Bath: 3-1/2	Depth: 45'0"
Foundation: Slab	
Exterior Walls: 2x6	

Main Level:	2,066 sq ft
Upper Level:	809 sq ft
Living Area:	2,875 sq ft

Price Code: **C4**

1-800-718-PLAN

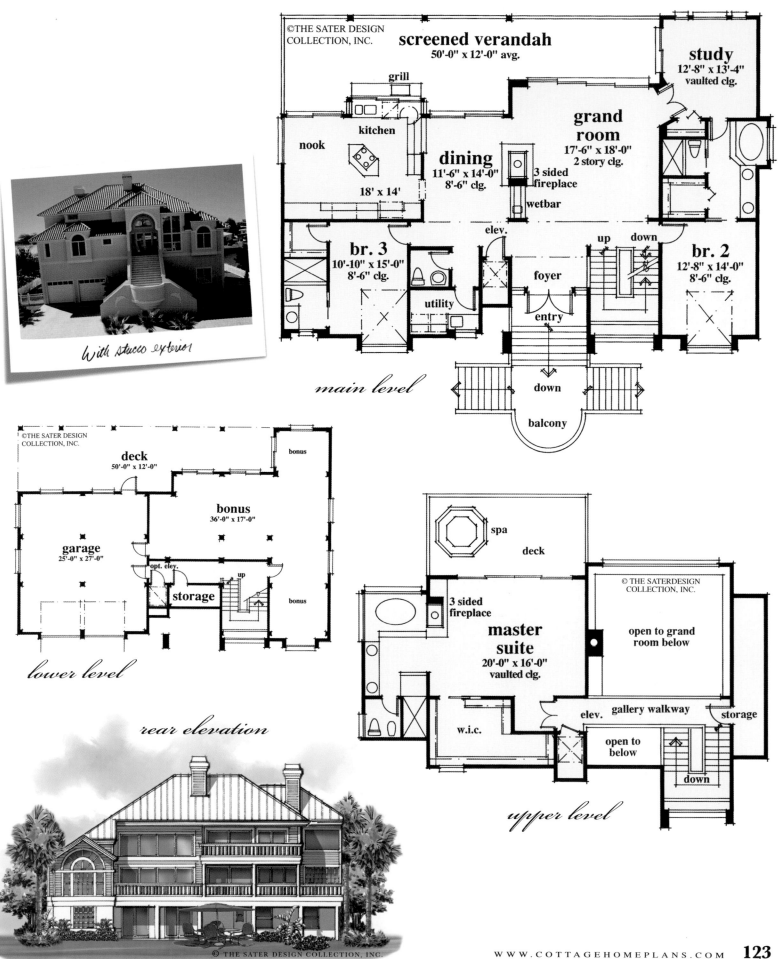

©THE SATER DESIGN COLLECTION, INC.

screened verandah
50'-0" x 12'-0" avg.

grill

study
12'-8" x 13'-4"
vaulted clg.

kitchen

nook

grand room
17'-6" x 18'-0"
2 story clg.

dining
11'-6" x 14'-0"
8'-6" clg.

18' x 14'

3 sided fireplace

wetbar

elev.

up   down

br. 3
10'-10" x 15'-0"
8'-6" clg.

foyer

br. 2
12'-8" x 14'-0"
8'-6" clg.

entry

utility

down

main level

balcony

With stucco exterior

©THE SATER DESIGN COLLECTION, INC.

deck
50'-0" x 12'-0"

bonus

bonus
36'-0" x 17'-0"

garage
25'-0" x 27'-0"

opt. elev.

up

storage

bonus

lower level

spa

deck

© THE SATERDESIGN COLLECTION, INC.

3 sided fireplace

master suite
20'-0" x 16'-0"
vaulted clg.

open to grand room below

elev.   gallery walkway   storage

w.i.c.

open to below

down

upper level

rear elevation

© THE SATER DESIGN COLLECTION, INC.

© THE SATER DESIGN COLLECTION, INC.

Savannah Sound

Stunning New South charm flavors this joyful reinterpretation of Key West island-style. Asymmetrical rooflines set off a grand turret and a two-story bay that allows glorious views within.

Glass doors open the great room to a sun-kissed deck, while arch-top clerestory windows enhance the casual atmosphere with natural light. A corner fireplace and a wet bar create warmth and coziness in the living and dining rooms. The gourmet kitchen boasts a center island with an eating bar for easy meals, plus a windowed wrapping counter.

A winding staircase leads to a luxurious upper-level master suite that opens to a private master balcony, while a morning kitchen offers juice and coffee service. A two-sided fireplace warms both the bedroom and a bath designed for two.

PLAN | *6698*

Bedroom: 3	Width: 45'0"
Bath: 3	Depth: 52'0"
Foundation: Island Basement	
Exterior Walls: 2x6	

Main Level:	1,684 sq ft
Upper Level:	1,195 sq ft
Living Area:	2,879 sq ft
Price Code:	**C3**

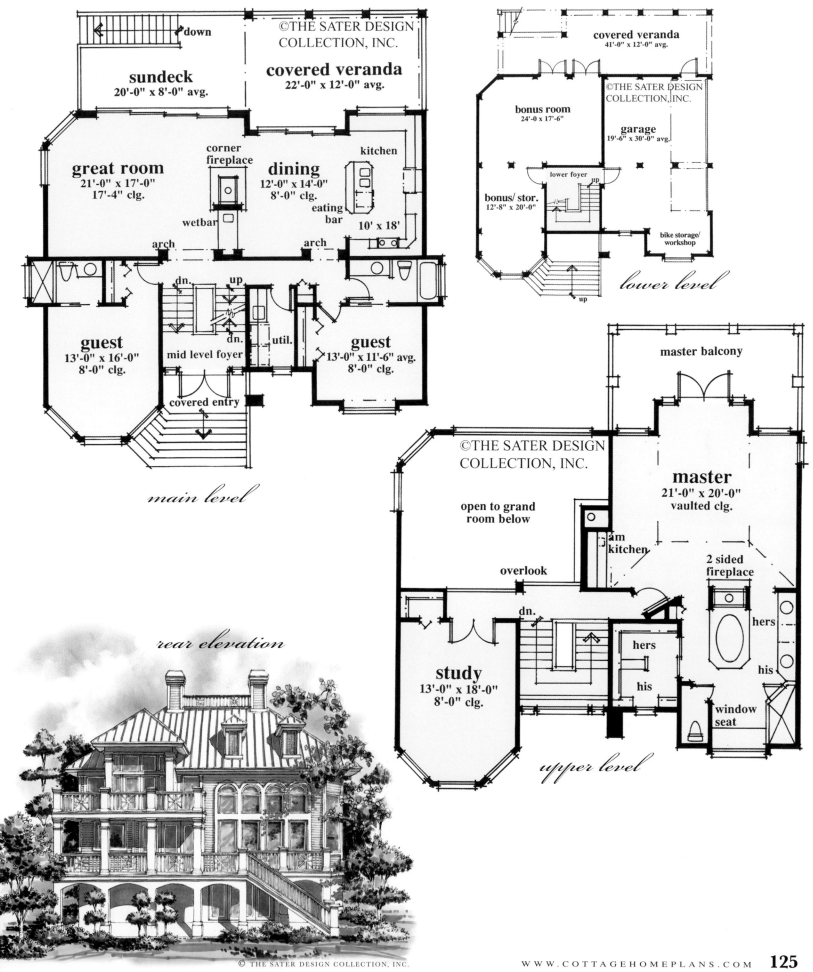

sundeck
20'-0" x 8'-0" avg.

down

©THE Sater Design
COLLECTION, INC.

covered veranda
22'-0" x 12'-0" avg.

great room
21'-0" x 17'-0"
17'-4" clg.

corner
fireplace

dining
12'-0" x 14'-0"
8'-0" clg.

kitchen

wetbar

eating
bar

10' x 18'

arch

arch

dn.

up

dn.

util.

guest
13'-0" x 16'-0"
8'-0" clg.

mid level foyer

guest
13'-0" x 11'-6" avg.
8'-0" clg.

covered entry

main level

rear elevation

covered veranda
41'-0" x 12'-0" avg.

©THE Sater Design
COLLECTION, INC.

bonus room
24'-0 x 17'-6"

garage
19'-6" x 30'-0" avg.

lower foyer

up

bonus/ stor.
12'-8" x 20'-0"

bike storage/
workshop

up

lower level

master balcony

©THE Sater Design
COLLECTION, INC.

open to grand
room below

km kitchen

master
21'-0" x 20'-0"
vaulted clg.

overlook

2 sided
fireplace

hers

dn.

hers

his

study
13'-0" x 18'-0"
8'-0" clg.

his

window
seat

upper level

© THE Sater Design Collection, Inc.

© THE SATER DESIGN COLLECTION, INC.

Hemingway Lane

Inspired by 19th-century Key West Island houses, the updated façade is heart-stoppingly beautiful with Doric columns and a glass-paneled arched entry. The mid-level foyer eases the trip from the ground level to living and dining areas.

Two sets of French doors lead out to the gallery and sundeck, and a two-story picture window invites natural light into the heart of the home. A dreamy, oversized kitchen has a walk-in pantry, a food preparation island and its own French door to the covered porch.

In the main-level master suite, French doors capture generous views and open to the covered porch. Upper-level sleeping quarters include four bedrooms, which take full advantage of their lofty placement. A central computer loft offers built-in desk space and a balcony overlook.

PLAN | 6689

Bedroom: 5   Width: 44'6"
Bath: 3-1/2   Depth: 58'0"
Foundation: Slab/Piling
Exterior Walls: 2x6

Main Level: 1,642 sq ft
Upper Level: 1,165 sq ft
Lower Level Entry: 168 sq ft

Living Area: 2,975 sq ft

Price Code: **C3**

1-800-718-PLAN

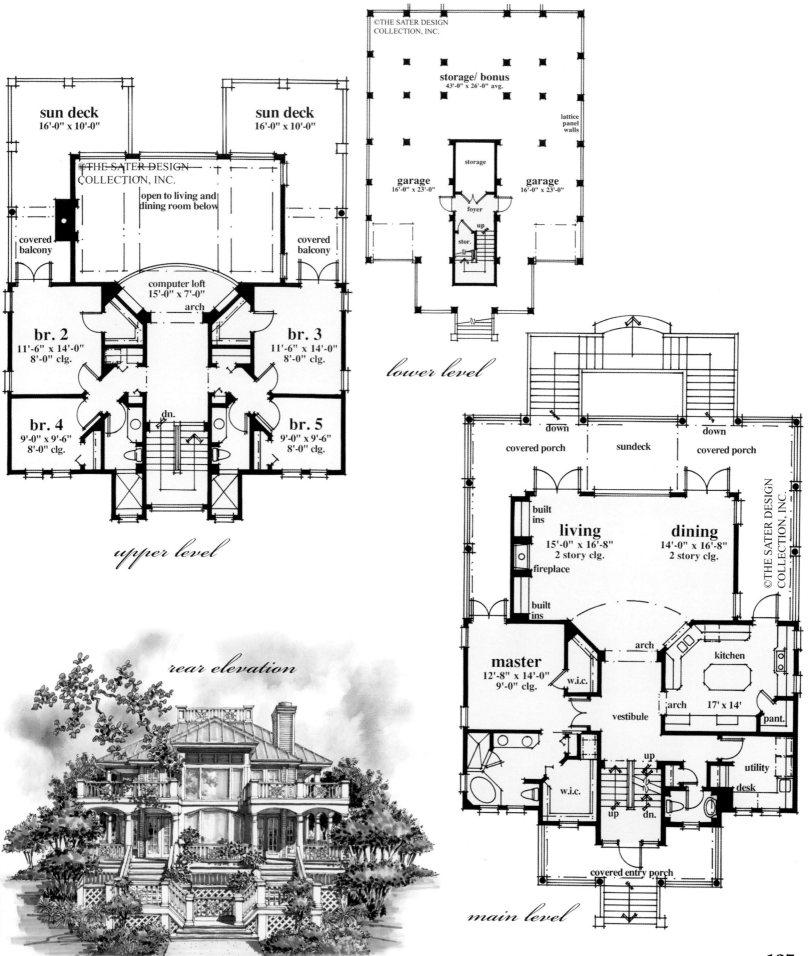

sun deck
16'-0" x 10'-0"

sun deck
16'-0" x 10'-0"

©THE SATER DESIGN
COLLECTION, INC.

open to living and
dining room below

covered
balcony

covered
balcony

computer loft
15'-0" x 7'-0"

arch

br. 2
11'-6" x 14'-0"
8'-0" clg.

br. 3
11'-6" x 14'-0"
8'-0" clg.

br. 4
9'-0" x 9'-6"
8'-0" clg.

dn.

br. 5
9'-0" x 9'-6"
8'-0" clg.

upper level

©THE SATER DESIGN
COLLECTION, INC.

storage/ bonus
43'-0" x 26'-0" avg.

lattice
panel
walls

storage

garage
16'-0" x 23'-0"

garage
16'-0" x 23'-0"

foyer

up

stor.

lower level

down

down

covered porch

sundeck

covered porch

built ins

living
15'-0" x 16'-8"
2 story clg.

dining
14'-0" x 16'-8"
2 story clg.

©THE SATER DESIGN
COLLECTION, INC.

fireplace

built ins

kitchen

arch

master
12'-8" x 14'-0"
9'-0" clg.

w.i.c.

arch

17' x 14'

pant.

vestibule

up

utility

desk

w.i.c.

up

dn.

covered entry porch

main level

rear elevation

© THE SATER DESIGN COLLECTION, INC.

© THE SATER DESIGN COLLECTION, INC.

Nantucket Sound

Vintage seaboard details gently flavor this Nantucket waterfront plan. A faux widow's walk creates a stunning complement to the observation balcony and two ocean-side sundecks, allowing panoramic views front and back. Two pairs of French doors, which frame a two-story wall of glass topped off by a graceful arch, define the open living and dining room area.

A cozy fireplace framed by built-ins invites gatherings of all kinds. A hard-working gourmet kitchen serves both family meals and planned events, with an island prep area, a walk-in pantry, a pass-through counter and its own French door to the covered porch.

Upstairs, a gallery loft leads to a computer area with a balcony overlook as well as built-in space for a desk.

PLAN | *6693*

Bedroom: 3	Width: 44'6"
Bath: 3-1/2	Depth: 58'0"
Foundation: Post/Pier/Slab	
Exterior Walls: 2x6	

Main Level: 1,642 sq ft
Upper Level: 1,165 sq ft
Lower Level Entry: 168 sq ft

Living Area: 2,975 sq ft

Price Code: **C3**

1-800-718-PLAN

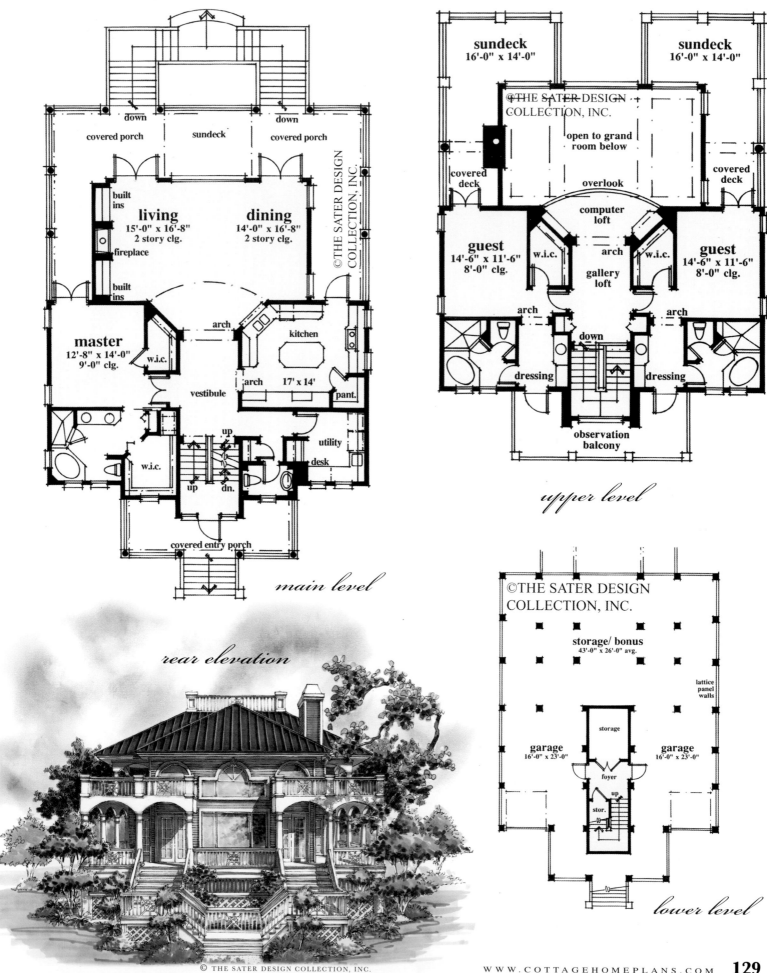

main level

down · covered porch · sundeck · down · covered porch

built ins
living
15'-0" x 16'-8"
2 story clg.
fireplace
built ins

dining
14'-0" x 16'-8"
2 story clg.

©THE SATER DESIGN COLLECTION, INC.

master
12'-8" x 14'-0"
9'-0" clg.
w.i.c.

arch

kitchen
17' x 14'

arch
pant.

vestibule

w.i.c.

up · up · dn.

utility
desk

covered entry porch

upper level

sundeck
16'-0" x 14'-0"

sundeck
16'-0" x 14'-0"

©THE SATER DESIGN COLLECTION, INC.

open to grand room below

covered deck

overlook

computer loft

covered deck

guest
14'-6" x 11'-6"
8'-0" clg.

w.i.c.

arch

w.i.c.

guest
14'-6" x 11'-6"
8'-0" clg.

gallery loft

arch

arch

dressing

down

dressing

observation balcony

rear elevation

© THE SATER DESIGN COLLECTION, INC.

lower level

©THE SATER DESIGN COLLECTION, INC.

storage/ bonus
43'-0" x 26'-0" avg.

lattice panel walls

garage
16'-0" x 23'-0"

storage

foyer

up

stor.

garage
16'-0" x 23'-0"

© THE SATER DESIGN COLLECTION, INC.

Montego Bay

This picturesque Key West Conch design displays the advantages of living in a warm climate. The windows welcome natural light and invigorating breezes into the snug interior. A wrap-around porch shelters the main entrance, making the transition from outdoors to indoors comfortable and inviting. A standing-seam metal roof, with simple balustrades, heritage columns and louvered shutters add authenticity to the classic cottage design.

A prominent great room stands apart with its cathedral ceiling, a central fireplace with adjoining entertainment center, and an entire wall of French doors which open to the spacious lanai. Arches and columns define the open areas between the formal dining room and kitchen. The master bedroom and luxurious bath are also on the main level with access to the verandah, while the upstairs hosts the guest suites.

PLAN | *6800*

Bedroom: 3   Width: 58'0"
Bath: 3-1/2   Depth: 54'0"
Foundation: Island basement
Exterior Walls: 2x6

Main Level: 2,096 sq ft
Upper Level: 892 sq ft

Living Area: 2,988 sq ft

Price Code: **C3**

FOR PHOTOGRAPHY
SEE PAGES 46-49

1-800-718-PLAN

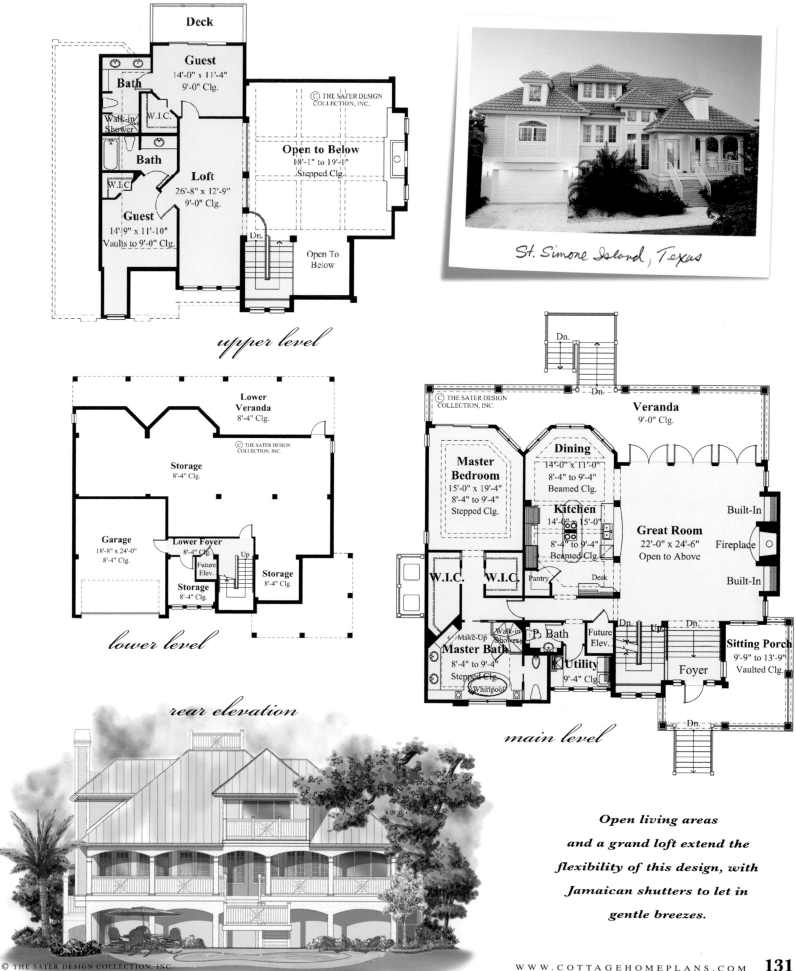

Deck

Guest
14'-0" x 11'-4"
9'-0" Clg.

Bath

Walk-in
Shower

W.I.C.

Bath

W.I.C.

Loft
26'-8" x 12'-9"
9'-0" Clg.

Guest
14'-9" x 11'-10"
Vaults to 9'-0" Clg.

© THE SATER DESIGN
COLLECTION, INC.

Open to Below
18'-1" to 19'-1"
Stepped Clg.

Dn.

Open To
Below

upper level

St. Simone Island, Texas

**Lower
Veranda**
8'-4" Clg.

Storage
8'-4" Clg.

© THE SATER DESIGN
COLLECTION, INC.

Garage
18'-8" x 24'-0"
8'-4" Clg.

Lower Foyer
8'-4" Clg.

Future
Elev.

Storage
8'-4" Clg.

Up

Storage
8'-4" Clg.

lower level

Dn.

Dn.

© THE SATER DESIGN
COLLECTION, INC.

Veranda
9'-0" Clg.

**Master
Bedroom**
15'-0" x 19'-4"
8'-4" to 9'-4"
Stepped Clg.

Dining
14'-0" x 11'-0"
8'-4" to 9'-4"
Beamed Clg.

Kitchen
14'-0" x 15'-0"
8'-4" to 9'-4"
Beamed Clg.

Built-In

Great Room
22'-0" x 24'-6"
Open to Above

Fireplace

Built-In

W.I.C.

W.I.C.

Pantry

Desk

Make-Up

Walk-in
Shower

P. Bath

Future
Elev.

Dn.

Up

Dn.

Sitting Porch
9'-9" to 13'-9"
Vaulted Clg.

Master Bath
8'-4" to 9'-4"
Stepped Clg

Whirlpool

Utility
9'-4" Clg.

Foyer

Dn.

main level

rear elevation

*Open living areas
and a grand loft extend the
flexibility of this design, with
Jamaican shutters to let in
gentle breezes.*

© THE SATER DESIGN COLLECTION, INC.

© THE SATER DESIGN COLLECTION, INC.

Sierra Vista

Sun-kissed porticos and wide-open decks capture views and permit breezes to whisper through rooms all around this coastal cottage. Inspired by Caribbean manors and refined in the architecture of Charleston Row houses, the style is brought into the 21st Century with a highly functional upside-down floor plan that is fully engaged with the outdoors.

The foyer links the entry with public living spaces as well as a private room that flexes to accommodate guests or harbor a quiet library or conservatory. Built-in cabinetry and a stepped ceiling subdue the scale of the media room. The central stairs create a fluid connection with the spacious living room, formal dining room and kitchen. An upper veranda features an alfresco kitchen that extends the function of the dining room.

PLAN | 6757

Bedroom: 5	Width: 50'0"
Bath: 5-1/2	Depth: 83'10"
Foundation: Pier	
Exterior Walls: 2x6	

Main Level:	1,372 sq ft
Upper Level:	1,617 sq ft
Living Area:	2,989 sq ft

Price Code: **C3**

1-800-718-PLAN

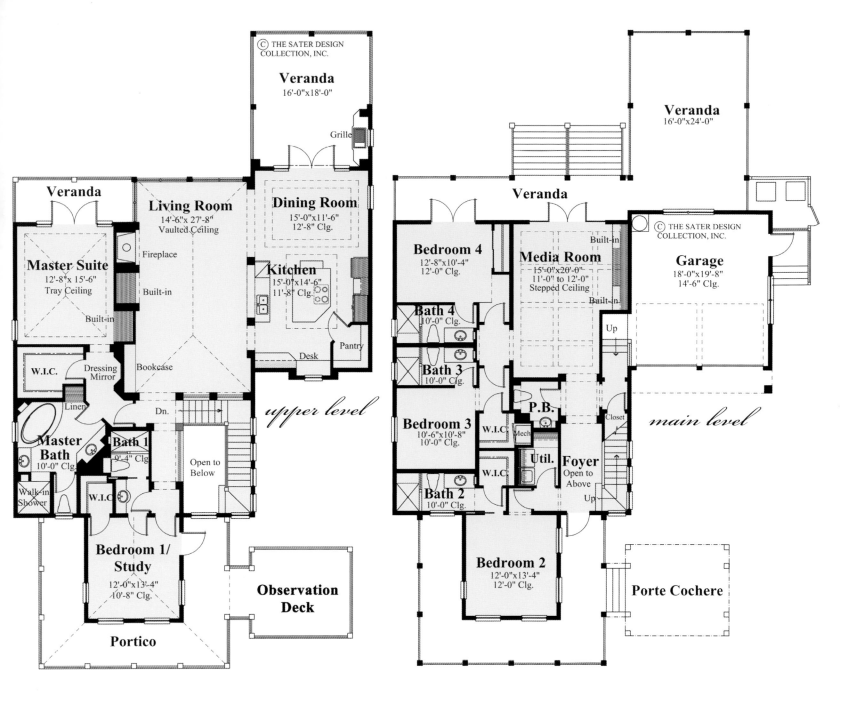

© THE SATER DESIGN COLLECTION, INC.

Veranda
16'-0"x18'-0"

Grille

Veranda
16'-0"x24'-0"

Veranda

© THE SATER DESIGN COLLECTION, INC.

Veranda

Living Room
14'-6." x 27'-8"
Vaulted Ceiling

Fireplace

Built-in

Dining Room
15'-0"x11'-6"
12'-8" Clg.

Kitchen
15'-0"x 14'-6"
11'-8" Clg.

Master Suite
12'-8" x 15'-6"
Tray Ceiling

Built-in

W.I.C.

Dressing
Mirror

Bookcase

Desk

Pantry

Linen

Dn.

upper level

Bedroom 4
12'-8"x10'-4"
12'-0" Clg.

Media Room
15'-0"x20'-0"
11'-0" to 12'-0"
Stepped Ceiling

Built-in

Built-in

Garage
18'-0"x19'-8"
14'-6" Clg.

Up

Bath 4
10'-0" Clg.

Bath 3
10'-0" Clg.

Bedroom 3
10'-6"x10'-8"
10'-0" Clg.

W.I.C.

P.B.

Mech.

Closet

main level

Master
Bath
10'-0" Clg.

Bath 1
9'-4" Clg.

Open to
Below

Bedroom 2
12'-0"x13'-4"
12'-0" Clg.

W.I.C.

Util.

Foyer
Open to
Above

Up

Walk-in
Shower

W.I.C.

Bedroom 1/
Study
12'-0"x13'-4"
10'-8" Clg.

Observation
Deck

Porte Cochere

Portico

---

rear elevation

© THE SATER DESIGN COLLECTION, INC.

© THE SATER DESIGN COLLECTION, INC.

Mimosa

This sensational cottage has natural beauty that blends a steep-pitched roof with a pleasing collection of prairie-style windows, a mix that feels like home in any region.

The portico opens to the foyer that rises to the living room with wrap-around views that extend to the back of the home. Kick up your feet and relax, this sprawling home offers plenty of space — just grab a drink from the wet bar and choose a spot. The formal dining room allows guests to mingle onto the patio through French doors. Nearby, the kitchen serves the leisure room and casual nook with ease.

The master suite extrends from front to back, and overlooks a rear-covered porch — providing seclusion and all the amenities that any fortunate owner will want.

PLAN | *6861*

Bedroom: 3   Width: 77'0"

Bath: 3-1/2   Depth: 66'8"

Foundation: Island basement

Exterior Walls: 2x6

Main Level: 3,074 sq ft

Living Area: 3,074 sq ft

Price Code: **C4**

1-800-718-PLAN

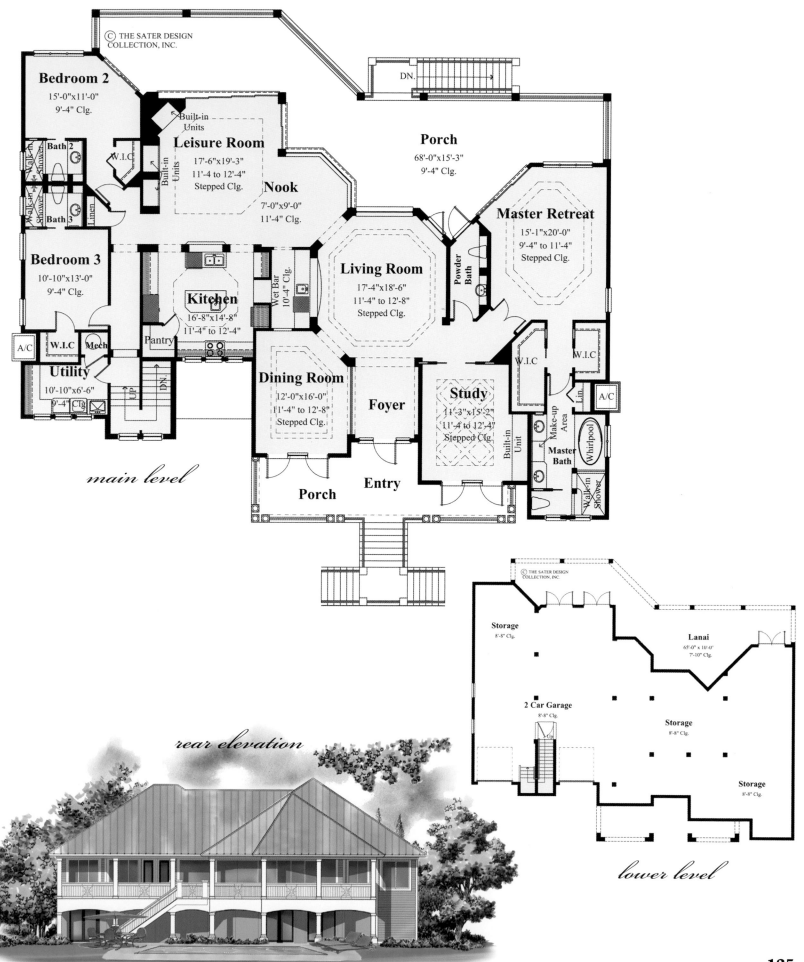

© THE SATER DESIGN COLLECTION, INC.

Bedroom 2
15'-0"x11'-0"
9'-4" Clg.

Bath 2

Bath 3

W.I.C

Linen

Built-in Units

Leisure Room
17'-6"x19'-3"
11'-4 to 12'-4"
Stepped Clg.

Built-in Units

Nook
7'-0"x9'-0"
11'-4" Clg.

Porch
68'-0"x15'-3"
9'-4" Clg.

DN.

Master Retreat
15'-1"x20'-0"
9'-4" to 11'-4"
Stepped Clg.

Bedroom 3
10'-10"x13'-0"
9'-4" Clg.

Kitchen
16'-8"x14'-8"
11'-4" to 12'-4"

Wet Bar
10'-4" Clg.

Living Room
17'-4"x18'-6"
11'-4" to 12'-8"
Stepped Clg.

Powder Bath

W.I.C

W.I.C

A/C

A/C

W.I.C

Mech

Pantry

Utility
10'-10"x6'-6"
9'-4" Clg.

UP

DN.

Dining Room
12'-0"x16'-0"
11'-4" to 12'-8"
Stepped Clg.

Foyer

Study
11'-3"x15'-2"
11'-4 to 12'-4"
Stepped Clg.

Built-in Unit

Make-up Area

Master Bath

Whirlpool

Walk-in Shower

main level

Porch

Entry

Lin

© THE SATER DESIGN COLLECTION, INC.

Storage
8'-8" Clg.

Lanai
65'-0" x 10'-0"
7'-10" Clg.

2 Car Garage
8'-8" Clg.

Up

Storage
8'-8" Clg.

Storage
8'-8" Clg.

rear elevation

lower level

Cottage | 3096 SQ. FT.

© THE SATER DESIGN COLLECTION, INC.

Alexandre

Full of character, this Victorian-inspired design blends a gazebo-style front porch and fish-scale siding with a metal roof, creating a timeless masterpiece.

An inviting entry opens to an impressive two-story circular foyer with a dome ceiling and hosts a radius staircase that hints at the amenities just beyond. The master wing, located at the front left, encases an ornate boudoir, private lanai and dual walk-in wardrobe closets. The plush bath is extended by a bay tub and enjoys the warmth of natural light.

A sweeping grand staircase rises to the upstairs loft, which circles views of the open foyer below. Three stylish bedrooms and a built-in computer center complete the beautiful upper level.

PLAN | *6849*

Bedroom: 4	Width: 74'0"
Bath: 3-1/2	Depth: 88'0"
Foundation: Crawlspace	
Exterior Walls: 2x6	

Main Level:	2,083 sq ft
Upper Level:	1,013 sq ft
Living Area:	3,096 sq ft
Price Code:	**C4**

1-800-718-PLAN

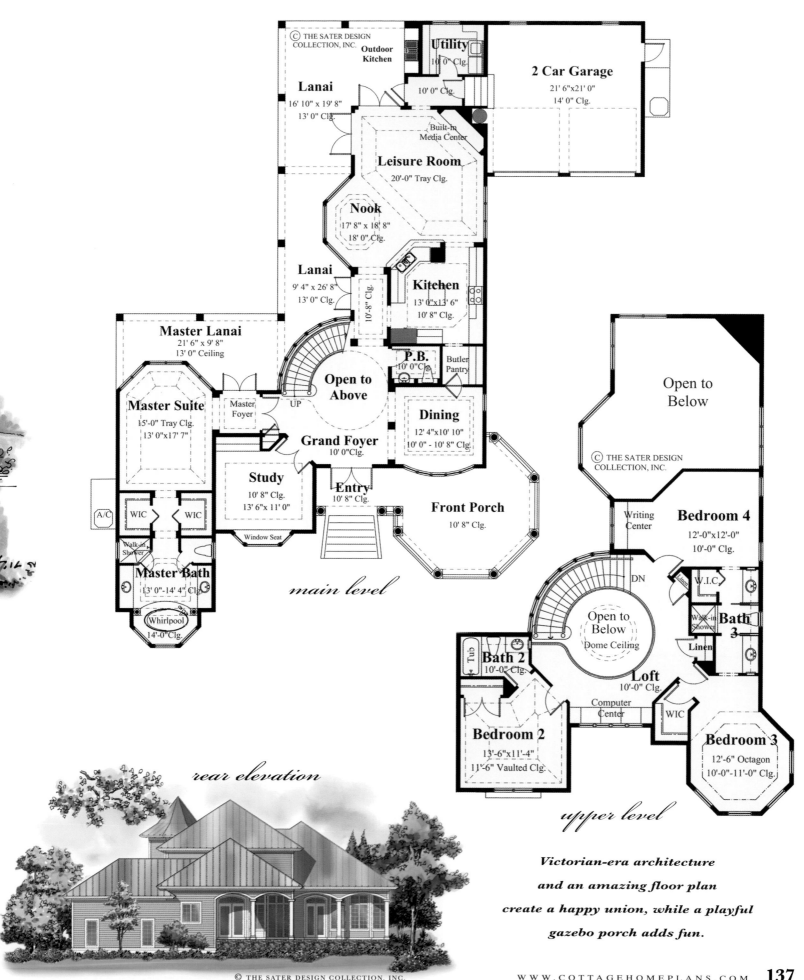

© THE SATER DESIGN COLLECTION, INC.

Outdoor Kitchen

Utility
10' 0" Clg.

2 Car Garage
21' 6"x21' 0"
14' 0" Clg.

Lanai
16' 10" x 19' 8"
13' 0" Clg.

Built-in Media Center

Leisure Room
20'-0" Tray Clg.

Nook
17' 8" x 18' 8"
18' 0" Clg.

Lanai
9' 4" x 26' 8"
13' 0" Clg.

10'-8" Clg.

Kitchen
13' 0"x13' 6"
10' 8" Clg.

Master Lanai
21' 6" x 9' 8"
13' 0" Ceiling

Master Suite
15'-0" Tray Clg.
13' 0"x17' 7"

Master Foyer

Open to Above

UP

P.B.
10' 0" Clg.

Butler Pantry

Open to Below

© THE SATER DESIGN COLLECTION, INC.

A/C

WIC WIC

Study
10' 8" Clg.
13' 6"x 11' 0"

Grand Foyer
10' 0"Clg.

Entry
10' 8" Clg.

Dining
12' 4"x10' 10"
10' 0" - 10' 8" Clg.

Writing Center

Bedroom 4
12'-0"x12'-0"
10'-0" Clg.

W.I.C.

Walk-in Shower

Bath 3

Walk-in Shower

Master Bath
13' 0"-14' 4" Clg.

Window Seat

Front Porch
10' 8" Clg.

DN

Linen

Whirlpool
14'-0" Clg.

Tub

Bath 2
10'-0" Clg.

Open to Below
Dome Ceiling

Loft
10'-0" Clg.

Linen

main level

Computer Center

WIC

Bedroom 2
13'-6"x11'-4"
11'-6" Vaulted Clg.

Bedroom 3
12'-6" Octagon
10'-0"-11'-0" Clg.

rear elevation

upper level

*Victorian-era architecture
and an amazing floor plan
create a happy union, while a playful
gazebo porch adds fun.*

© THE SATER DESIGN COLLECTION, INC.

© THE SATER DESIGN COLLECTION, INC.

Edgewood Trail

A splendid waterfront manor melds an established sense of luxury with a sand-between-the-toes mentality. Outdoor spaces frame an open floor plan that takes on planned events with ease, yet offers views of nature and great places to relax.

The plan unfolds progressively, with the great room providing a transition from the well-defined rooms of the public zone to the private realm. Two broad porches extend the living spaces of the house, and transform the boundaries of the interior when retreating glass walls allow indoors and out to mingle.

Dominated by a bay window, the master suite offers a spacious sitting area and access to the rear porch. An upper-level overlook leads to a computer loft that links three secondary bedrooms—two with bay windows.

PLAN | 6667

Bedroom: 4   Width: 69'8"
Bath: 2-1/2   Depth: 61'10"
Foundation: Slab/Opt. Basement
Exterior Walls: 2x6

Main Level: 2,241 sq ft
Upper Level: 949 sq ft
Living Area: 3,190 sq ft
Price Code: **C4**

FOR PHOTOGRAPHY
SEE PAGES 16-21

1-800-718-PLAN

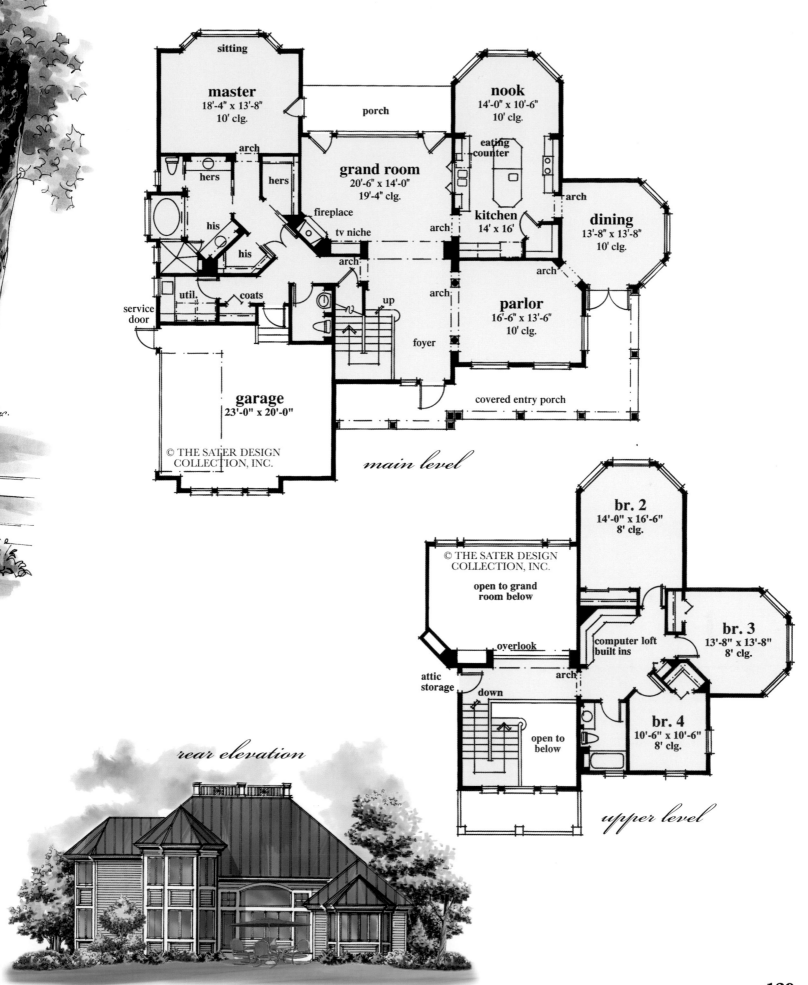

master
18'-4" x 13'-8"
10' clg.

sitting

porch

nook
14'-0" x 10'-6"
10' clg.

eating counter

arch

hers   hers

grand room
20'-6" x 14'-0"
19'-4" clg.

fireplace

his

tv niche

kitchen
14' x 16'

arch

arch

dining
13'-8" x 13'-8"
10' clg.

his

arch

up

util.   coats

service door

foyer

arch

parlor
16'-6" x 13'-6"
10' clg.

garage
23'-0" x 20'-0"

covered entry porch

© THE SATER DESIGN COLLECTION, INC.

main level

br. 2
14'-0" x 16'-6"
8' clg.

© THE SATER DESIGN COLLECTION, INC.

open to grand room below

overlook

computer loft built ins

br. 3
13'-8" x 13'-8"
8' clg.

attic storage

down

arch

br. 4
10'-6" x 10'-6"
8' clg.

open to below

upper level

rear elevation

© THE SATER DESIGN COLLECTION, INC.

Cottage | 3285 SQ. FT.

© THE SATER DESIGN COLLECTION, INC.

Les Anges

A sensational wrap-around porch and additional outdoor spaces extend the living areas of this adorable cottage. Summer breezes find their way though picturesque rooms by a wall of French doors that access the verandah. Highlighted in the two-story great room is a central fireplace, built-in custom cabinetry and a convenient wet bar. The well-designed kitchen includes a sunny breakfast nook, a center island and plenty of storage.

To the front, the formal dining room hosts traditional events graciously. Upstairs boasts two bedrooms complete with baths and bountiful views shared from the spacious deck. A great spot to study, the unique work centers located outside each bedroom complete both wings.

PLAN | 6825

Bedroom: 3   Width: 56'0"
Bath: 3-1/2   Depth: 64'0"
Foundation: Island basement
Exterior Walls: 2x6

Main Level: 2,146 sq ft
Upper Level: 952 sq ft
Lower Level Foyer: 187 sq ft

Living Area: 3,285 sq ft

Price Code: **C4**

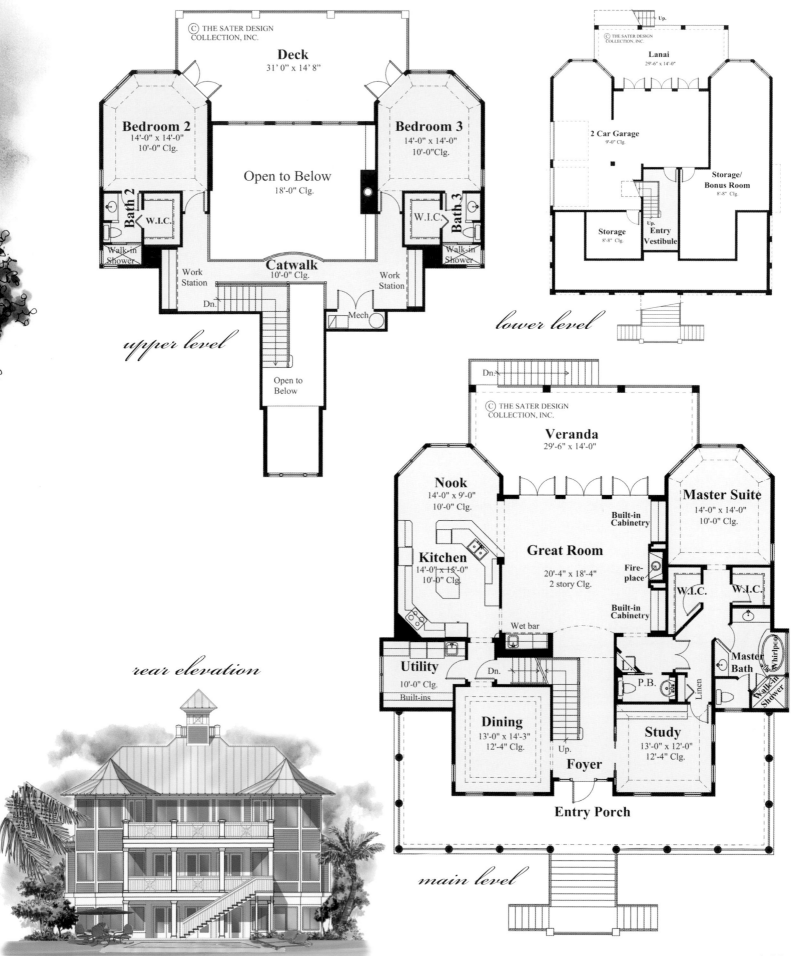

Deck
31' 0" x 14' 8"

© THE SATER DESIGN COLLECTION, INC.

Bedroom 2
14'-0" x 14'-0"
10'-0" Clg.

Bedroom 3
14'-0" x 14'-0"
10'-0"Clg.

Open to Below
18'-0" Clg.

Bath 2

W.I.C.

W.I.C.

Bath 3

Walk-in Shower

Walk-in Shower

Work Station

Catwalk
10'-0" Clg.

Work Station

Dn.

Mech

Open to Below

upper level

Lanai
29'-6" x 14'-0"

Up.

© THE SATER DESIGN COLLECTION, INC.

2 Car Garage
9'-0" Clg.

Storage/ Bonus Room
8'-8" Clg.

Storage
8'-8" Clg.

Up. **Entry Vestibule**

lower level

Dn.

Veranda
29'-6" x 14'-0"

© THE SATER DESIGN COLLECTION, INC.

Nook
14'-0" x 9'-0"
10'-0" Clg.

Kitchen
14'-0" x 15'-0"
10'-0" Clg.

Built-in Cabinetry

Great Room
20'-4" x 18'-4"
2 story Clg.

Fire-place

Built-in Cabinetry

Master Suite
14'-0" x 14'-0"
10'-0" Clg.

W.I.C.

W.I.C.

Master Bath

Whirlpool

Walk-in Shower

Wet bar

Utility
10'-0" Clg.
Built-ins

Dn.

P.B.

Linen

Dining
13'-0" x 14'-3"
12'-4" Clg.

Up.

Study
13'-0" x 12'-0"
12'-4" Clg.

Foyer

Entry Porch

main level

rear elevation

© THE SATER DESIGN COLLECTION, INC.

Gaspirilla Bay

The raised multi-level wrap-around porch captures fantastic views from three sides. Through arches and columns, the great room opens to expansive views. Planned events are a cinch in the gourmet kitchen, where ample storage and counters circle a culinary island.

Upstairs, a rambling master suite enjoys a luxury bath with separate vanities and a walk-in closet with dressing area. With generous outdoor views from the private deck, homeowners may easily be persuaded to sit and watch the sunset.

On the opposite wing, a study or additional bedroom leads to an open deck, enabling wide views and breezes to mingle. A gallery overlooks the great room and foyer below.

PLAN | 6618

Bedroom: 4	Width: 68'0"
Bath: 4-1/2	Depth: 54'0"
Foundation: Island basement	
Exterior Walls: 2x6	

Main Level:	1,944 sq ft
Upper Level:	1,196 sq ft
Lower Level Entry:	195 sq ft
Living Area:	3,335 sq ft

Price Code: **C4**

1-800-718-PLAN

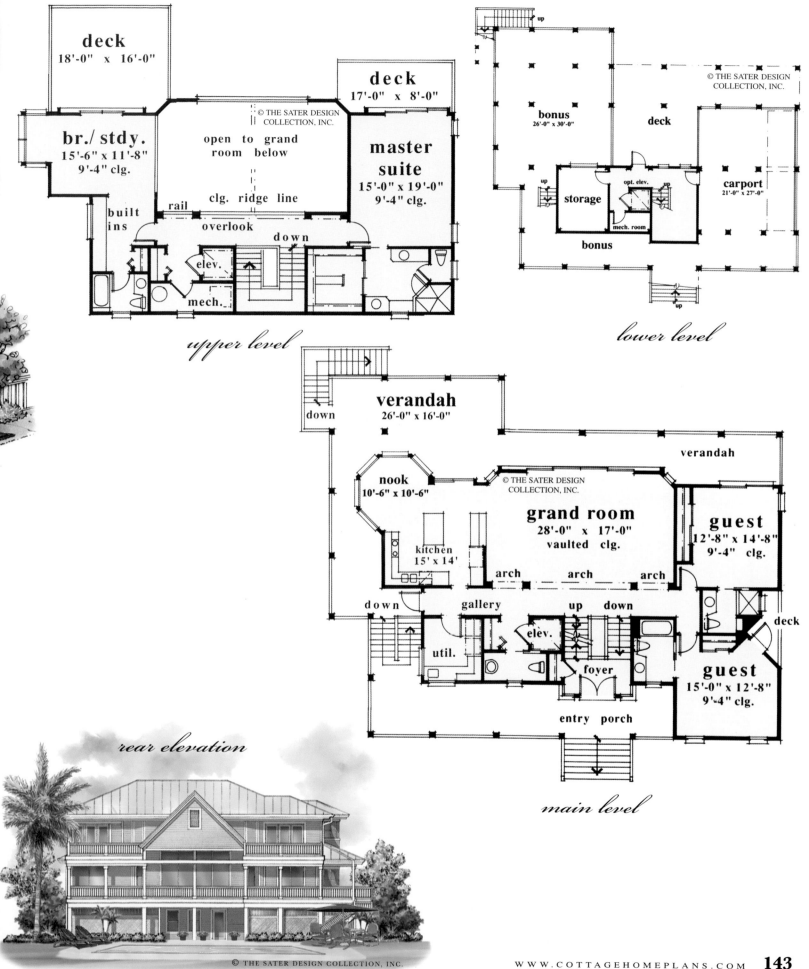

deck
18'-0" x 16'-0"

deck
17'-0" x 8'-0"

© THE SATER DESIGN
COLLECTION, INC.

br./stdy.
15'-6" x 11'-8"
9'-4" clg.

open to grand
room below

**master
suite**
15'-0" x 19'-0"
9'-4" clg.

clg. ridge line

built
ins

rail

overlook

down

elev.

mech.

upper level

up

© THE SATER DESIGN
COLLECTION, INC.

bonus
26'-0" x 30'-0"

deck

carport
21'-0" x 27'-0"

up

storage

opt. elev.

up

mech. room

bonus

up

lower level

down

verandah
26'-0" x 16'-0"

verandah

nook
10'-6" x 10'-6"

© THE SATER DESIGN
COLLECTION, INC.

grand room
28'-0" x 17'-0"
vaulted clg.

guest
12'-8" x 14'-8"
9'-4" clg.

kitchen
15' x 14'

arch   arch   arch

down

gallery

up   down

elev.

deck

guest
15'-0" x 12'-8"
9'-4" clg.

util.

foyer

entry porch

main level

rear elevation

© THE SATER DESIGN COLLECTION, INC.

Cottage | 3348 SQ. FT.

© THE SATER DESIGN COLLECTION, INC.

Carlile Bay

Wide verandas and a double portico enrich the sidewalk presentation of this coastal cottage. Influenced by the raffish dialects of breezy Key West styles, this Revival home integrates regional elements with world-class components, such as a cathedral ceiling in the gathering room and a gallery loft that links to the forward portico.

The entry hall leads through a centered gallery, defined by columns and graceful arches, which eases the transition from the outdoors to a space-age media room, equipped with an up-to-the-minute entertainment center and built-in cabinetry. A flex room connects the service entry and utility zone with an angled hall and luxe bedroom suite. On the upper level, French doors open the gathering room to a wide veranda allowing the upside-down plan to take advantage of the views.

PLAN | 6755

Bedroom: 5   Width: 56'0"
Bath: 5-1/2   Depth: 80'0"
Foundation: Pier
Exterior Walls: 2x6

Main Level: 1,766 sq ft
Upper Level: 1,582 sq ft

Living Area: 3,348 sq ft
Bonus Room: 434 sq ft

Price Code: **C4**

1-800-718-PLAN

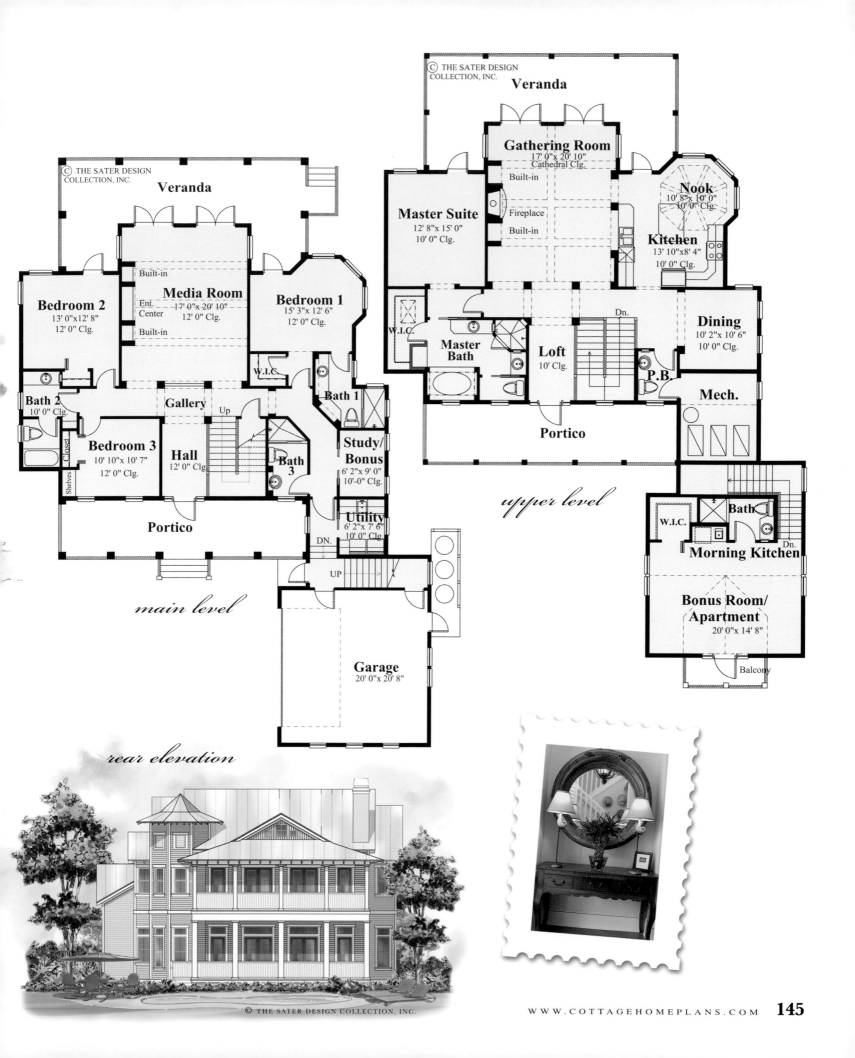

© THE SATER DESIGN
COLLECTION, INC.

Veranda

Gathering Room
17' 0"x 20' 10"
Cathedral Clg.

Built-in

Master Suite
12' 8"x 15' 0"
10' 0" Clg.

Fireplace

Built-in

Nook
10' 8" x 10' 0"
10' 0" Clg.

Kitchen
13' 10"x8' 4"
10' 0" Clg.

Dining
10' 2"x 10' 6"
10' 0" Clg.

W.I.C.

Master Bath

Dn.

Loft
10' Clg.

P.B.

Mech.

Portico

upper level

W.I.C.

Bath

Morning Kitchen

Dn.

**Bonus Room/
Apartment**
20' 0"x 14' 8"

Balcony

© .THE SATER DESIGN
COLLECTION, INC.

Veranda

Built-in

Media Room
17' 0"x 20' 10"
12' 0" Clg.

Ent.
Center

Built-in

Bedroom 2
13' 0"x12' 8"
12' 0" Clg.

Bedroom 1
15' 3"x 12' 6"
12' 0" Clg.

W.I.C.

Bath 2
10' 0" Clg.

Gallery

Up

Bath 1

Shelves Closet

Bedroom 3
10' 10"x 10' 7"
12' 0" Clg.

Hall
12' 0" Clg

Bath 3

**Study/
Bonus**
6' 2"x 9' 0"
10'-0" Clg.

Portico

Utility
6' 2"x 7' 6"
10' 0" Clg.

DN.

UP

main level

Garage
20' 0"x 20' 8"

rear elevation

© THE SATER DESIGN COLLECTION, INC.

© THE SATER DESIGN COLLECTION, INC.

Marquilla

Triple dormers and a widow's walk set off the standing-seam roof of this New South cottage, inspired by island plantation houses of the early 20th Century. Horizontal siding lends an informal character to the stately façade, which is set off by massive columns and tall shuttered windows.

A mid-level landing eases the transition to an L-shaped plan anchored by a forward arrangement of the great room and study. The foyer creates a fluid boundary by connecting the entry veranda with the wrapping rear veranda, pool and spa.

Toward the center of the plan, a winding staircase defines a progression from the public realm, which includes a high-tech kitchen, formal dining room, and the private sleeping quarters. Luxe amenities highlight the master retreat, which offers its own access to the solana and pool.

PLAN | *6865*

Bedroom: 5	Width: 63'0"
Bath: 5	Depth: 114'10"
Foundation: Piling	
Exterior Walls: 2x6	

Main Level:	2,159 sq ft
Upper Level:	1,160 sq ft
Guest Suite:	317 sq ft
Living Area:	3,636 sq ft

Price Code: **C3**

1-800-718-PLAN

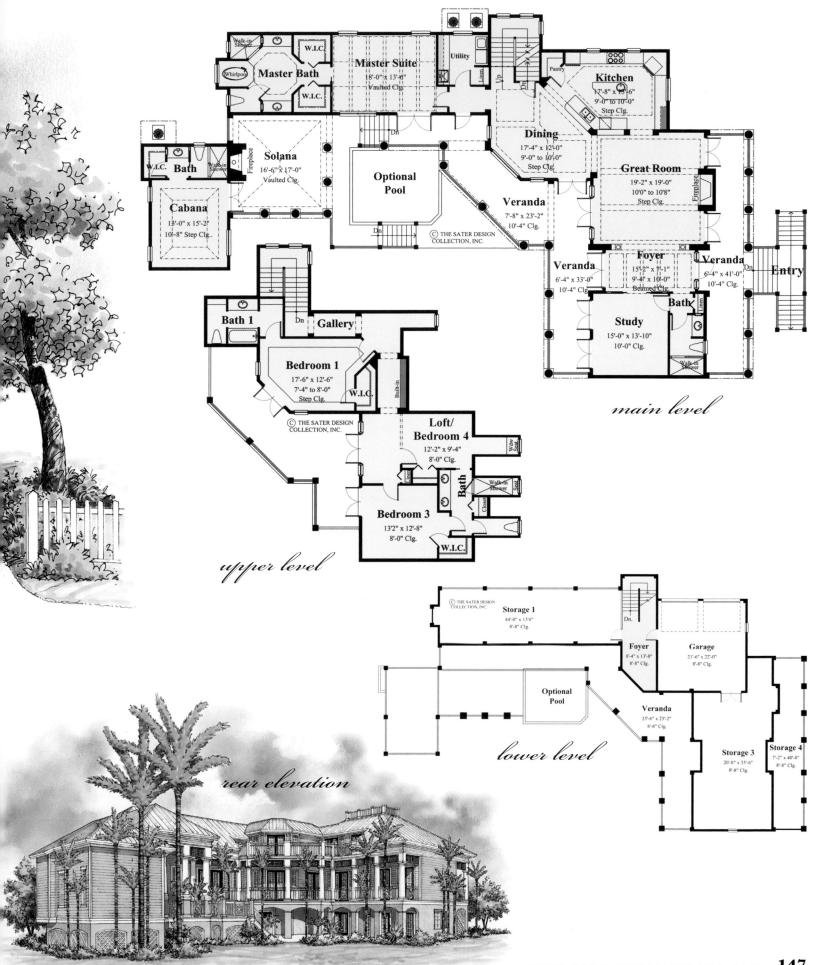

Walk-in Shower
Whirlpool

Master Bath

W.I.C.
W.I.C.

Master Suite
18'-0" x 13'-6"
Vaulted Clg.

Utility

Pantry

Up

Dn

Kitchen
17'-8" x 13'-6"
9'-0" to 10'-0"
Step Clg.

W.I.C.
Bath
Walk-in Shower

Fireplace

Solana
16'-6" x 17'-0"
Vaulted Clg.

Optional Pool

Dining
17'-4" x 12'-0"
9'-0" to 10'-0"
Step Clg.

Great Room
19'-2" x 19'-0"
10'-0" to 10'-8"
Step Clg.

Fireplace

Cabana
13'-0" x 15'-2"
10'-8" Step Clg.

Dn

Veranda
7'-8" x 23'-2"
10'-4" Clg.

© THE SATER DESIGN COLLECTION, INC.

Veranda
6'-4" x 33'-0"
10'-4" Clg.

Foyer
15'-2" x 7'-1"
9'-4" x 10'-0"
Beamed Clg.

Veranda
6'-4" x 41'-0"
10'-4" Clg.

Entry

Bath
Linen

Study
15'-0" x 13'-10"
10'-0" Clg.

Walk-in Shower

main level

Bath 1

Dn

Gallery

Bedroom 1
17'-6" x 12'-6"
7'-4" to 8'-0"
Step Clg.

W.I.C.

Built-in

© THE SATER DESIGN COLLECTION, INC.

Loft/ Bedroom 4
12'-2" x 9'-4"
8'-0" Clg.

Wdw Seat

Linen

Bath

Walk-in Shower
Seat

Closet

Bedroom 3
13'2" x 12'-8"
8'-0" Clg.

W.I.C.

upper level

© THE SATER DESIGN COLLECTION, INC.

Storage 1
44'-0" x 13'4"
8'-8" Clg.

Dn

Foyer
8'-4" x 13'-8"
8'-8" Clg.

Garage
21'-6" x 22'-0"
8'-8" Clg.

Optional Pool

Veranda
25'-6" x 23'-2"
8'-8" Clg.

Storage 3
20'-8" x 33'-6"
8'-8" Clg.

Storage 4
7'-2" x 40'-8"
8'-8" Clg.

lower level

rear elevation

© THE SATER DESIGN COLLECTION, INC.

Cottage | 3839 SQ. FT.

© THE SATER DESIGN COLLECTION, INC.

Savona Cove

This impressive Bahamian-styled design emphasizes peerless style. You will feel you've arrived when you are greeted by the magnificent three-story staircase. The front door opens into the grand foyer, exposing the great room and winding staircase. The formal dining room, defined by a three-sided fireplace and wet bar, continues into the kitchen.

Two bedrooms, each with a full bath, along with a spacious verandah and outdoor kitchen, complete the main level. The sumptuous master suite occupies the entire upstairs and includes an elevator for transferring between floors. The three-sided fireplace extended from the lower level provides a warm, intimate atmosphere, perfect for privacy and relaxation.

PLAN | *6816*

Bedroom: 3   Width: 56'0"
Bath: 4   Depth: 54'0"
Foundation: Island basement
Exterior Walls: 2x6

Main Level: 2,039 sq ft
Upper Level: 1,426 sq ft
Lower Level Entry: 374 sq ft

Living Area: 3,839 sq ft

Price Code: **L1**

1-800-718-PLAN

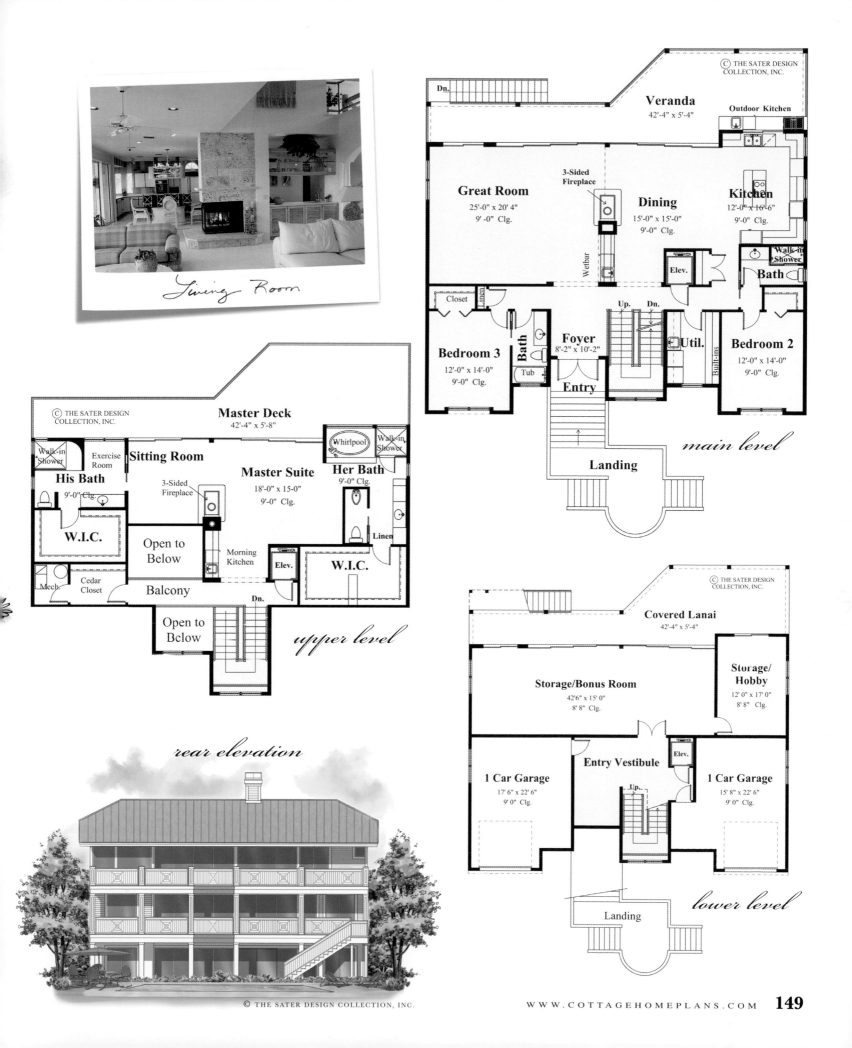

Living Room

© THE SATER DESIGN COLLECTION, INC.

Veranda
42'-4" x 5'-4"

Outdoor Kitchen

Dn.

Great Room
25'-0" x 20' 4"
9'-0" Clg.

3-Sided Fireplace

Dining
15'-0" x 15'-0"
9'-0" Clg.

Kitchen
12'-0" x 16'-6"
9'-0" Clg.

Wetbar

Elev.

Walk-in Shower

Bath

Closet

Linen

Up.   Dn.

Util.

Built-ins

Bedroom 3
12'-0" x 14'-0"
9'-0" Clg.

Bath

Tub

Foyer
8'-2" x 10'-2"

Entry

Bedroom 2
12'-0" x 14'-0"
9'-0" Clg.

Landing

main level

Master Deck
42'-4" x 5'-8"

© THE SATER DESIGN COLLECTION, INC.

Whirlpool

Walk-in Shower

Walk-in Shower

Exercise Room

Sitting Room

Master Suite
18'-0" x 15'-0"
9'-0" Clg.

Her Bath
9'-0" Clg.

His Bath
9'-0" Clg.

3-Sided Fireplace

W.I.C.

Linen

Open to Below

Morning Kitchen

Elev.

W.I.C.

Mech.

Cedar Closet

Balcony

Dn.

Open to Below

upper level

rear elevation

© THE SATER DESIGN COLLECTION, INC.

Covered Lanai
42'-4" x 5'-4"

© THE SATER DESIGN COLLECTION, INC.

Storage/Bonus Room
42'6" x 15' 0"
8' 8" Clg.

Storage/ Hobby
12' 0" x 17' 0"
8' 8" Clg.

1 Car Garage
17' 6" x 22' 6"
9' 0" Clg.

Entry Vestibule

Elev.

Up.

1 Car Garage
15' 8" x 22' 6"
9' 0" Clg.

Landing

lower level

© THE SATER DESIGN COLLECTION, INC.

Cottage | 3946 SQ. FT.

© THE SATER DESIGN COLLECTION, INC.

Anna Belle

A mixture of shiplap board and batten siding adorns this comfortable waterfront coastal retreat in a formal style. The cupola sits atop the main structure between two gabled wings of this plantation-inspired home. Two-story round tapered columns support the large front porch and roof above, creating shade and security.

Oriented towards views from the rear, this plan allows spectacular vistas, even from the front door. Square columns and French doors define the great room, which hosts an extended-hearth fireplace and built-in cabinetry. To the right of the plan, the study maintains privacy for the master wing. The owners' retreat sports a walk-in closet designed for two, and a luxurious bath with dual vanities and a soaking tub.

PLAN | *6782*

Bedroom: 4   Width: 98'0"
Bath: 4   Depth: 60'0"
Foundation: Slab or Crawlspace
Exterior Walls: 2x6

Main Level: 2,705 sq ft
Upper Level: 1,241 sq ft
Living Area: 3,946 sq ft
Price Code: **L1**

1-800-718-PLAN

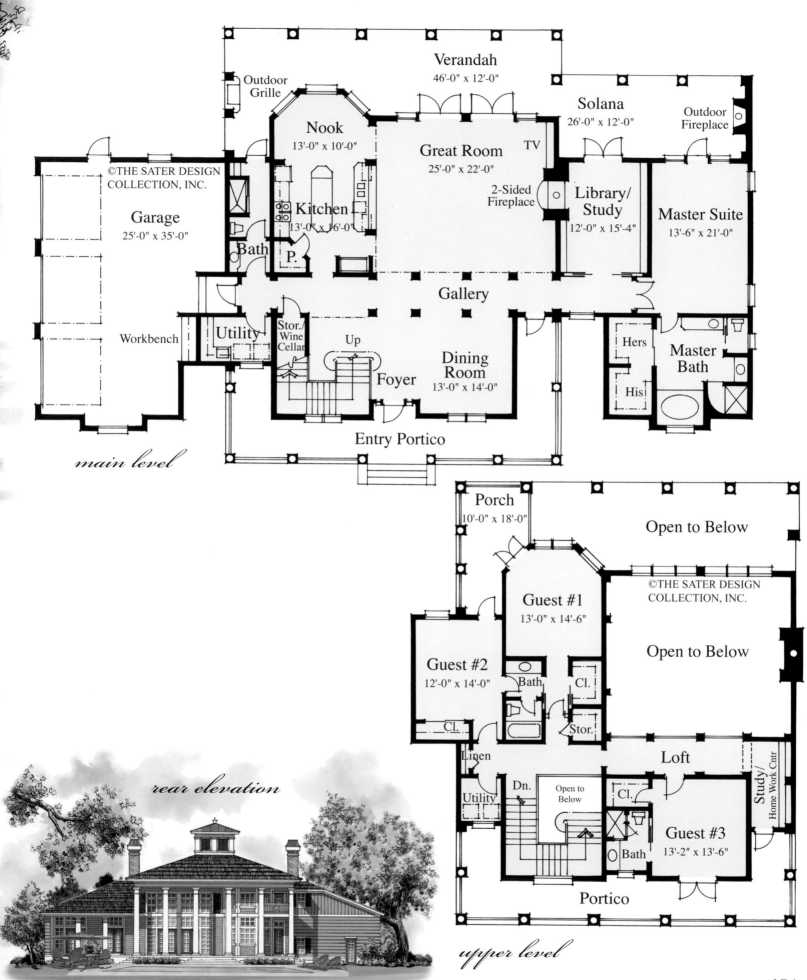

Verandah 46'-0" x 12'-0"

Outdoor Grille

Solana 26'-0" x 12'-0"

Outdoor Fireplace

Nook 13'-0" x 10'-0"

Great Room 25'-0" x 22'-0"

TV

©THE SATER DESIGN COLLECTION, INC.

Garage 25'-0" x 35'-0"

Kitchen 13'-0" x 16'-0"

2-Sided Fireplace

Library/ Study 12'-0" x 15'-4"

Master Suite 13'-6" x 21'-0"

Bath

P.

Gallery

Workbench

Utility

Stor./ Wine Cellar

Up

Foyer

Dining Room 13'-0" x 14'-0"

Hers

His

Master Bath

Entry Portico

main level

Porch 10'-0" x 18'-0"

Open to Below

Guest #1 13'-0" x 14'-6"

©THE SATER DESIGN COLLECTION, INC.

Guest #2 12'-0" x 14'-0"

Bath

Cl.

Open to Below

Cl.

Stor.

Linen

Utility

Dn.

Open to Below

Loft

Cl.

Study/ Home Work Cntr

Guest #3 13'-2" x 13'-6"

Bath

Portico

rear elevation

upper level

© THE SATER DESIGN COLLECTION, INC.

Cottage | 4037 SQ. FT.

© THE SATER DESIGN COLLECTION, INC.

Sunburst Parkway

A magnificent two-story entry with circle-head window takes center stage on this stately coastal design. The arrangement of the third and fourth car garage makes storing a boat easy.

Inside, the two-story great room offers a three-sided fireplace, a wet bar and a niche for an entertainment center. Pocket sliding glass doors open to an expansive veranda allowing outdoor breezes to mingle with the interior.

A food preparation island and cooktop highlight a well-planned kitchen, which provides double ovens, plenty of storage and a pass-thru to the porch cooking area. Serving formal events is easy with the open arrangement to the dining room, which allows guests to enjoy the views from the veranda and glimpses of the sunset.

PLAN | **6741**

Bedroom: 5   Width: 76'0"

Bath: 4-1/2   Depth: 56'0"

Foundation: Slab

Exterior Walls: 2x6

Main Level: 2,162 sq ft

Upper Level: 1,585 sq ft

Lower Level Entry: 290 sq ft

Living Area: 4,037 sq ft

Price Code: **L2**

1-800-718-PLAN

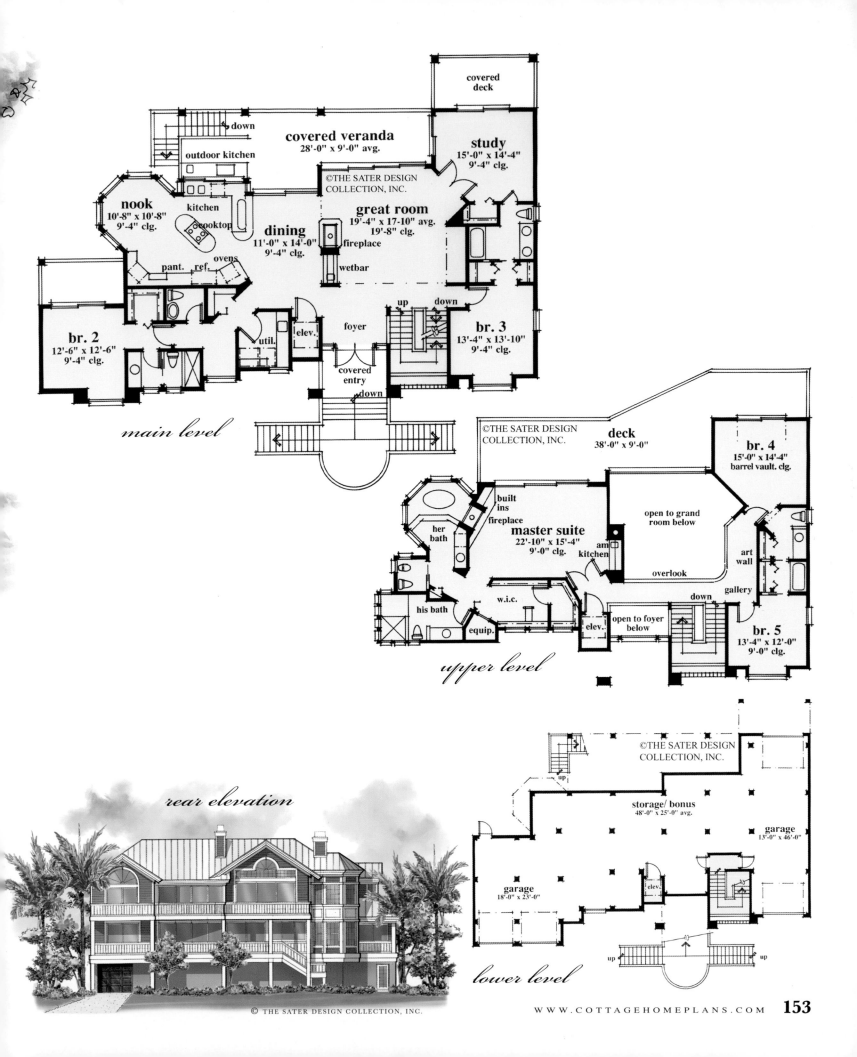

main level

covered deck

covered veranda
28'-0" x 9'-0" avg.

study
15'-0" x 14'-4"
9'-4" clg.

outdoor kitchen

down

©THE SATER DESIGN
COLLECTION, INC.

nook
10'-8" x 10'-8"
9'-4" clg.

kitchen

cooktop

great room
19'-4" x 17-10" avg.
19'-8" clg.

dining
11'-0" x 14'-0"
9'-4" clg.

fireplace

wetbar

ovens

pant. ref.

up

down

foyer

util.

elev.

br. 2
12'-6" x 12'-6"
9'-4" clg.

br. 3
13'-4" x 13'-10"
9'-4" clg.

covered
entry

down

upper level

©THE SATER DESIGN
COLLECTION, INC.

deck
38'-0" x 9'-0"

br. 4
15'-0" x 14'-4"
barrel vault. clg.

built
ins

fireplace

her
bath

master suite
22'-10" x 15'-4"
9'-0" clg.

am
kitchen

open to grand
room below

w.i.c.

overlook

his bath

elev.

open to foyer
below

down

gallery

art
wall

equip.

br. 5
13'-4" x 12'-0"
9'-0" clg.

rear elevation

©THE SATER DESIGN
COLLECTION, INC.

storage/ bonus
48'-0" x 25'-0" avg.

up

garage
13'-0" x 46'-0"

garage
18'-0" x 23'-0"

elev.

up

up

lower level

© THE SATER DESIGN COLLECTION, INC.

© THE SATER DESIGN COLLECTION, INC.

Madra

A centered cupola sets off the clean, simple lines of this New South cottage. Horizontal siding and history-rich details rethink tradition in a thoroughly modern plan drawn for livability and a deep level of comfort.

At the front of the home, massive square columns line the wrapping entry porch. Inside, an unrestrained floor plan permits public and casual spaces to flex, with rooms that facilitate planned events as easily as they do family gatherings. Graceful arches define the dining room and parlor, which complements an informal nook adjacent to the great room. Pocket doors seclude a library or study, which sports a beamed ceiling and grants private access to the solana.

A main-level master suite features a tray ceiling, while upper-level secondary bedrooms access separate sun decks.

PLAN | *6864*

Bedroom: 5	Width: 92'0"
Bath: 4	Depth: 63'0"
Foundation: Slab or Crawlspace	
Exterior Walls: 2x6	

Main Level:	2,642 sq ft
Upper Level:	1,420 sq ft
Living Area:	4,062 sq ft
Price Code:	**L2**

1-800-718-PLAN

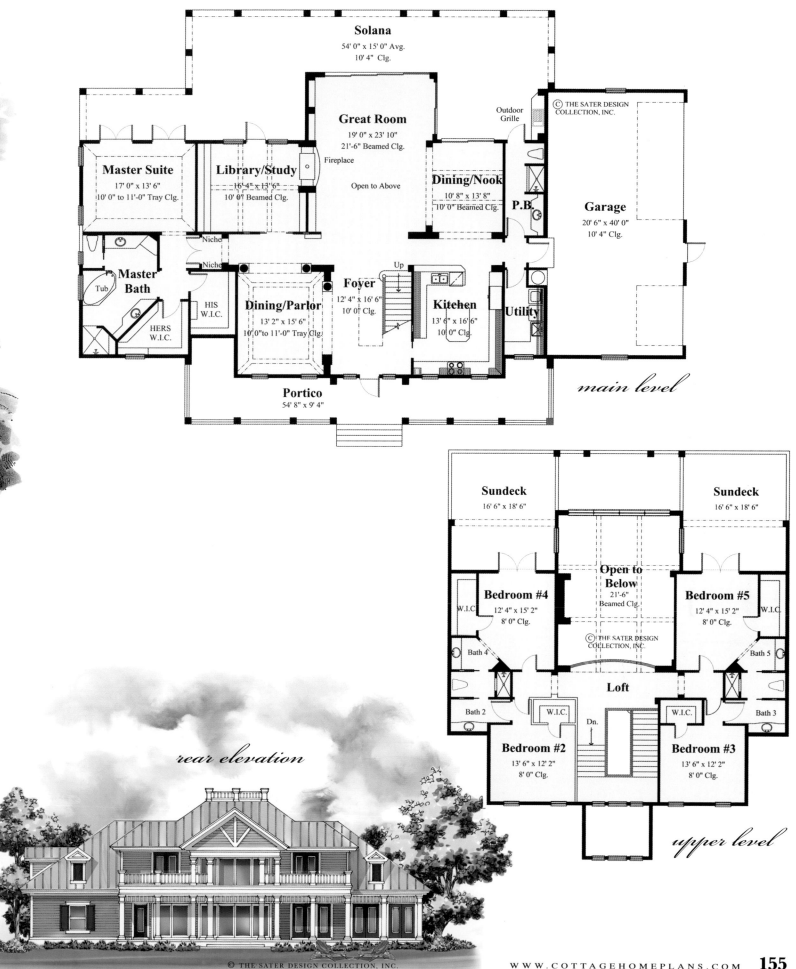

Solana
54' 0" x 15' 0" Avg.
10' 4" Clg.

Great Room
19' 0" x 23' 10"
21'-6" Beamed Clg.

Fireplace

Open to Above

Outdoor Grille

© THE SATER DESIGN COLLECTION, INC.

Master Suite
17' 0" x 13' 6"
10' 0" to 11'-0" Tray Clg.

Library/Study
16' 4" x 13' 6"
10' 0" Beamed Clg.

Dining/Nook
10' 8" x 13' 8"
10' 0" Beamed Clg.

P.B.

Garage
20' 6" x 40' 0"
10' 4" Clg.

Niche

Niche

Master Bath

Tub

HIS W.I.C.

HERS W.I.C.

Dining/Parlor
13' 2" x 15' 6"
10' 0" to 11'-0" Tray Clg.

Up

Foyer
12' 4" x 16' 6"
10' 0" Clg.

Kitchen
13' 6" x 16' 6"
10' 0" Clg.

Utility

Portico
54' 8" x 9' 4"

main level

Sundeck
16' 6" x 18' 6"

Sundeck
16' 6" x 18' 6"

Open to Below
21'-6" Beamed Clg.

Bedroom #4
12' 4" x 15' 2"
8' 0" Clg.

Bedroom #5
12' 4" x 15' 2"
8' 0" Clg.

W.I.C.

W.I.C.

Bath 4

© THE SATER DESIGN COLLECTION, INC.

Bath 5

Bath 2

Bath 3

Loft

W.I.C.

W.I.C.

Dn.

Bedroom #2
13' 6" x 12' 2"
8' 0" Clg.

Bedroom #3
13' 6" x 12' 2"
8' 0" Clg.

rear elevation

upper level

© THE SATER DESIGN COLLECTION, INC.

© THE SATER DESIGN COLLECTION, INC.

La Palma

Charming stick-work frames tall windows in the two-story grand entry, giving this impressive cottage Southern appeal.

Inside, the gallery expands the entry to the great room, revealing a cathedral ceiling, two-sided fireplace and custom cabinetry. Glass sliders open the interior to a wrap-around verandah and outdoor kitchen, which hosts a servery for planned events. The main floor also provides three bedrooms, one facing the back property that shares the fireplace and opens to a private verandah allowing breezes to mingle.

The secluded upstairs master suite enjoys an open fireplace shared with an extraordinary bath. A large wardrobe closet and dressing area make starting the day pleasurable — simply take a break, open the doors and watch the sun rise.

PLAN | *6819*

Bedroom: 5	Width: 62'0"
Bath: 4-1/2	Depth: 67'0"
Foundation: Island basement	
Exterior Walls: 2x6	

Main Level:	2,491 sq ft
Upper Level:	1,290 sq ft
Lower Level Entry:	358 sq ft
Living Area:	4,139 sq ft
Price Code:	**L2**

1 - 8 0 0 - 7 1 8 - P L A N

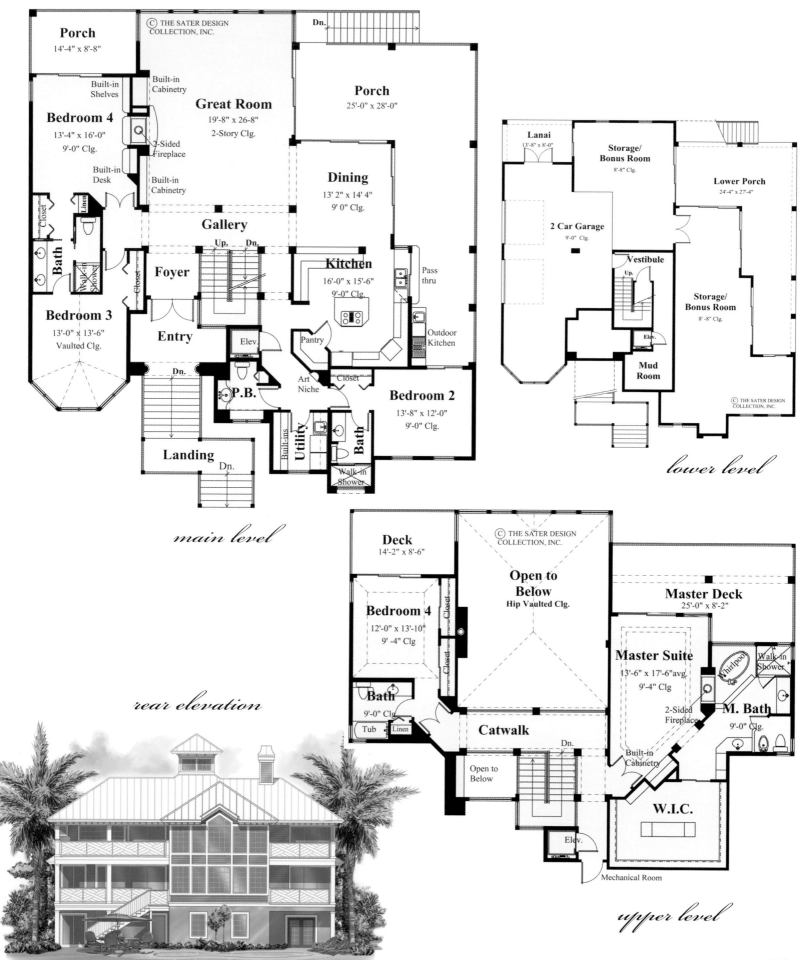

Porch
14'-4" x 8'-8"

© THE SATER DESIGN COLLECTION, INC.

Dn.

Built-in Shelves

Built-in Cabinetry

Great Room
19'-8" x 26-8"
2-Story Clg.

Porch
25'-0" x 28'-0"

Bedroom 4
13'-4" x 16'-0"
9'-0" Clg.

2-Sided Fireplace

Built-in Desk

Built-in Cabinetry

Dining
13' 2" x 14' 4"
9' 0" Clg.

Gallery

Linen

Closet

Bath

Walk-in Shower

Up. Dn.

Foyer

Kitchen
16'-0" x 15'-6"
9'-0" Clg.

Pass thru

Bedroom 3
13'-0" x 13'-6"
Vaulted Clg.

Closet

Entry

Elev.

Pantry

Outdoor Kitchen

Dn.

P.B.

Art Niche

Closet

Bedroom 2
13'-8" x 12'-0"
9'-0" Clg.

Landing

Dn.

Built-ins

Utility

Bath

Walk-in Shower

Dn.

main level

Lanai
13'-8" x 8'-0"

Storage/ Bonus Room
8'-8" Clg.

Lower Porch
24'-4" x 27'-4"

2 Car Garage
9'-0" Clg.

Vestibule

Up.

Storage/ Bonus Room
8'-8" Clg.

Elev.

Mud Room

© THE SATER DESIGN COLLECTION, INC.

lower level

rear elevation

Deck
14'-2" x 8'-6"

© THE SATER DESIGN COLLECTION, INC.

Open to Below
Hip Vaulted Clg.

Master Deck
25'-0" x 8'-2"

Bedroom 4
12'-0" x 13'-10"
9'-4" Clg

Closet

Closet

Master Suite
13'-6" x 17'-6"avg.
9'-4" Clg

Whirlpool

Walk-in Shower

Bath
9'-0" Clg.

Tub

Linen

Catwalk

Dn.

2-Sided Fireplace

M. Bath
9'-0" Clg.

Open to Below

Built-in Cabinetry

W.I.C.

Elev.

Mechanical Room

upper level

© THE SATER DESIGN COLLECTION, INC.

Cottage | 4143 SQ. FT.

© THE SATER DESIGN COLLECTION, INC.

Cutlass Key

Graceful living abounds in this splendid and very livable design. Turreted roofs and a three-story glass staircase highlight the front of the home. The exterior blends siding, wood lattice and a metal roof, making it perfect for any region.

Upon entering the home, you're instantly impressed by the openness. A two-story grand room gains attention as a superb entertaining area, with a wet bar and a see-through fireplace. Glass doors open to the screened veranda, which allows for great rear vistas.

The eat-in kitchen has a center island cooktop, a huge walk-in pantry, and a pass-thru to the dining room and to the outdoor grill. The bayed nook is great for family eating. A multitude of windows offer spectacular rear yard views.

PLAN | *6619*

Bedroom: 4   Width: 61'4"
Bath: 5-1/2   Depth: 62'0"
Foundation: Piling with slab
Exterior Walls: 2x6

Main Level: 2,725 sq ft
Upper Level: 1,418 sq ft

Living Area: 4,143 sq ft

Price Code: **L 2**

1 - 8 0 0 - 7 1 8 - P L A N

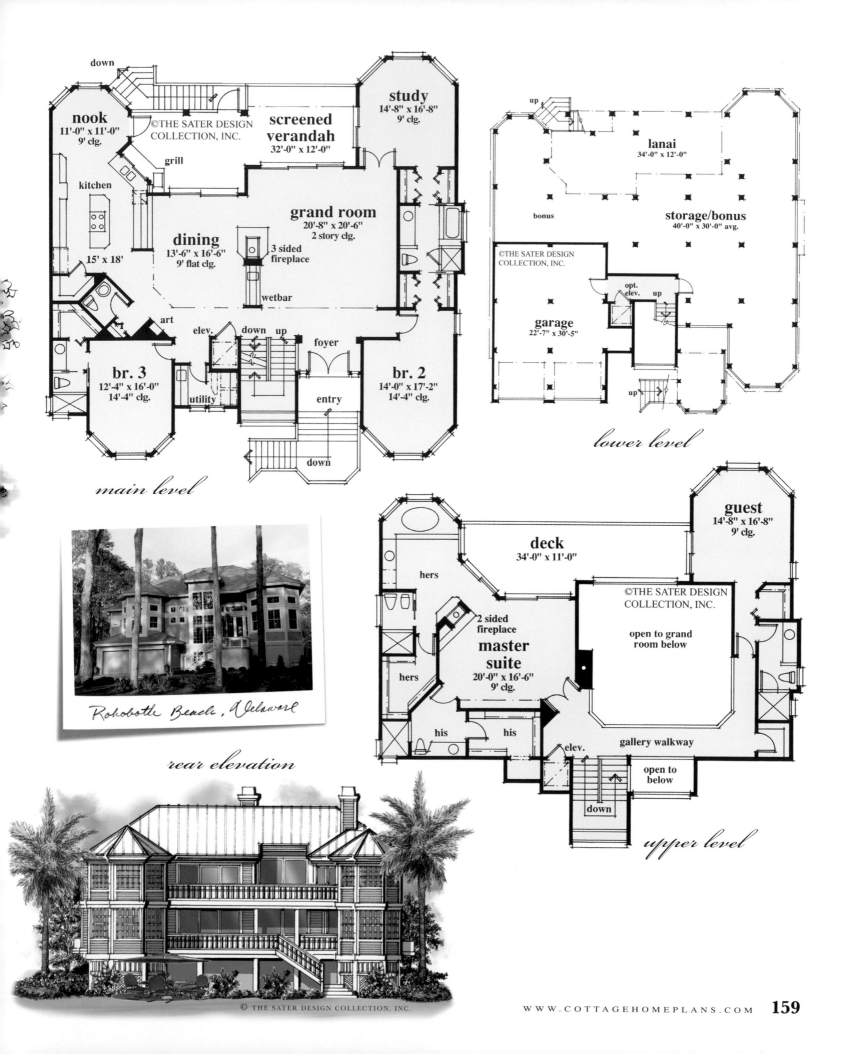

main level

down

nook
11'-0" x 11'-0"
9' clg.

©THE SATER DESIGN COLLECTION, INC.

screened verandah
32'-0" x 12'-0"

study
14'-8" x 16'-8"
9' clg.

grill

kitchen

15' x 18'

grand room
20'-8" x 20'-6"
2 story clg.

dining
13'-6" x 16'-6"
9' flat clg.

3 sided fireplace

wetbar

art

elev.

down

up

foyer

br. 3
12'-4" x 16'-0"
14'-4" clg.

utility

entry

br. 2
14'-0" x 17'-2"
14'-4" clg.

down

lower level

up

lanai
34'-0" x 12'-0"

bonus

storage/bonus
40'-0" x 30'-0" avg.

©THE SATER DESIGN COLLECTION, INC.

opt. elev.

up

garage
22'-7" x 30'-5"

up

rear elevation

Rehoboth Beach, Delaware

upper level

deck
34'-0" x 11'-0"

guest
14'-8" x 16'-8"
9' clg.

hers

hers

2 sided fireplace

master suite
20'-0" x 16'-6"
9' clg.

©THE SATER DESIGN COLLECTION, INC.

open to grand room below

his

his

elev.

gallery walkway

open to below

down

© THE SATER DESIGN COLLECTION, INC.

© THE SATER DESIGN COLLECTION, INC.

Cottage | 4359 SQ. FT.

Saint Croix

This enchanting Caribbean-style home combines a collection of windows, stately columns and tin roof, as well as a quaint porte-cochere. Once inside, columns open the great room to vast window views. Sliding glass doors allow a cool breeze to filter through. The kitchen is designed to be accessible to all serving areas, including a breakfast nook, verandah, and formal dining room. On the opposite wing, the hall ending in a whimsical window seat adjoins a bedroom and study.

An elevator eases the transition upstairs to a catwalk that overlooks the formal areas below. Featured in the master bedroom is a two-sided fireplace facing the luxurious tub, double vanities, a divided walk-in closet and an open shower flooded by natural light.

PLAN | 6822

Bedroom: 3   Width: 71'0"
Bath: 3-1/2   Depth: 69'0"
Foundation: Island basement
Exterior Walls: 2x6

Main Level: 2,391 sq ft
Upper Level: 1,539 sq ft
Lower Level Entry: 429 sq ft

Living Area: 4,359 sq ft

Price Code: **L2**

1-800-718-PLAN

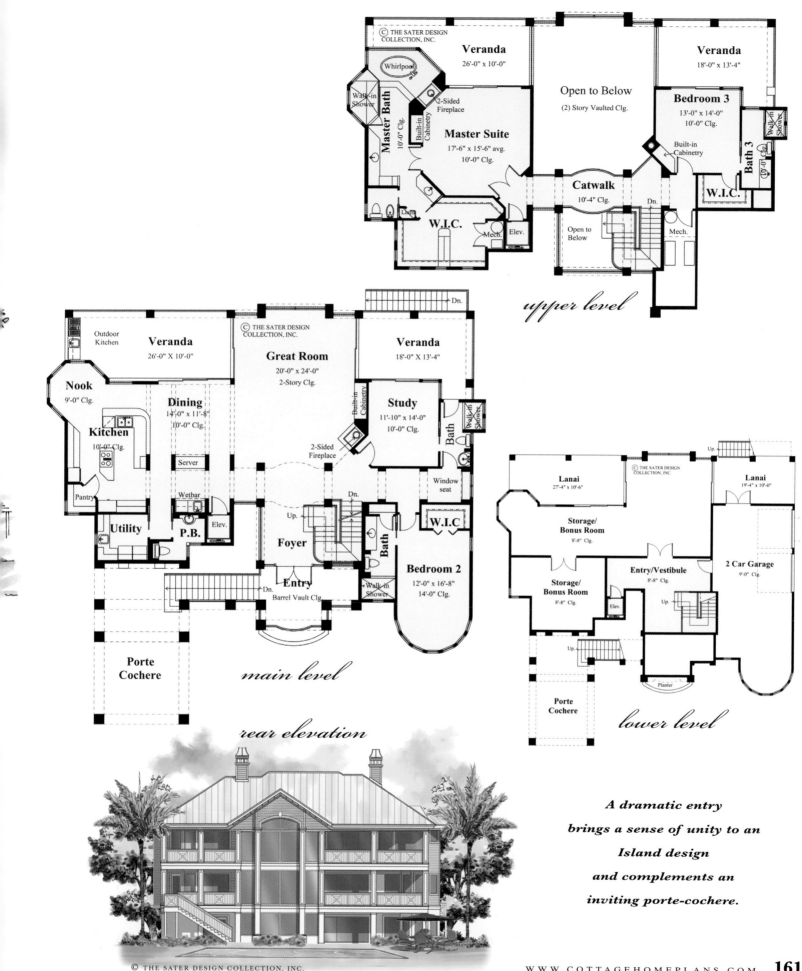

© THE SATER DESIGN COLLECTION, INC.

Veranda
26'-0" x 10'-0"

Whirlpool

Walk-in Shower

Veranda
18'-0" x 13'-4"

2-Sided Fireplace

Open to Below
(2) Story Vaulted Clg.

Bedroom 3
13'-0" x 14'-0"
10'-0" Clg.

Built-in Cabinetry

Walk-in Shower

Master Bath
10'-0" Clg.

Built-in Cabinetry

Master Suite
17'-6" x 15'-6" avg.
10'-0" Clg.

Bath 3

Linen

W.I.C.

Mech. Elev.

Catwalk
10'-4" Clg.

Dn.

W.I.C.

Open to Below

Dn.

Mech.

upper level

Dn.

Outdoor Kitchen

Veranda
26'-0" X 10'-0"

© THE SATER DESIGN COLLECTION, INC.

Great Room
20'-0" x 24'-0"
2-Story Clg.

Veranda
18'-0" X 13'-4"

Nook
9'-0" Clg.

Dining
14'-0" x 11'-8"
10'-0" Clg.

Built-in Cabinetry

Study
11'-10" x 14'-0"
10'-0" Clg.

Bath

Walk-in Shower

Kitchen
10'-0" Clg.

Server

2-Sided Fireplace

Pantry

Wetbar

Utility

Elev.

P.B.

Dn.

Up.

Foyer

Window seat

W.I.C

Bath

Entry
Barrel Vault Clg.

Walk-in Shower

Bedroom 2
12'-0" x 16'-8"
14'-0" Clg.

Dn.

Porte Cochere

main level

Up.

Lanai
27'-4" x 10'-6"

© THE SATER DESIGN COLLECTION, INC.

Lanai
19'-4" x 10'-0"

Storage/ Bonus Room
8'-8" Clg.

Storage/ Bonus Room
8'-8" Clg.

Entry/Vestibule
8'-8" Clg.

2 Car Garage
9'-0" Clg.

Elev.

Up.

Up.

Planter

Porte Cochere

lower level

rear elevation

© THE SATER DESIGN COLLECTION, INC.

A dramatic entry brings a sense of unity to an Island design and complements an inviting porte-cochere.

Photograph by: Laurence Taylor

Villas

Rambling loggias, hip roofs and dreamy archways make a beautiful statement about everyday life with the romantic houses of this collection. Drawn from the rugged yet refined villas carved into Mediterranean cliffsides, these are grand retreats designed to build in any region. Cast-stone moldings, smooth stucco and bold Moorish, English and Italianate details charge up the Euro flavor of the dramatic exteriors. Spare, sleek lines set off by terracotta tile, varied gables and classic columns conceal high-performance interiors that boast flex spaces, lofts, luxe wings for the homeowners, and bold links to the outdoors. Rows of French doors open to breezy decks and rambling porticos that invite lingering. Savory amenities such as garden tubs, secluded porches and do-everything kitchens step into the 21st Century.

© THE SATER DESIGN COLLECTION, INC.

Saint Basque

Reminiscent of early European styles, this villa boasts an array of windows, detailed masonry and a gabled roof. A recessed entryway acts as the main corridor that links the living spaces.

Take-your-breath-away views are captured in the great room from a wall of glass that protrudes into nature. Double doors open to a romantic deck, which wraps around the entire rear. Also residing on the main floor is a guest bedroom with a private bath, a powder room and a convenient laundry room. Upstairs, the loft overlooks the great room below. The master suite is a quiet refuge with rear decks to enjoy the evening air.

PLAN | *6851*

Bedroom: 2   Width: 32'0"

Bath: 2-1/2   Depth: 57'0"

Foundation: Island basement

Exterior Walls: 2x6

Main Level: 1,143 sq ft

Upper Level: 651 sq ft

Living Area: 1,794 sq ft

Price Code: **C1**

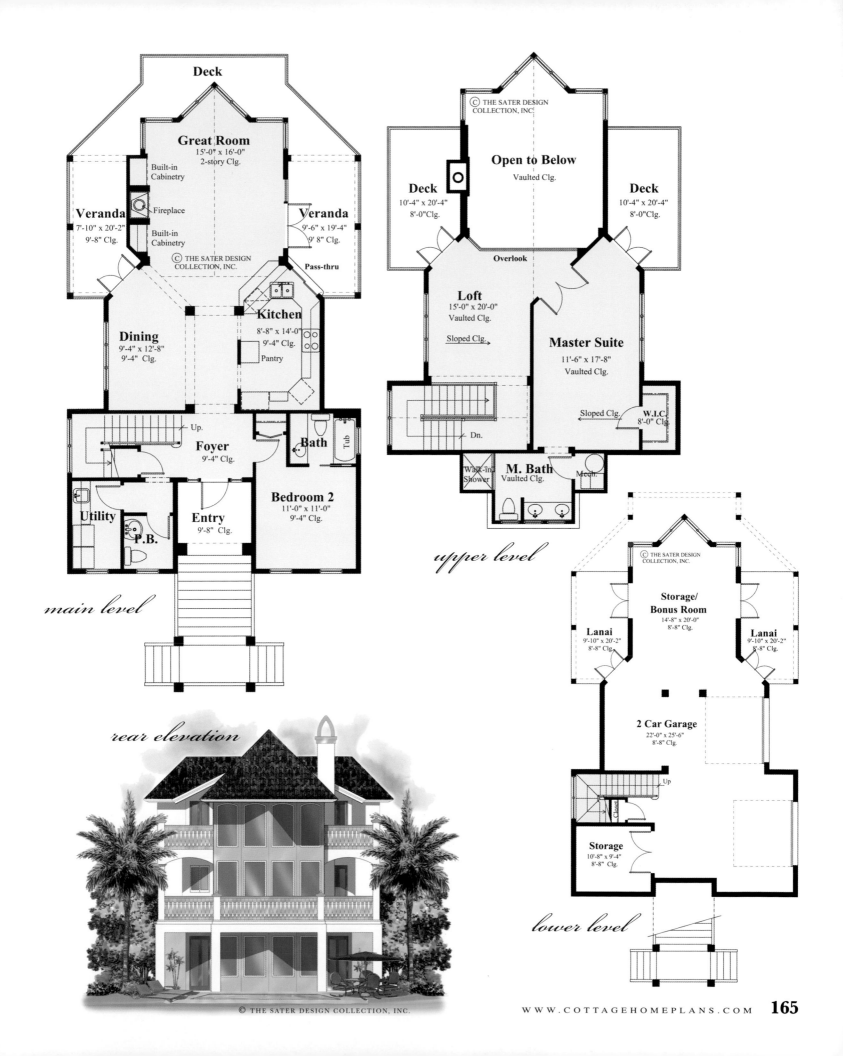

Deck

Great Room
15'-0" x 16'-0"
2-story Clg.

Built-in Cabinetry

Veranda
7'-10" x 20'-2"
9'-8" Clg.

Fireplace

Built-in Cabinetry

© THE SATER DESIGN COLLECTION, INC.

Veranda
9'-6" x 19'-4"
9' 8" Clg.

Pass-thru

Kitchen
8'-8" x 14'-0"
9'-4" Clg.

Pantry

Dining
9'-4" x 12'-8"
9'-4" Clg.

Up.

Foyer
9'-4" Clg.

Bath

Tub

Utility

P.B.

Entry
9'-8" Clg.

Bedroom 2
11'-0" x 11'-0"
9'-4" Clg.

main level

rear elevation

© THE SATER DESIGN COLLECTION, INC.

© THE SATER DESIGN COLLECTION, INC.

Open to Below
Vaulted Clg.

Deck
10'-4" x 20'-4"
8'-0" Clg.

Deck
10'-4" x 20'-4"
8'-0" Clg.

Overlook

Loft
15'-0" x 20'-0"
Vaulted Clg.

Sloped Clg.

Master Suite
11'-6" x 17'-8"
Vaulted Clg.

Sloped Clg.

W.I.C.
8'-0" Clg.

Dn.

Walk-in Shower

M. Bath
Vaulted Clg.

Mech.

upper level

© THE SATER DESIGN COLLECTION, INC.

**Storage/
Bonus Room**
14'-8" x 20'-0"
8'-8" Clg.

Lanai
9'-10" x 20'-2"
8'-8" Clg.

Lanai
9'-10" x 20'-2"
8'-8" Clg.

2 Car Garage
22'-0" x 25'-6"
8'-8" Clg.

Up

Closet

Storage
10'-8" x 9'-4"
8'-8" Clg.

lower level

© THE SATER DESIGN COLLECTION, INC.

© THE SATER DESIGN COLLECTION, INC.

Vittorio Terrace

Bold forms, keystone arches and exposed brackets indicate an Italianate influence with this stunning villa. Smooth earthen-hued stucco creates a striking counterpoint to detailed fretwork, which encases a ground-level arcade. A tall, arch-top window grants natural light to a centered winding staircase and repeats the graceful curves of the fanlight entry. The foyer provides interior vistas that extend through the great room and an open arrangement of the dining room and kitchen.

French doors open the central living space and the master bedroom to separate rear porches. The upper level features a computer loft with plenty of space for books, and an overlook to the great room. One of two secondary bedrooms opens to a sun deck with wide views beyond.

PLAN | *6866*

Bedroom: 3   Width: 44'0"
Bath: 2-1/2   Depth: 40'0"
Foundation: Island Basement
Exterior Walls: 2x6

Main Level: 1,342 sq ft
Upper Level: 511 sq ft
Lower Entry Level: 33 sq ft

Living Area: 1,886 sq ft

Price Code: **C1**

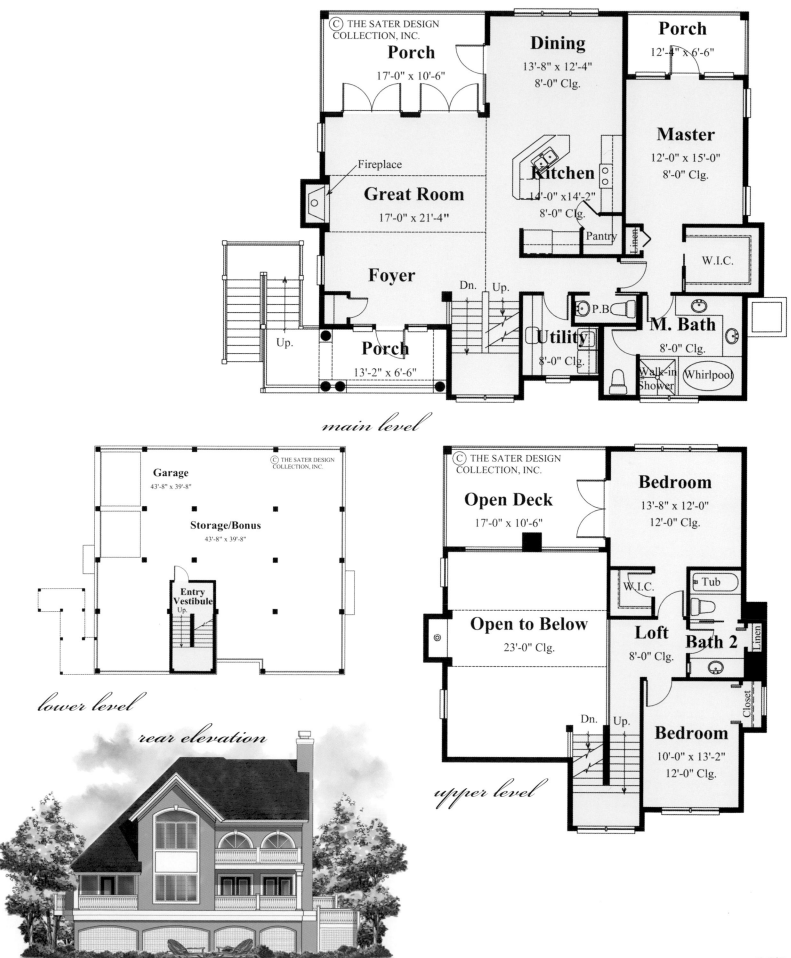

main level

© THE SATER DESIGN COLLECTION, INC.

Porch
17'-0" x 10'-6"

Dining
13'-8" x 12'-4"
8'-0" Clg.

Porch
12'-4" x 6'-6"

Fireplace

Kitchen
14'-0" x14'-2"
8'-0" Clg.

Master
12'-0" x 15'-0"
8'-0" Clg.

Great Room
17'-0" x 21'-4"

Pantry

Linen

W.I.C.

Foyer

Dn.   Up.

P.B

M. Bath
8'-0" Clg.

Up.

Porch
13'-2" x 6'-6"

Utility
8'-0" Clg.

Walk-in Shower

Whirlpool

lower level

© THE SATER DESIGN COLLECTION, INC.

Garage
43'-8" x 39'-8"

Storage/Bonus
43'-8" x 39'-8"

Entry Vestibule
Up.

upper level

© THE SATER DESIGN COLLECTION, INC.

Open Deck
17'-0" x 10'-6"

Bedroom
13'-8" x 12'-0"
12'-0" Clg.

W.I.C.

Tub

Open to Below
23'-0" Clg.

Loft
8'-0" Clg.

Bath 2

Linen

Closet

Dn.   Up.

Bedroom
10'-0" x 13'-2"
12'-0" Clg.

rear elevation

© THE SATER DESIGN COLLECTION, INC.

© THE SATER DESIGN COLLECTION, INC.

Terra di Mare

Classic columns and an enchanting double portico lend a sense of grandeur and romance to this impressive entry. The foyer leads up to an open, free-flowing interior where columns separate rooms and a bounty of windows provides unrestrained views. The vaulted ceiling in the great room adds volume to the room but the warming fireplace keeps it cozy.

To the left of the plan, two secondary bedrooms lead onto a private area of the porch. Fresh breezes invigorate the spirit through French doors opening to a balcony off the stairs leading up to the master suite. Wake up to bright and cheery mornings and the sun peeking through the doors from the rear deck. This breathtaking space offers a walk-in wardrobe closet and pampering bath.

PLAN | *6806*

Bedroom: 3   Width: 48'0"
Bath: 2   Depth: 48'0"
Foundation: Island basement
Exterior Walls: 2x6

Main Level: 1,383 sq ft
Upper Level: 595 sq ft

Living Area: 1,978 sq ft

Price Code: **C 1**

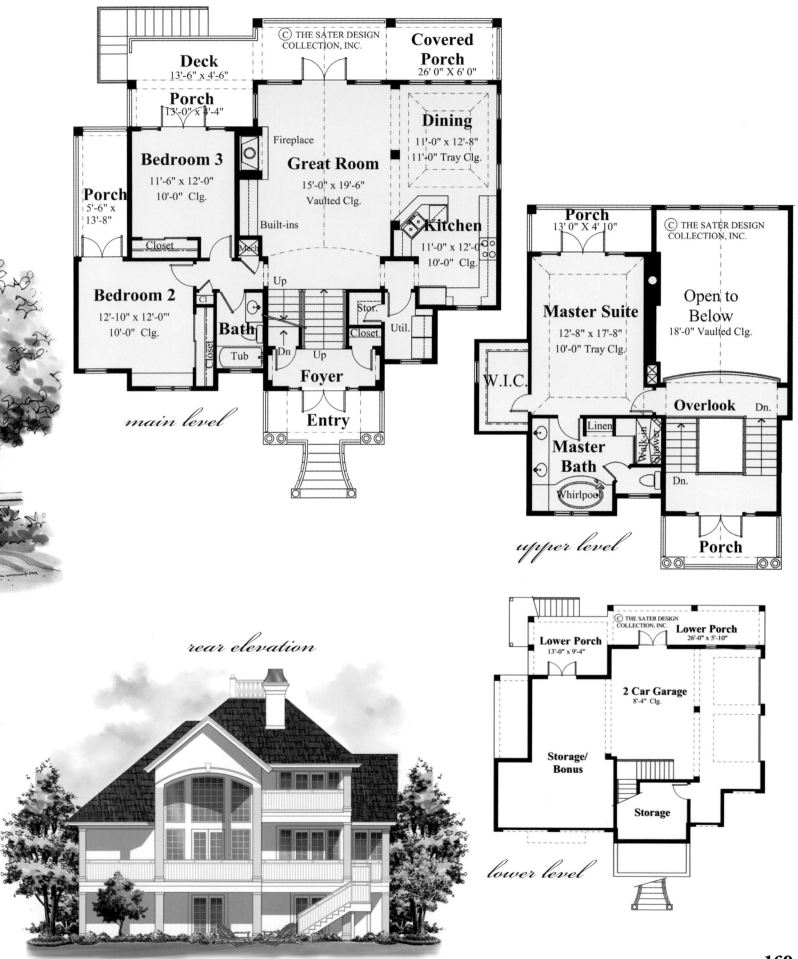

Deck
13'-6" x 4'-6"

© THE SATER DESIGN
COLLECTION, INC.

Covered Porch
26' 0" X 6' 0"

Porch
13'-0" x 4'-4"

Fireplace

Dining
11'-0" x 12'-8"
11'0" Tray Clg.

Bedroom 3
11'-6" x 12'-0"
10'-0" Clg.

Great Room
15'-0" x 19'-6"
Vaulted Clg.

Porch
5'-6" x
13'-8"

Built-ins

Kitchen
11'-0" x 12'-0"
10'-0" Clg.

Closet

Mech.

Up

Stor.

Bedroom 2
12'-10" x 12'-0"
10'-0" Clg.

Cl.

Closet

Util.

Bath

Tub

Dn.

Up

Closet

Foyer

Entry

main level

Porch
13' 0" X 4' 10"

© THE SATER DESIGN
COLLECTION, INC.

Master Suite
12'-8" x 17'-8"
10'-0" Tray Clg.

Open to Below
18'-0" Vaulted Clg.

W.I.C.

Linen

Overlook

Dn.

Master Bath

Walk-in Shower

Whirlpool

Dn.

Porch

upper level

rear elevation

Lower Porch
13'-0" x 9'-4"

© THE SATER DESIGN
COLLECTION, INC.

Lower Porch
26'-0" x 5'-10"

2 Car Garage
8'-4" Clg.

Storage/ Bonus

Storage

lower level

© THE SATER DESIGN COLLECTION, INC.

© THE SATER DESIGN COLLECTION, INC.

Villa Caprini

Vintage details such as a high-pitched roof, faux widow's walk and corner quoins look absolutely stunning on this Mediterranean villa. Well-planned rooms and wide-open spaces reside inside. Throughout the home, the creative use of columns soften the space and French doors brighten the rooms with daylight. All decked out, the back has full-length porches on every level for outdoor enjoyment.

Window seats in the great room not only offer a decorative touch but a cozy spot to chill-out. The gourmet kitchen is a chef's dream. Pull a couple of chairs around the center island and enjoy the company and conversation of family and friends while preparing meals.

PLAN | *6854*

Bedroom: 3   Width: 34'0"
Bath: 2-1/2   Depth: 40'6"
Foundation: Island basement
Exterior Walls: 2x6

Main Level: 874 sq ft
Upper Level: 880 sq ft
Lower Level Entry: 242 sq ft

Living Area: 1,996 sq ft

Price Code: **C1**

1 - 8 0 0 - 7 1 8 - P L A N

© THE SATER DESIGN COLLECTION, INC.

Veranda
39'-0" x 7'-6"
10'-6" Clg.

Window Seat

Built-in Cabinetry

Great Room
18'-0" x 20'-0"
10'-0" Clg.

Fireplace

Built-in Cabinetry

Window Seat

Dining
10'-0" x 13'-0"
10'-0" Clg.

Kitchen
15'-0" x 15'-0"
10'-0" Clg.

Dn.

Up.

Utility

P.B
9'-0" Clg

main level

© THE SATER DESIGN COLLECTION, INC.

Deck
39'-0" x 7'-6"
8'-4" Clg.

Walk-in Shower

Bedroom 3
10'-0" x 13'-0"
9'-4" Clg.

Master Bath

Master Suite
13'-0" x 13'-0"
10'-4" Clg.

W.I.C

Linen

W.I.C

Bedroom 2
12'-8" x 11'-0"
9'-4" Clg.

Dn.

Walk-in Shower

Bath 2

Closet

upper level

---

rear elevation

© THE SATER DESIGN COLLECTION, INC.

© THE SATER DESIGN COLLECTION, INC.

Lanai
39'-0" x 7'-6"
9'-4" Clg.

2 1/2 Car Garage
20'-0" x 29'-0"
10'-0" Clg.

Optional Utility

Mech.

W.I.C.

Up.

Foyer

Entry Porch

lower level

Villa | 2137 SQ. FT.

© THE SATER DESIGN COLLECTION, INC.

Via Pascoli

Lovely architecture and brilliant windows adorn this inside-out villa that enjoys light and scenic views from all sides. This floor plan offers all the necessary amenities, gently mixed with a distinctive touch of elegant extras, such as interesting ceilings, a central fireplace and decorative columns.

The master suite, secluded to the back of this treasure, allows many views from inside with carefully placed windows. Downstairs has ample storage with two colossal bonus rooms that provide for future development and triple sets of French doors that invite family and friends to watch a scenic water view.

PLAN | 6842

Bedroom: 3   Width: 44'0"
Bath: 2   Depth: 61'0"
Foundation: Island basement
Exterior Walls: 2x6

Main Level: 2,137 sq ft
Living Area: 2,137 sq ft
Price Code: **C2**

1-800-718-PLAN

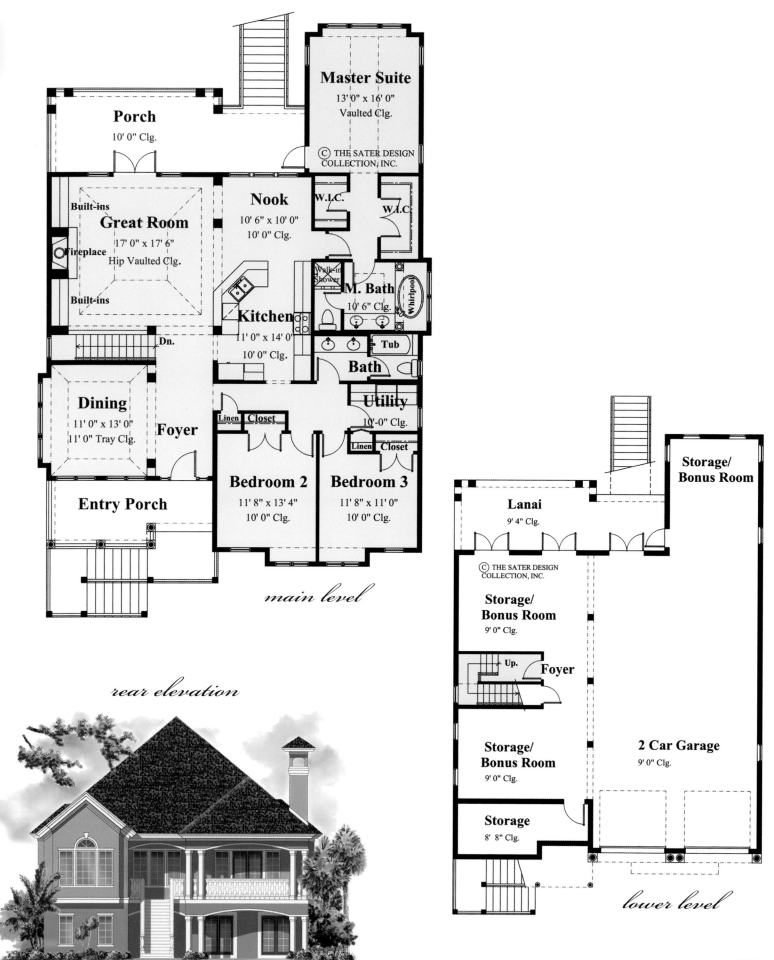

Porch
10' 0" Clg.

Master Suite
13' 0" x 16' 0"
Vaulted Clg.

© THE SATER DESIGN
COLLECTION, INC.

Great Room
17' 0" x 17' 6"
Hip Vaulted Clg.

Built-ins

Fireplace

Built-ins

Nook
10' 6" x 10' 0"
10' 0" Clg.

W.I.C.

W.I.C.

Walk-in Shower

M. Bath
10' 6" Clg.

Whirlpool

Kitchen
11' 0" x 14' 0"
10' 0" Clg.

Dn.

Tub

Bath

Dining
11' 0" x 13' 0"
11' 0" Tray Clg.

Foyer

Linen | Closet

Utility
10'-0" Clg.

Linen | Closet

Entry Porch

Bedroom 2
11' 8" x 13' 4"
10' 0" Clg.

Bedroom 3
11' 8" x 11' 0"
10' 0" Clg.

main level

rear elevation

Lanai
9' 4" Clg.

Storage/ Bonus Room

© THE SATER DESIGN
COLLECTION, INC.

Storage/ Bonus Room
9' 0" Clg.

Up. **Foyer**

Storage/ Bonus Room
9' 0" Clg.

2 Car Garage
9' 0" Clg.

Storage
8' 8" Clg.

lower level

© THE SATER DESIGN COLLECTION, INC.

© THE SATER DESIGN COLLECTION, INC.

Chelsea Passage

A stunning entrance is only the beginning to what awaits in this lovely villa home. Inside, the formal gallery announces the spacious interior. A vaulted ceiling above the great room, which hosts a center fireplace and French doors, carries on into the master bedroom. Comfortable elegance in the suite is provided by a garden soaking tub and vanities for two. During the cool season, French doors allow simple pleasures like fresh breezes to mingle.

Taking center stage, the gallery kitchen is extended to the great room by a snack bar and views of the warming fireplace. Secondary bedrooms are found upstairs along with a den and a loft that overlooks the great room below.

PLAN | *6812*

Bedroom: 3	Width: 45'4"
Bath: 2-1/2	Depth: 50'0"
Foundation: Island basement	
Exterior Walls: 2x6	

Main Level:	1,537 sq ft
Upper Level:	812 sq ft
Living Area:	2,349 sq ft
Price Code:	**C2**

1-800-718-PLAN

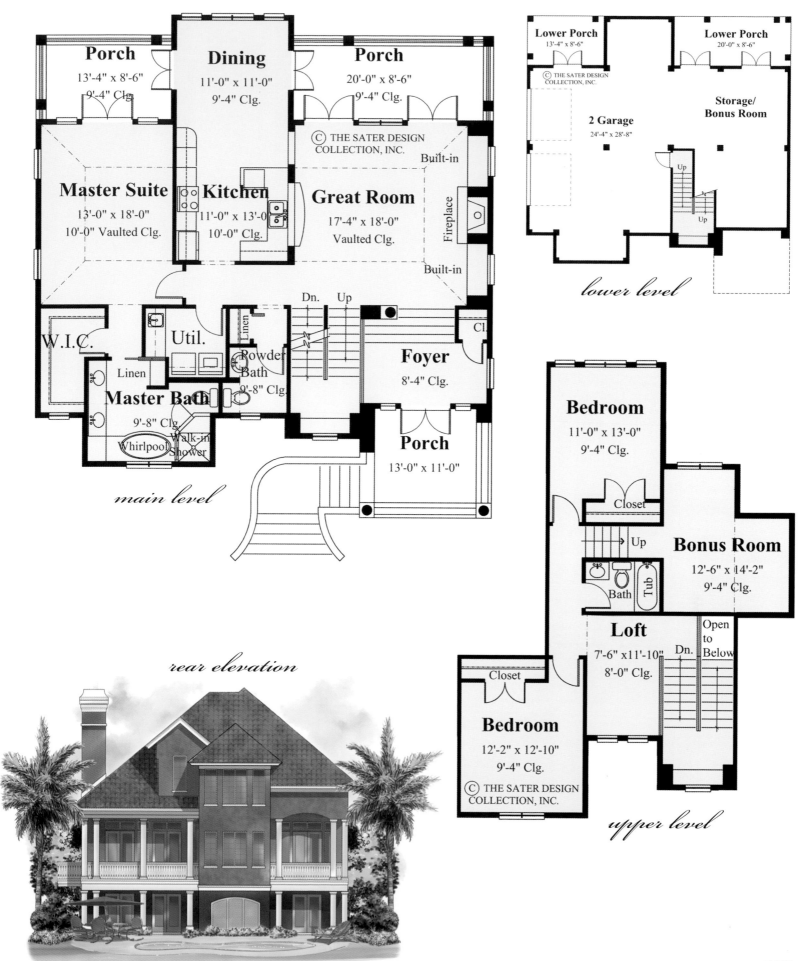

Porch
13'-4" x 8'-6"
9'-4" Clg.

Dining
11'-0" x 11'-0"
9'-4" Clg.

Porch
20'-0" x 8'-6"
9'-4" Clg.

© THE SATER DESIGN COLLECTION, INC.

Built-in

Master Suite
13'-0" x 18'-0"
10'-0" Vaulted Clg.

Kitchen
11'-0" x 13'-0"
10'-0" Clg.

Great Room
17'-4" x 18'-0"
Vaulted Clg.

Fireplace

Built-in

W.I.C.

Util.

Linen

Linen

Dn. Up

Cl.

Foyer
8'-4" Clg.

Powder Bath
9'-8" Clg.

Master Bath
9'-8" Clg.

Whirlpool

Walk-in Shower

Porch
13'-0" x 11'-0"

main level

Lower Porch
13'-4" x 8'-6"

Lower Porch
20'-0" x 8'-6"

© THE SATER DESIGN COLLECTION, INC.

2 Garage
24'-4" x 28'-8"

Storage/ Bonus Room

Up

Up

lower level

Bedroom
11'-0" x 13'-0"
9'-4" Clg.

Closet

Up

Bath

Tub

Bonus Room
12'-6" x 14'-2"
9'-4" Clg.

Loft
7'-6" x 11'-10"
8'-0" Clg.

Open to Below

Dn.

Closet

Bedroom
12'-2" x 12'-10"
9'-4" Clg.

© THE SATER DESIGN COLLECTION, INC.

upper level

rear elevation

© THE SATER DESIGN COLLECTION, INC.

Villa | 2374 SQ. FT.

© THE SATER DESIGN COLLECTION, INC.

Nicholas Park

An elaborate entry porch with bold columns sets off this chic villa. An array of windows brings in light, guiding the way to a mid-level foyer that invites you to see what awaits. No one is ever left out with an open arrangement of the two-story great room, gallery kitchen and casual dining. Overlooks to the rear deck are to be enjoyed by all — perfect for summertime entertainment.

An art niche in the gallery hall leads to the master suite and French doors open the master bedroom to the rear porch. A tray ceiling highlights the suite, which enjoys a spacious bath and garden tub. Upstairs, two ample bedrooms have tray ceilings and open to the rear observation deck.

PLAN | *6804*

Bedroom: 3	Width: 44'0"
Bath: 3-1/2	Depth: 49'0"
Foundation: Island basement	
Exterior Walls: 2x6	

Main Level:	1,510 sq ft
Upper Level:	864 sq ft
Living Area:	2,374 sq ft
Price Code:	**C 2**

Open Deck
30'-10" x 12'-8"

Porch
8' Clg.

Bedroom 3
12'-2" x 15'-0"
8'-0" - 9'-4" Clg.

Porch
8' Clg

© THE SATER DESIGN
COLLECTION, INC.

Open to Below

Bedroom 2
13'-2" x 12'-0"
8'-0" - 9'-4" clg.

Cl. Cl.

Tub **Bath 3**
10'-0" Clg.

WIC

Down

Tub

Loft
10'-4" x 11'-4"
8" Clg

Open to Below

Bath 2
10'-0" Clg.

Window Seat

upper level

© THE SATER DESIGN
COLLECTION, INC.

Lower Porch
30' 0" x 7' 2"

Storage/Bonus

Garage
24'-0" x 25'-6"

UP

Storage

lower level

© THE SATER DESIGN
COLLECTION, INC.

Porch
30'-10" - 12'-8"
10 Clg.

Dining
12'-0" x 11'-4"
10'-0" Clg.

Great Room
16'-4" x 18'-0"
19'-4" - 20'-0" Clg.
Fireplace

Kitchen
12'-2" x 13'-4"
10'-0" Clg.

Master Suite
13'-0" x 16'-0"
9'-0" - 10'-0" Clg.

Entertainment Center

Linen

Ref.

Niche

Linen

Walk-in Shower

Master Bath
10'-0" Clg.

Powder
10'-0" Clg.

Utility

Whirlpool **WIC**

Foyer
9'-10" clg.

UP

Porch
12'-0" clg.

main level

rear elevation

© THE SATER DESIGN COLLECTION, INC.

© THE SATER DESIGN COLLECTION, INC.

San Marino

This hip chateau is redefined, extending its indoor to outdoor spaces, combining nature-inspired comfort with character and beauty. A fashionable sunburst transom adorns the entryway and pillars introduce the lavish interior. Cathedral ceilings in the great room and formal dining areas extend the sense of spaciousness and allow for an easy transition to the outdoor living space. From the entry to the rear balcony, the wide-open vistas allow the warm gentle breezes to flow through the house.

The formal dining room opens through a colonnade from the gallery hall and shares the comfort of the central fireplace. A kitchen buffet counter can be used for casual serving or can accommodate formal entertaining. Common areas separate easily maintained guestrooms from the private master suite.

PLAN | *6833*

Bedroom: 3   Width: 70'2"
Bath: 3   Depth: 53'0"
Foundation: Island basement
Exterior Walls: 2x6

Main Level: 2,433 sq ft

Living Area: 2,433 sq ft

Price Code: **C2**

1-800-718-PLAN

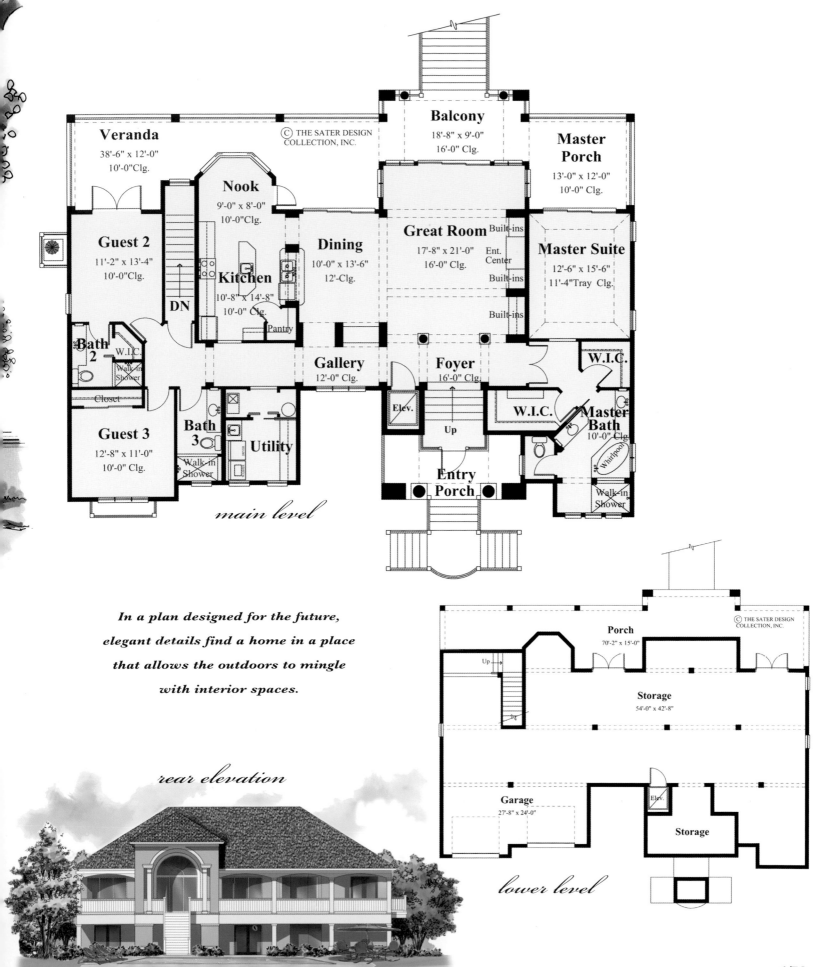

Veranda
38'-6" x 12'-0"
10'-0"Clg.

© THE SATER DESIGN
COLLECTION, INC.

Balcony
18'-8" x 9'-0"
16'-0" Clg.

Master Porch
13'-0" x 12'-0"
10'-0" Clg.

Nook
9'-0" x 8'-0"
10'-0"Clg.

Great Room
17'-8" x 21'-0"
16'-0" Clg.

Built-ins

Guest 2
11'-2" x 13'-4"
10'-0"Clg.

Dining
10'-0" x 13'-6"
12'-Clg.

Ent. Center

Master Suite
12'-6" x 15'-6"
11'-4"Tray Clg.

Kitchen
10'-8" x 14'-8"
10'-0" Clg.

Built-ins

Built-ins

DN

Pantry

Bath 2

W.I.C.

Walk in Shower

W.I.C.

Gallery
12'-0" Clg.

Foyer
16'-0" Clg.

Elev.

Master Bath
10'-0" Clg.

Closet

W.I.C.

Up

Whirlpool

Guest 3
12'-8" x 11'-0"
10'-0" Clg.

Bath 3

Utility

Walk in Shower

Entry Porch

Walk-in Shower

main level

*In a plan designed for the future,
elegant details find a home in a place
that allows the outdoors to mingle
with interior spaces.*

rear elevation

Porch
70'-2" x 15'-0"

© THE SATER DESIGN
COLLECTION, INC.

Up

Storage
54'-0" x 42'-8"

Garage
27'-8" x 24'-0"

Elev.

Storage

lower level

© THE SATER DESIGN COLLECTION, INC.

Villa | 2465 SQ. FT.

© THE SATER DESIGN COLLECTION, INC.

Southhampton Bay

A cupola on this gorgeous coastal design tops a classic pediment and low-pitched roof. Inside, the beauty and warmth of natural light splash the spacious living area with a sense of the outdoors.

A stunning sunburst sets off the entry and announces the foyer's impressive staircase. The great room features a wall of built-ins designed for even the most technology-savvy entertainment buff. Dazzling views through great walls of glass are enlivened by the presence of a breezy portico, set off by European-style arches.

The master suite features a luxurious bath, a dressing area and his and hers walk-in closets. Lower-level space includes a game room, a bonus room, extra storage and plans for an optional elevator.

PLAN | 6684

Bedroom: 3   Width: 60'4"

Bath: 2-1/2   Depth: 59'4"

Foundation: Slab

Exterior Walls: 2x6 and 8"CBS

Main Level: 2,385 sq ft

Upper Level: 80 sq ft

Living Area: 2,465 sq ft

Price Code: **C2**

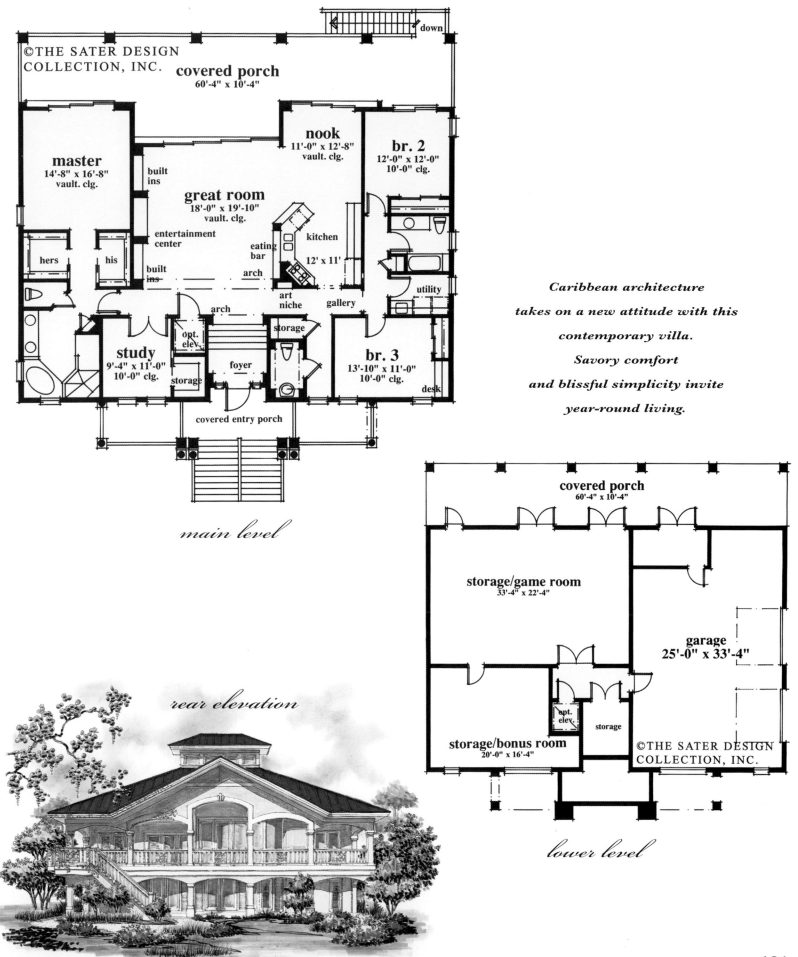

©THE SATER DESIGN COLLECTION, INC.

covered porch
60'-4" x 10'-4"

master
14'-8" x 16'-8"
vault. clg.

built ins

nook
11'-0" x 12'-8"
vault. clg.

br. 2
12'-0" x 12'-0"
10'-0" clg.

great room
18'-0" x 19'-10"
vault. clg.

entertainment center

hers

his

built ins

kitchen

eating bar

arch

utility

art niche

gallery

arch

storage

study
9'-4" x 11'-0"
10'-0" clg.

opt. elev.

storage

foyer

br. 3
13'-10" x 11'-0"
10'-0" clg.

desk

covered entry porch

main level

*Caribbean architecture
takes on a new attitude with this
contemporary villa.
Savory comfort
and blissful simplicity invite
year-round living.*

covered porch
60'-4" x 10'-4"

storage/game room
33'-4" x 22'-4"

garage
25'-0" x 33'-4"

opt. elev.

storage

storage/bonus room
20'-0" x 16'-4"

©THE SATER DESIGN COLLECTION, INC.

lower level

rear elevation

© THE SATER DESIGN COLLECTION, INC.

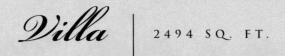

© THE SATER DESIGN COLLECTION, INC.

Mission Hills

This classy European villa combines Mediterranean influences with Italian design. Rising a few steps, this home offers banded stucco, columns and an arched-glassed entry leading into the main corridor, linking two wings that spread outward from the central great room. The kitchen with casual dining blends into the great room, with an eating bar that defines the spaces, still joined by expansive vaulted ceilings. Up front, both a study and utility room open onto covered balconies, capturing sunshine and fresh breezes.

Guest quarters are on the right, and enjoy ample baths and lovely views. On the other side, the master bedroom provides stylish comfort, with separate closets and a totally indulgent bath with dual vanities, corner whirlpool-tub, walk-in shower and windows that filter in natural light.

PLAN | *6845*

Bedroom: 3	Width: 60'0"
Bath: 3	Depth: 52'0"

Foundation: Island basement
Exterior Walls: 2x6

Main Level:	2,385 sq ft
Lower Level Entry:	109 sq ft
Living Area:	2,494 sq ft

Price Code: **C2**

1-800-718-PLAN

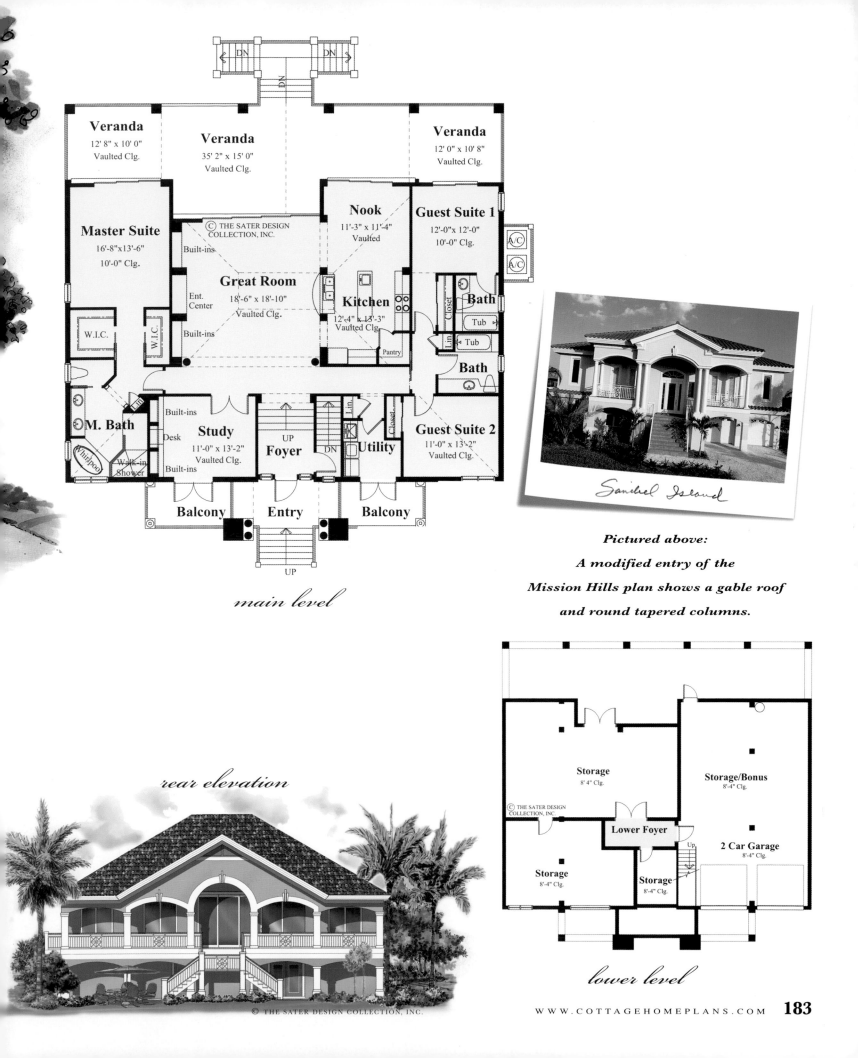

Veranda
12' 8" x 10' 0"
Vaulted Clg.

Veranda
35' 2" x 15' 0"
Vaulted Clg.

Veranda
12' 0" x 10' 8"
Vaulted Clg.

Master Suite
16'-8"x13'-6"
10'-0" Clg.

© THE SATER DESIGN COLLECTION, INC.

Built-ins

Nook
11'-3" x 11'-4"
Vaulted

Guest Suite 1
12'-0"x 12'-0"
10'-0" Clg.

Ent.
Center

Great Room
18'-6" x 18'-10"
Vaulted Clg.

Kitchen
12'-4" x 13'-3"
Vaulted Clg.

A/C

A/C

Bath

Tub

W.I.C.

W.I.C.

Built-ins

Pantry

Closet

Lin.

Tub

Bath

M. Bath

Built-ins

Desk

Study
11'-0" x 13'-2"
Vaulted Clg.

Built-ins

UP

Foyer

DN

Lin.

Utility

Closet

Guest Suite 2
11'-0" x 13'-2"
Vaulted Clg.

Whirlpool

Walk-in
Shower

Balcony

Entry

Balcony

UP

main level

Pictured above:

A modified entry of the

Mission Hills plan shows a gable roof

and round tapered columns.

Sanibel Island

rear elevation

Storage
8' 4" Clg.

Storage/Bonus
8'-4" Clg.

© THE SATER DESIGN
COLLECTION, INC.

Lower Foyer

Up

2 Car Garage
8'-4" Clg.

Storage
8'-4" Clg.

Storage
8'-4" Clg.

lower level

© THE SATER DESIGN COLLECTION, INC.

© THE SATER DESIGN COLLECTION, INC.

Riviera dei Fiori

Inspired by Mediterranean architecture, sun-splashed columns and balustrades call to mind an earlier era. Sidelights and transoms enrich the elevation and offer a warm welcome. Gentle breezes flow through the interior of very comfortable rooms. The kitchen is a dream for any culinary chef. Ample counters allow the cook needed space to prepare a masterpiece. The convenient butler's pantry is a nice place for a coffee station during family events.

The third floor master suite is just dreamy. The plush bath has a relaxing soaking tub and dual vanities, while the sitting area allows spectacular views and French doors to an observation deck.

PLAN | 6809

Bedroom: 4   Width: 46'0"

Bath: 3   Depth: 51'0"

Foundation: Island basement

Exterior Walls: 2x6

Main Level: 1,542 sq ft

Upper Level: 971 sq ft

Living Area: 2,513 sq ft

Price Code: **C3**

1-800-718-PLAN

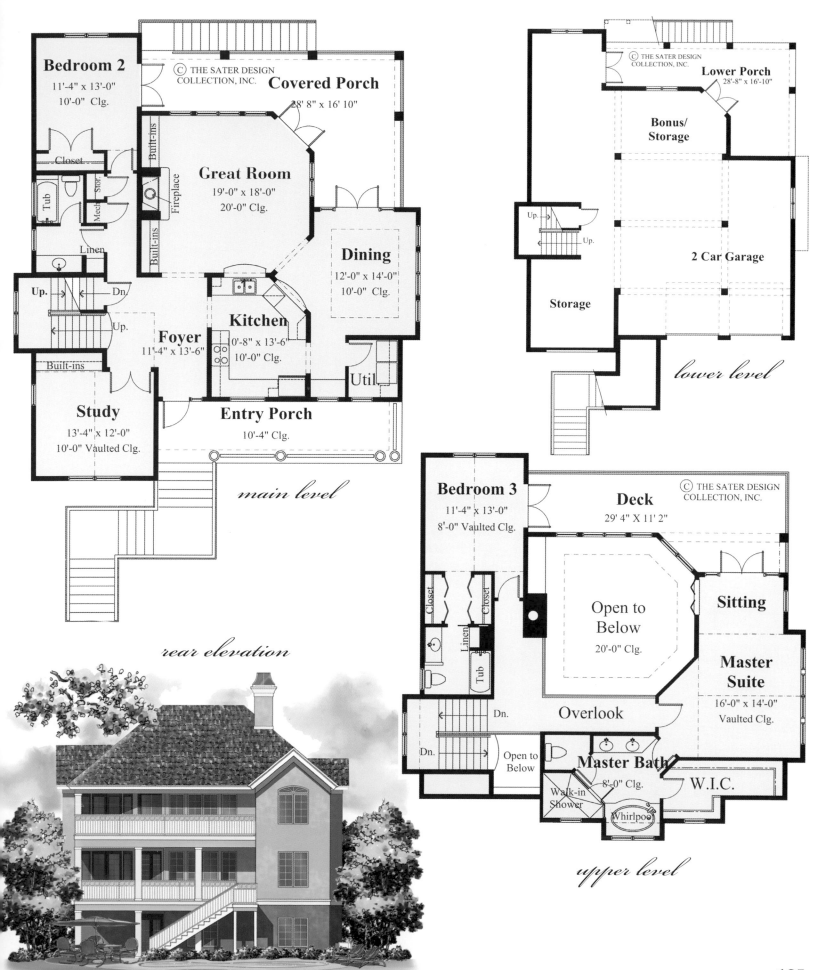

Bedroom 2
11'-4" x 13'-0"
10'-0" Clg.

Closet

Tub

Mech. Stor.

Linen

Covered Porch
28' 8" x 16' 10"

Built-ins

Great Room
19'-0" x 18'-0"
20'-0" Clg.

Fireplace

Built-ins

Up.   Dn.

Up.

Built-ins

Foyer
11'-4" x 13'-6"

Kitchen
0'-8" x 13'-6"
10'-0" Clg.

Dining
12'-0" x 14'-0"
10'-0" Clg.

Util.

Study
13'-4" x 12'-0"
10'-0" Vaulted Clg.

Entry Porch
10'-4" Clg.

main level

© THE SATER DESIGN COLLECTION, INC.

© THE SATER DESIGN COLLECTION, INC.

Lower Porch
28'-8" x 16'-10"

Bonus/ Storage

Up.   Up.

Storage

2 Car Garage

lower level

rear elevation

Bedroom 3
11'-4" x 13'-0"
8'-0" Vaulted Clg.

Closet   Closet

Linen

Deck
29' 4" X 11' 2"

© THE SATER DESIGN COLLECTION, INC.

Open to Below
20'-0" Clg.

Sitting

Master Suite
16'-0" x 14'-0"
Vaulted Clg.

Dn.

Dn.

Open to Below

Overlook

Master Bath
8'-0" Clg.

Walk-in Shower

Whirlpool

W.I.C.

upper level

© THE SATER DESIGN COLLECTION, INC.

© THE SATER DESIGN COLLECTION, INC.

Charleston Place

PLAN | *6700*

Louvered shutters, balustered railings and a Spanish tile roof blend with stucco-and-quoins in this Row House-style plan, infused with a Mediterranean flavor. Breezes whisper through plantation-style galleries, defining a new look that marries past and present. Interior spaces that are long on views achieve a narrow footprint, perfect for slender lots.

Entry stairs lead to the main-level living areas, defined by arches and columns that blend Old World craftsmanship with modern space. A wall of built-ins and a warming fireplace lend a cozy feeling to the open, contemporary great room. Four sets of French doors expand the living area to the gallery and extend an invitation to gentle afternoon breezes.

Bedroom: 3   Width: 30'6"
Bath: 2-1/2   Depth: 77'6"
Foundation: Slab/Island basement
Exterior Walls: 2x6

Main Level: 1,305 sq ft
Upper Level: 1,215 sq ft

Living Area: 2,520 sq ft

Price Code: **C3**

1-800-718-PLAN

©THE SATER DESIGN COLLECTION, INC.

covered porch
30'-0" x 12'-0" avg.

bonus space
19'-0" x 19'-0" avg.
8'-0" clg.

optional fireplace

covered porch

arch

garden courtyard

bonus space
24'-6" x 14'-0" avg.
8'-0" clg.

entry

foyer

up

down

privacy wall

entry gate

garage
21'-4" x 21'-0"

lower level

©THE SATER DESIGN COLLECTION, INC.

observation deck
30'-0" x 12'-0" avg.

master
19'-0" x 13'-8"
10'-0" tray clg.

sundeck

his

hers

his

hers

br. 2
9'-6" x 12'-8"
9'-0" clg.

arch

gallery

down

equip.

guest
10'-4" x 15'-8"
9'-0" clg.

upper level

rear elevation

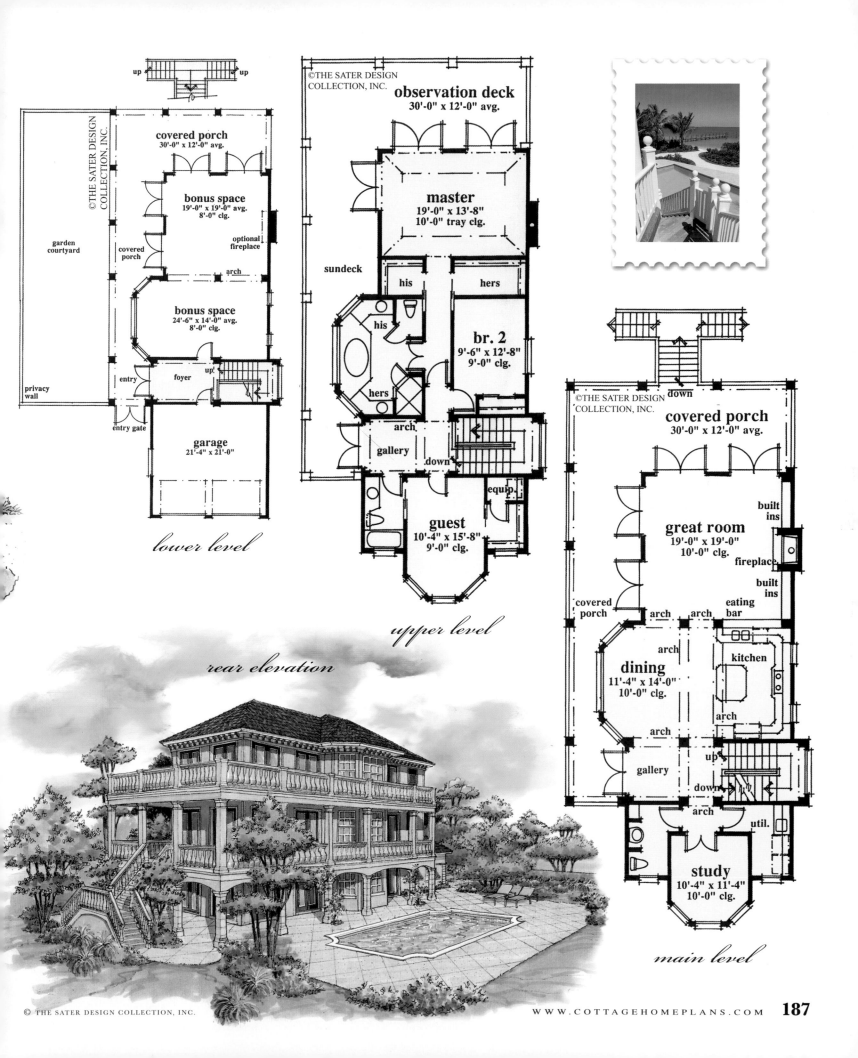

©THE SATER DESIGN COLLECTION, INC.

covered porch
30'-0" x 12'-0" avg.

down

built ins

great room
19'-0" x 19'-0"
10'-0" clg.

fireplace

built ins

covered porch

arch

arch

eating bar

kitchen

arch

dining
11'-4" x 14'-0"
10'-0" clg.

arch

arch

gallery

up

down

arch

util.

study
10'-4" x 11'-4"
10'-0" clg.

main level

Villa | 2650 SQ. FT.

© THE SATER DESIGN COLLECTION, INC.

Sommerset

A Spanish tile roof and an elegant portico combine to create this captivating Mediterranean villa. Tall windows and deep porches invite shade and cool breezes to linger. The easy spirit of the interior is reminiscent of a true Southern plantation with spans of French doors that fold onto the wrap-around porch.

The kitchen hugs the back of the house. Angled counters, a center island and built-in desk or message center overlook the breakfast nook and offer views of the rear property.

Upstairs, the luxurious master suite has an octagonal sitting area and French doors to the wrapping deck. At the other end of the deck are two more bedrooms and a study.

PLAN | *6827*

Bedroom: 3	Width: 34'0"
Bath: 2-1/2	Depth: 63'2"
Foundation: Slab	
Exterior Walls: 2x6	

Main Level:	1,296 sq ft
Upper Level:	1,354 sq ft
Living Area:	2,650 sq ft
Price Code:	**C3**

Master Bath

Whirlpool

Walk-in Shower

W.I.C.

W.I.C.

Master Suite
12'-5" x 22'-4"
10'-0" Clg.

Dn.

Sitting Area
13'-0" Octagon
Vaulted Clg.

Optional Vent-Free Fireplace

Bedroom 3
13'-2" x 12'-0"
10'-0" Clg.

W.I.C.

Bath 2

Tub

Loft

Mech.

Bedroom 2
15'-6" x 12'-0"
10'-0" Clg.

Deck
8'-2" x 42'-4"

Study
9'-0" x 14'-6"
11'-4" Clg.

Deck
26'-4" x 10'-0"

© THE SATER DESIGN COLLECTION, INC.

upper level

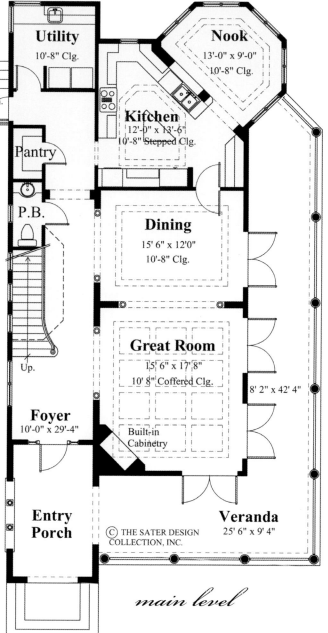

Utility
10'-8" Clg.

Nook
13'-0" x 9'-0"
10'-8" Clg.

Kitchen
12'-0" x 13'-6"
10'-8" Stepped Clg.

Pantry

P.B.

Dining
15'6" x 12'0"
10'-8" Clg.

Dn.

Up.

Great Room
15'6" x 17'8"
10'8" Coffered Clg.

8'2" x 42'4"

Foyer
10'-0" x 29'-4"

Built-in Cabinetry

Entry Porch

Veranda
25'6" x 9'4"

© THE SATER DESIGN COLLECTION, INC.

main level

rear elevation

© THE SATER DESIGN COLLECTION, INC.

© THE SATER DESIGN COLLECTION, INC.

Rue Nouveau

This sun-drenched villa sports a Spanish tiled roof, stucco exterior and arch-top windows. Inside, the great room highlights a vaulted ceiling, a warming fireplace and a built-in entertainment center. A spacious kitchen with wrapping counters serves the heart of the home. Two linen closets line the gallery hall to the secondary bedrooms. This wing also has a convenient laundry room and guest bath.

Secluded upstairs is the spacious master suite. The unique layout accommodates large furniture and takes full advantage of the untamed views. The master bath is made for two with dual vanities and a large soaking tub.

PLAN | *6836*

Bedroom: 3   Width: 44'0"
Bath: 2   Depth: 55'0"
Foundation: Island basement
Exterior Walls: 2x6

Main Level: 1,671 sq ft
Upper Level: 846 sq ft
Lower Level Entry: 140 sq ft

Living Area: 2,657 sq ft

Price Code: **C3**

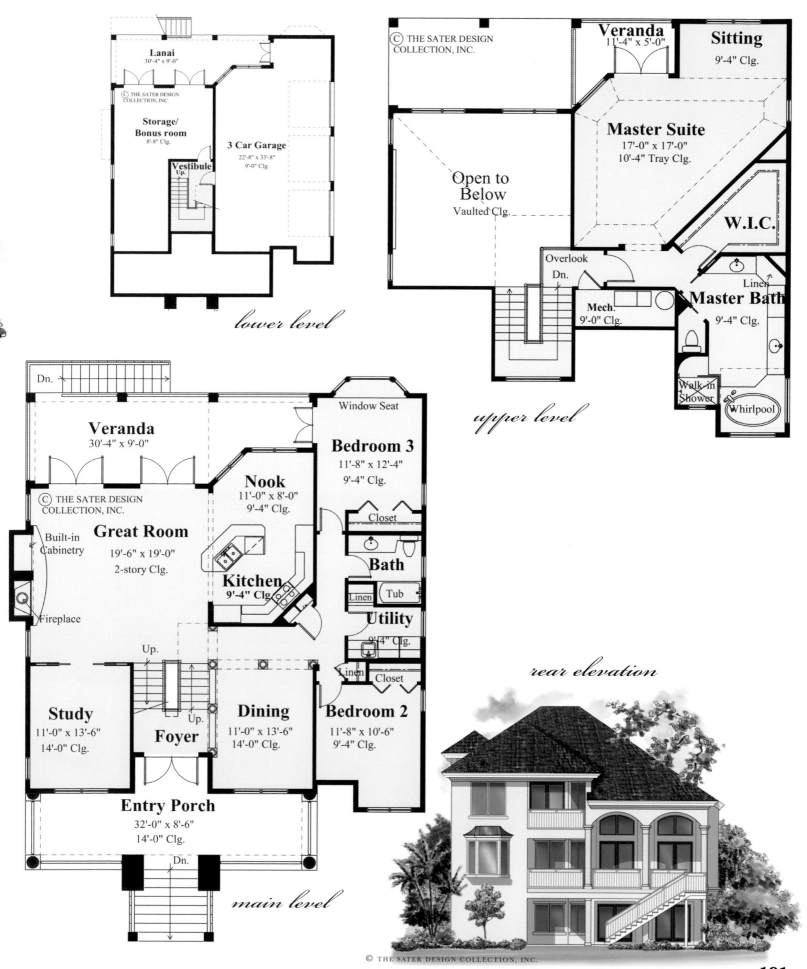

Lanai
30'-4" x 9'-0"

© THE SATER DESIGN
COLLECTION, INC.

**Storage/
Bonus room**
8'-8" Clg.

3 Car Garage
22'-8" x 33'-8"
9'-0" Clg.

Vestibule
Up.

lower level

© THE SATER DESIGN
COLLECTION, INC.

Veranda
11'-4" x 5'-0"

Sitting
9'-4" Clg.

Master Suite
17'-0" x 17'-0"
10'-4" Tray Clg.

**Open to
Below**
Vaulted Clg.

W.I.C.

Overlook
Dn.

Linen

Mech.
9'-0" Clg.

Master Bath
9'-4" Clg.

**Walk-in
Shower**

Whirlpool

upper level

Dn.

Veranda
30'-4" x 9'-0"

Window Seat

© THE SATER DESIGN
COLLECTION, INC.

Nook
11'-0" x 8'-0"
9'-4" Clg.

Bedroom 3
11'-8" x 12'-4"
9'-4" Clg.

Closet

Great Room
19'-6" x 19'-0"
2-story Clg.

Built-in
Cabinetry

Kitchen
9'-4" Clg.

Bath

Linen   Tub

Fireplace

Utility
9'-4" Clg.

Up.

Linen

Up.

Closet

Study
11'-0" x 13'-6"
14'-0" Clg.

Dining
11'-0" x 13'-6"
14'-0" Clg.

Bedroom 2
11'-8" x 10'-6"
9'-4" Clg.

Foyer

Entry Porch
32'-0" x 8'-6"
14'-0" Clg.

Dn.

main level

rear elevation

© THE SATER DESIGN COLLECTION, INC.

© THE SATER DESIGN COLLECTION, INC.

Biscayne Bay

Styled for coastal perfection, this home has soaring interior vistas and ample rooms — each offering hospitality to family and friends. Elegant and ambient, the stately great room hosts three French doors, warm built-in cabinetry and a strategically placed two-sided fireplace shared with the formal dining room. Whether cooking for a group or preparing a personal meal, this kitchen is spacious, well organized and open to the main areas.

A formal study with a dramatic stepped ceiling precedes the master suite that contains walk-in closets, a separate bath with garden tub and a glass walk-in shower. The second floor takes full advantage of the space with two large bedrooms with walk-in closets and their own private baths.

PLAN | *6830*

Bedroom: 3   Width: 54'0"
Bath: 3   Depth: 57'0"
Foundation: Crawlspace
Exterior Walls: 2x6

Main Level: 1,798 sq ft
Upper Level: 900 sq ft
Living Area: 2,698 sq ft
Price Code: **C3**

1-800-718-PLAN

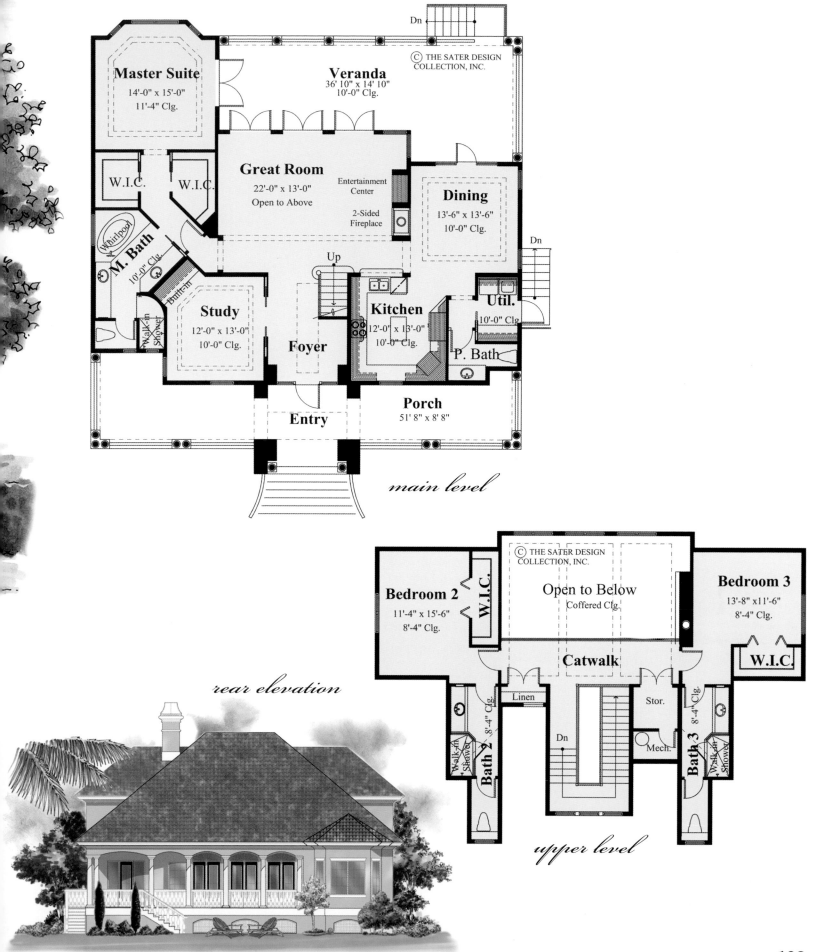

Master Suite
14'-0" x 15'-0"
11'-4" Clg.

Veranda
36' 10" x 14' 10"
10'-0" Clg.

© THE SATER DESIGN
COLLECTION, INC.

Dn

W.I.C.

W.I.C.

Great Room
22'-0" x 13'-0"
Open to Above

Entertainment
Center

2-Sided
Fireplace

Dining
13'-6" x 13'-6"
10'-0" Clg.

Whirlpool

M. Bath
10'-0" Clg.

Walk-in Shower

Built-in

Study
12'-0" x 13'-0"
10'-0" Clg.

Up

Foyer

Kitchen
12'-0" x 13'-0"
10'-0" Clg.

Util.
10'-0" Clg.

Dn

P. Bath

Porch
51' 8" x 8' 8"

Entry

main level

rear elevation

© THE SATER DESIGN
COLLECTION, INC.

Bedroom 2
11'-4" x 15'-6"
8'-4" Clg.

W.I.C.

Open to Below
Coffered Clg.

Bedroom 3
13'-8" x 11'-6"
8'-4" Clg.

Catwalk

W.I.C.

Bath 2
8'-4" Clg.

Walk-in Shower

Linen

Dn

Stor.

Mech.

Bath 3
8'-4" Clg.

Walk-in Shower

upper level

© THE SATER DESIGN COLLECTION, INC.

Villa | 2756 SQ. FT.

© THE SATER DESIGN COLLECTION, INC.

Royal Marco

A wrap-around porch, paned windows and stately columns enhance a prominent entry. Inside, colonnades frame an octagon-shaped great room, which illuminates the entire floor plan. This room offers a fireplace, an entertainment center and three sets of French doors opening outside to a vaulted lanai, bringing in extended views. Next to the foyer is an executive study and formal dining area. To the side is the kitchen, equipped with a pass-thru server to the outdoor patio.

A winding staircase leads upstairs to a loft, which overlooks the great room. A computer center and a morning kitchen hug the hallway that opens to an observation deck. Completing this level, two family bedrooms have private baths.

PLAN | *6857*

Bedroom: 3	Width: 66'0"
Bath: 3-1/2	Depth: 50'0"
Foundation: Island basement	
Exterior Walls: 2x6	

Main Level: 1,855 sq ft
Upper Level: 901 sq ft
Living Area: 2,756 sq ft
Price Code: **C 3**

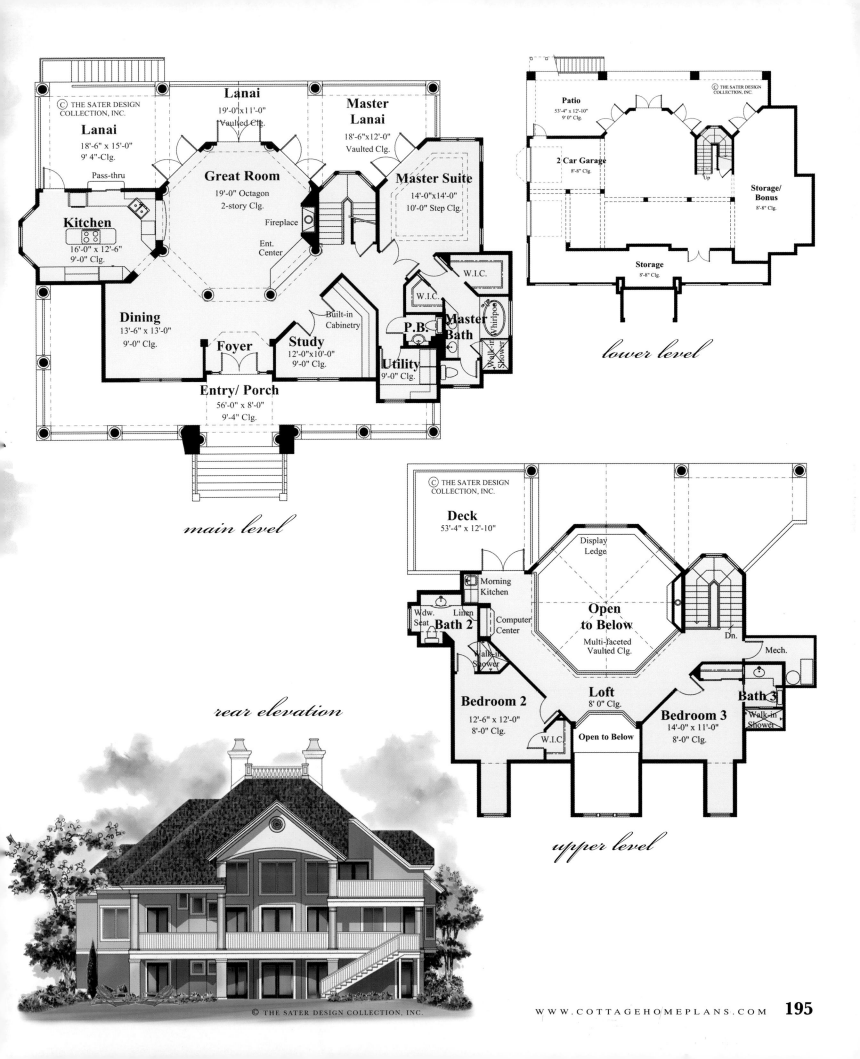

© THE SATER DESIGN COLLECTION, INC.

Lanai
18'-6" x 15'-0"
9' 4"-Clg.

Pass-thru

Lanai
19'-0"x11'-0"
Vaulted Clg.

Master Lanai
18'-6"x12'-0"
Vaulted Clg.

Kitchen
16'-0" x 12'-6"
9'-0" Clg.

Great Room
19'-0" Octagon
2-story Clg.

Fireplace

Ent. Center

Master Suite
14'-0"x14'-0"
10'-0" Step Clg.

W.I.C.

W.I.C.

Dining
13'-6" x 13'-0"
9'-0" Clg.

Built-in Cabinetry

P.B.

Master Bath

Whirlpool

Foyer

Study
12'-0"x10'-0"
9'-0" Clg.

Utility
9'-0" Clg.

Walk-in Shower

Entry/ Porch
56'-0" x 8'-0"
9'-4" Clg.

main level

rear elevation

© THE SATER DESIGN COLLECTION, INC.

Patio
53'-4" x 12'-10"
9'-0" Clg.

2 Car Garage
8'-8" Clg.

Up

Storage/ Bonus
8'-8" Clg.

Storage
8'-8" Clg.

lower level

© THE SATER DESIGN COLLECTION, INC.

Deck
53'-4" x 12'-10"

Display Ledge

Morning Kitchen

Wdw. Seat

Linen

Bath 2

Computer Center

Open to Below

Multi-faceted Vaulted Clg.

Dn.

Mech.

Walk-in Shower

Bedroom 2
12'-6" x 12'-0"
8'-0" Clg.

Loft
8' 0" Clg.

Bedroom 3
14'-0" x 11'-0"
8'-0" Clg.

Bath 3

Walk-in Shower

W.I.C.

Open to Below

upper level

© THE SATER DESIGN COLLECTION, INC.

Sandel Island

© THE SATER DESIGN COLLECTION, INC.

Wulfert Point

The romantic Charleston coast is rich with the timeless serenity of quiet island communities, where a relaxed attitude and architectural styles blend.

This Charleston-inspired home sports louvered shutters and circle-head windows that speak softly of the past, while French doors extend the living areas and welcome sunlight and balmy breezes inside.

Gentle arches and decorative columns announce interior vistas as well as multi-directional views. Three sets of French doors extend an invitation to the covered porch, sundeck and courtyard. A beautiful bayed formal dining room is open to the gourmet kitchen.

The second level includes two secondary bedrooms, a bath and a grand master suite with walls of glass that bring the outside in. A bonus room over the garage has a morning kitchen and a full bath.

PLAN | *6688*

Bedroom: 4	Width: 50'0"
Bath: 3-1/2	Depth: 90'0"
Foundation: Slab	
Exterior Walls: 2x6	

Main Level:	1,293 sq ft
Upper Level:	1,154 sq ft
Bonus Room:	426 sq ft
Living Area:	2,873 sq ft

Price Code: **C3**

FOR PHOTOGRAPHY
SEE PAGES

10-15 & 40-45

1-800-718-PLAN

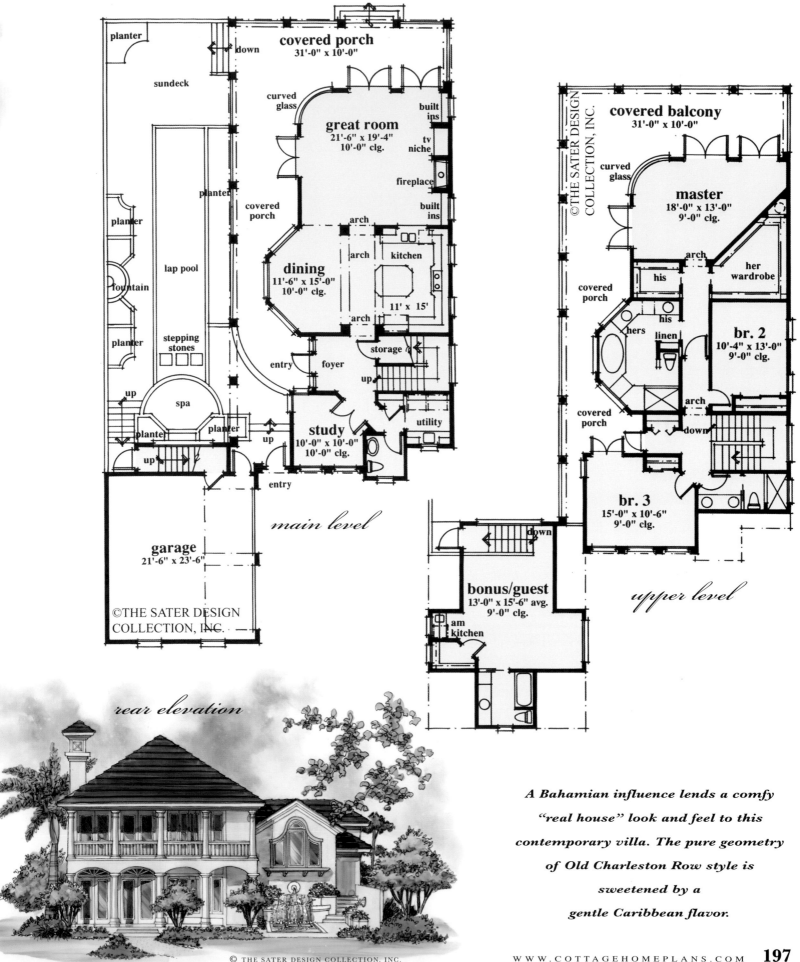

covered porch
31'-0" x 10'-0"

planter

down

sundeck

curved glass

great room
21'-6" x 19'-4"
10'-0" clg.

built ins

tv niche

fireplace

built ins

planter

covered porch

arch

planter

arch

kitchen

lap pool

dining
11'-6" x 15'-0"
10'-0" clg.

arch

11' x 15'

planter

fountain

arch

stepping stones

storage

planter

entry

foyer

up

up

spa

up

planter

planter

up

study
10'-0" x 10'-0"
10'-0" clg.

utility

entry

main level

garage
21'-6" x 23'-6"

©THE SATER DESIGN COLLECTION, INC.

covered balcony
31'-0" x 10'-0"

©THE SATER DESIGN COLLECTION, INC.

curved glass

master
18'-0" x 13'-0"
9'-0" clg.

arch

her wardrobe

covered porch

his

his

hers

linen

br. 2
10'-4" x 13'-0"
9'-0" clg.

covered porch

arch

down

br. 3
15'-0" x 10'-6"
9'-0" clg.

upper level

down

bonus/guest
13'-0" x 15'-6" avg.
9'-0" clg.

am kitchen

rear elevation

A Bahamian influence lends a comfy "real house" look and feel to this contemporary villa. The pure geometry of Old Charleston Row style is sweetened by a gentle Caribbean flavor.

© THE SATER DESIGN COLLECTION, INC.

© THE SATER DESIGN COLLECTION, INC.

Château-sur-Mer

An imaginative Mediterranean-style villa flirts with the past to create a design with a timeless future. The front porch boasts rich Doric columns, arch-top openings and an assortment of windows that border an enchanting façade and an astounding entryway.

Inside the foyer, the open floor plan is sophisticated yet casual and comfortable. A two-story great room, warmed by a fireplace and hosts of French doors, opens onto the verandah and allows natural light and gentle breezes into the main gathering space. An island kitchen with spacious dining area provides for great entertaining.

The impressive master suite and private bath complete the main floor. Upstairs, the loft overlook leads to the secondary bedrooms. Both have full baths and one opens out to a viewing deck.

PLAN | *6801*

Bedroom: 3   Width: 58'2"
Bath: 3-1/2   Depth: 54'2"
Foundation: Island basement
Exterior Walls: 2x6

Main Level: 2,096 sq ft
Upper Level: 892 sq ft
Living Area: 2,988 sq ft
Price Code: **C3**

1-800-718-PLAN

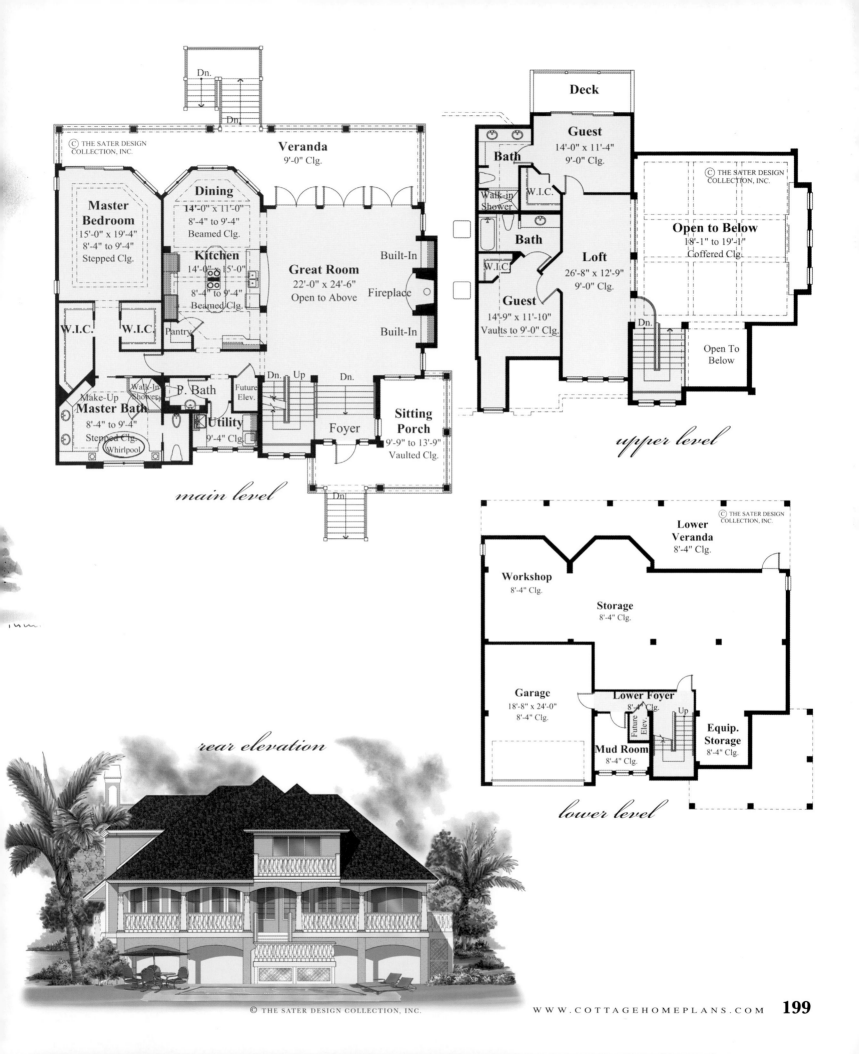

main level

Veranda
9'-0" Clg.

© THE SATER DESIGN
COLLECTION, INC.

Master Bedroom
15'-0" x 19'-4"
8'-4" to 9'-4"
Stepped Clg.

Dining
14'-0" x 11'-0"
8'-4" to 9'-4"
Beamed Clg.

Kitchen
14'-0" x 15'-0"
8'-4" to 9'-4"
Beamed Clg.

Great Room
22'-0" x 24'-6"
Open to Above

Built-In

Fireplace

Built-In

W.I.C.

W.I.C.

Pantry

Make-Up
Walk-In
Shower
P. Bath

Master Bath
8'-4" to 9'-4"
Stepped Clg.
Whirlpool

Utility
9'-4" Clg.

Future
Elev.

Dn. Up

Dn.

Foyer

Sitting Porch
9'-9" to 13'-9"
Vaulted Clg.

Dn.

main level

upper level

Deck

Guest
14'-0" x 11'-4"
9'-0" Clg.

Bath

Walk-in
Shower

W.I.C.

Bath

W.I.C.

Loft
26'-8" x 12'-9"
9'-0" Clg.

Guest
14'-9" x 11'-10"
Vaults to 9'-0" Clg.

Dn.

© THE SATER DESIGN
COLLECTION, INC.

Open to Below
18'-1" to 19'-1"
Coffered Clg.

Open To
Below

upper level

lower level

Lower Veranda
8'-4" Clg.

© THE SATER DESIGN
COLLECTION, INC.

Workshop
8'-4" Clg.

Storage
8'-4" Clg.

Garage
18'-8" x 24'-0"
8'-4" Clg.

Lower Foyer
8'-4" Clg.

Future
Elev.

Up

Mud Room
8'-4" Clg.

Equip. Storage
8'-4" Clg.

lower level

rear elevation

© THE SATER DESIGN COLLECTION, INC.

© THE SATER DESIGN COLLECTION, INC.

Barcelona Harbor

A stunning Mediterranean villa that gracefully combines Spanish and French influences creates an elegant exterior that includes a portico entry, fanlight transoms and colossal columns. The mid-level foyer welcomes friends and family to the grand salon that allows for casual or formal gatherings.

Adjacent to one another, the kitchen, dining nook and leisure room allow for entertaining in comfort — where the host can still be a part of the fun. This split floor plan provides two handsome and private guest suites, offering spacious walk-in closets and private bathrooms.

A regal master retreat is host to a full bath, sizable wardrobe closets and sliding glass doors that invite comfortable breezes. A lower level provides a two-car garage, storage and a porch.

PLAN | 6860

Bedroom: 3   Width: 77'0"
Bath: 3-1/2   Depth: 74'6"
Foundation: Island basement
Exterior Walls: 2x6

Main Level: 3,074 sq ft
Living Area: 3,074 sq ft
Price Code: **C4**

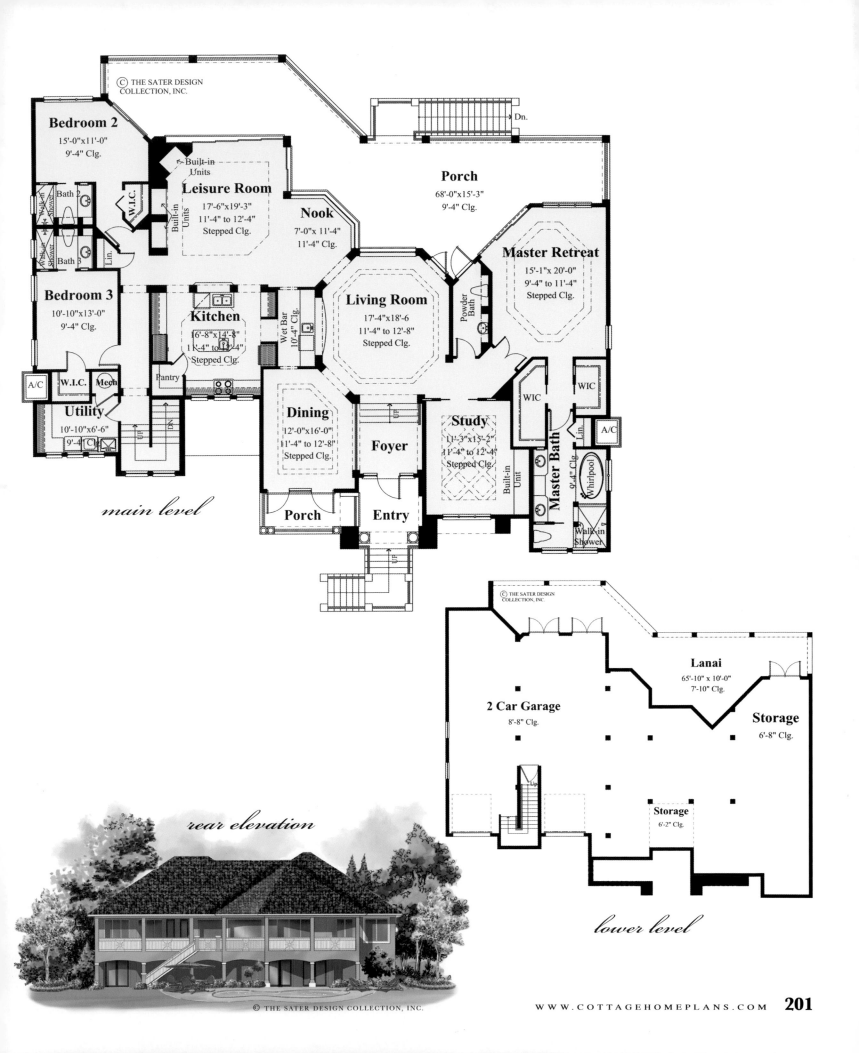

© THE SATER DESIGN COLLECTION, INC.

Bedroom 2
15'-0"x11'-0"
9'-4" Clg.

Bath 2

Bath 3

W.I.C.

Walk-in Shower

Lin.

Leisure Room
17'-6"x19'-3"
11'-4" to 12'-4"
Stepped Clg.

Built-in Units

Built-in Units

Nook
7'-0"x 11'-4"
11'-4" Clg.

Porch
68'-0"x15'-3"
9'-4" Clg.

Dn.

Master Retreat
15'-1"x 20'-0"
9'-4" to 11'-4"
Stepped Clg.

Bedroom 3
10'-10"x13'-0"
9'-4" Clg.

Kitchen
16'-8"x14'-8"
11'-4" to 12'-4"
Stepped Clg.

Wet Bar
10'-4" Clg.

Living Room
17'-4"x18'-6
11'-4" to 12'-8"
Stepped Clg.

Powder Bath

WIC

WIC

A/C

W.I.C.

Mech.

Pantry

Utility
10'-10"x6'-6"
9'-4" Clg.

DN.

UP

DN

Dining
12'-0"x16'-0"
11'-4" to 12'-8"
Stepped Clg.

Foyer

UP

Study
11'-3"x15'-2"
11'-4" to 12'-4"
Stepped Clg.

Built-in Unit

WIC

Lin.

A/C

Master Bath
9'-4" Clg.

Whirlpool

Walk-in Shower

Porch

Entry

UP

main level

rear elevation

© THE SATER DESIGN COLLECTION, INC.

2 Car Garage
8'-8" Clg.

Lanai
65'-10" x 10'-0"
7'-10" Clg.

Storage
6'-8" Clg.

Up

Storage
6'-2" Clg.

lower level

© THE SATER DESIGN COLLECTION, INC.

© THE SATER DESIGN COLLECTION, INC.

Sunset Beach

Just beautiful, this elegant manor of perfect proportion is long on views with a gazebo-styled front porch. A dramatic foyer opens to a sweeping circular staircase and views that extend the length of the house.

Corridors lead to the study, where built-in cabinetry holds the finest collection of books and a window seat longs to enjoy them. A butler's pantry serves the kitchen and dining areas with ease and a swinging door, that can be bumped open, is handy when your hands are full. The leisure room, with a built-in media center, opens to an outdoor lanai and kitchen, ideal for alfresco dining and casual entertaining.

PLAN | *6848*

Bedroom: 4   Width: 74'0"
Bath: 3-1/2   Depth: 88'0"
Foundation: Crawlspace/Slab
Exterior Walls: 2x6

Main Level: 2,083 sq ft
Upper Level: 1,013 sq ft
Living Area: 3,096 sq ft
Price Code: **C4**

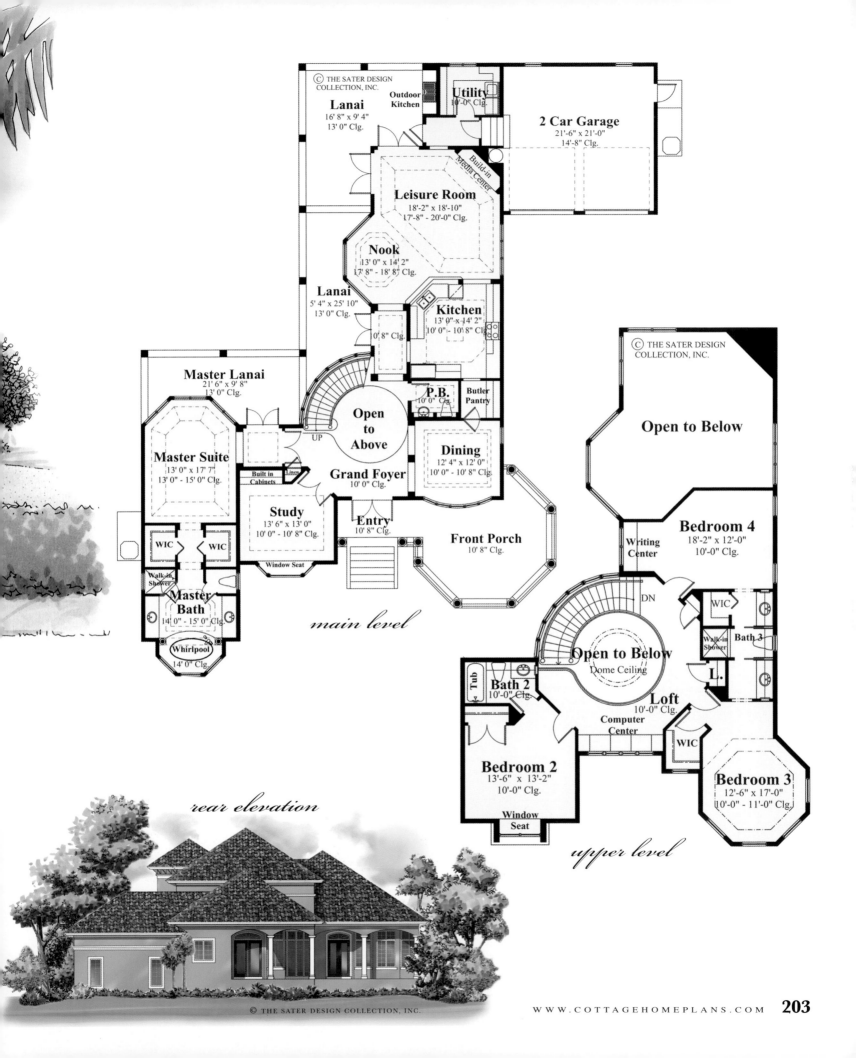

© THE SATER DESIGN COLLECTION, INC.

Lanai
16' 8" x 9' 4"
13' 0" Clg.

Outdoor Kitchen

Utility
10' 0" Clg.

2 Car Garage
21'-6" x 21'-0"
14'-8" Clg.

Build-in Media Center

Leisure Room
18'-2" x 18'-10"
17'-8" - 20'-0" Clg.

Nook
13' 0" x 14' 2"
17' 8" - 18' 8" Clg.

Lanai
5' 4" x 25' 10"
13' 0" Clg.

10' 8" Clg.

Kitchen
13' 0" x 14' 2"
10' 0" - 10' 8" Clg.

Master Lanai
21' 6" x 9' 8"
13' 0" Clg.

Open to Above

P.B.
10' 0"

Butler Pantry

Master Suite
13' 0" x 17' 7"
13' 0" - 15' 0" Clg.

UP

Built in Cabinets

Linen

Dining
12' 4" x 12' 0"
10' 0" - 10' 8" Clg.

Grand Foyer
10' 0" Clg.

WIC   WIC

Walk-in Shower

Study
13' 6" x 13' 0"
10' 0" - 10' 8" Clg.

Entry
10' 8" Clg.

Window Seat

Front Porch
10' 8" Clg.

Master Bath
14' 0" - 15' 0" Clg.

Whirlpool
14' 0" Clg.

main level

© THE SATER DESIGN COLLECTION, INC.

Open to Below

Bedroom 4
18'-2" x 12'-0"
10'-0" Clg.

Writing Center

Open to Below
Dome Ceiling

DN

WIC

Walk-in Shower

Bath 3

L.

Bath 2
10'-0" Clg.

Tub

Loft
10'-0" Clg.

Computer Center

WIC

Bedroom 2
13'-6" x 13'-2"
10'-0" Clg.

Bedroom 3
12'-6" x 17'-0"
10'-0" - 11'-0" Clg.

Window Seat

upper level

rear elevation

© THE SATER DESIGN COLLECTION, INC.

Villa | 3285 SQ. FT.

© THE SATER DESIGN COLLECTION, INC.

Coconut Grove

Old-world Mediterranean architecture inspires this contemporary villa. Graced with a steeply pitched tile roof with deep overhangs and a wrap-around porch, this home is adorned with exquisite detail.

Inside, modern amenities mix with casual free-flowing living. The wrapping kitchen with prep island pours into the nook and sneaks a peek at the generous outdoor vistas provided by the great room. Pull a book off the shelf, curl up next to the crackling fireplace and enjoy the views.

The grand foyer staircase leads to the upper level bedrooms. Each suite has a full bath and walk-in closet. French doors lead out to an adjoining sundeck, a great place to catch the sunset. Built-in work centers outside of the rooms offer a place to get away to work or study.

PLAN | *6824*

Bedroom: 3   Width: 52'0"
Bath: 3-1/2   Depth: 65'4"
Foundation: Island basement
Exterior Walls: 2x6

Main Level: 2,146 sq ft
Upper Level: 952 sq ft
Lower Level Entry: 187 sq ft

Living Area: 3,285 sq ft

Price Code: **C4**

1-800-718-PLAN

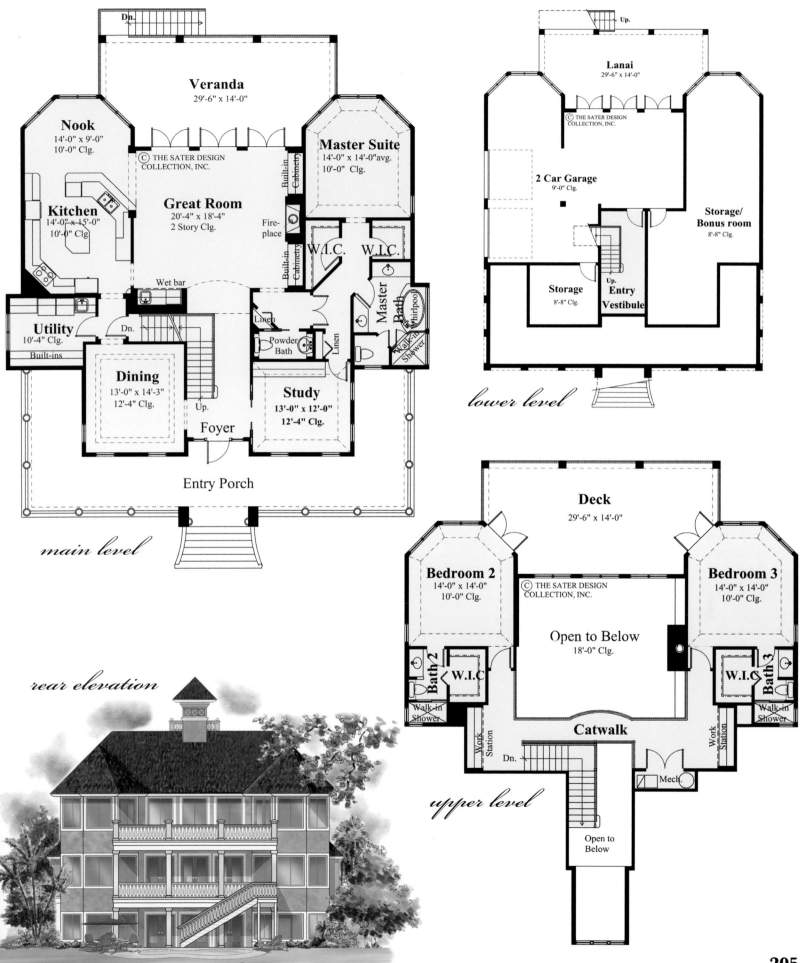

main level

Dn.

Veranda
29'-6" x 14'-0"

Nook
14'-0" x 9'-0"
10'-0" Clg.

Master Suite
14'-0" x 14'-0"avg.
10'-0" Clg.

© THE SATER DESIGN COLLECTION, INC.

Great Room
20'-4" x 18'-4"
2 Story Clg.

Kitchen
14'-0" x 15'-0"
10'-0" Clg

Built-in Cabinetry

Fire-place

Built-in Cabinetry

W.I.C.

W.I.C.

Wet bar

Master Bath

Whirlpool

Walk-in Shower

Utility
10'-4" Clg.
Built-ins

Dn.

Linen

Linen

Powder Bath

Dining
13'-0" x 14'-3"
12'-4" Clg.

Up.

Study
13'-0" x 12'-0"
12'-4" Clg.

Foyer

Entry Porch

lower level

Up.

Lanai
29'-6" x 14'-0"

© THE SATER DESIGN COLLECTION, INC.

2 Car Garage
9'-0" Clg.

Storage/ Bonus room
8'-8" Clg.

Storage
8'-8" Clg.

Entry Vestibule

Up.

upper level

Deck
29'-6" x 14'-0"

Bedroom 2
14'-0" x 14'-0"
10'-0" Clg.

© THE SATER DESIGN COLLECTION, INC.

Bedroom 3
14'-0" x 14'-0"
10'-0" Clg.

Open to Below
18'-0" Clg.

Bath 2

W.I.C

Walk-in Shower

Bath 3

W.I.C

Walk-in Shower

Work Station

Catwalk

Work Station

Dn.

Mech.

Open to Below

rear elevation

© THE SATER DESIGN COLLECTION, INC.

Villa | 3 8 3 9   S Q .   F T .

© THE SATER DESIGN COLLECTION, INC.

Villa Tucano

A masterpiece in design, this villa presents a fascinating façade, reflecting a variety of architectural styles that are timeless, yet fresh. Inside, the foyer opens to the main great room and the views beyond, creating a feeling of freedom and comfort, further enhanced by a full-length balcony, three-sided fireplace and a wet bar.

The formal dining room is open to the kitchen that has counter seating and a pass-through to the outdoor verandah. Two bedrooms facing the front have window views and private baths.

Take the elevator to the third level, which is dedicated to the spacious master suite. An open fireplace, exercise room, morning kitchen, separate baths and private deck supply ultimate relaxation in this romantic retreat.

PLAN | *6815*

Bedroom: 3   Width: 56'0"
Bath: 4   Depth: 54'0"
Foundation: Island basement
Exterior Walls: 2x6

Main Level: 2,039 sq ft
Upper Level: 1,426 sq ft
Lower Level Entry: 374 sq ft
Living Area: 3,839 sq ft
Price Code: **L1**

1 - 8 0 0 - 7 1 8 - P L A N

upper level

© THE SATER DESIGN COLLECTION, INC.

Master Deck
55' 4" X 5' 8"

Walk-in Shower

Exercise Room

Sitting Room

His Bath
9'-0" Clg.

W.I.C.

3-Sided Fireplace

Open to below

Morning Kitchen

Mech.

Cedar Closet

Balcony

Open to Below

Dn.

Whirlpool

Walk-in Shower

Her Bath

Master Suite
18' 0" x 15' 0"
9' 0" Clg.

9'-0" Clg.

Elev.

Linen

W.I.C.

lower level

© THE SATER DESIGN COLLECTION, INC.

Covered Lanai
55'-4" x 5'-4"

Storage/Bonus
42' 6" x 15' 0"
8' 8" Clg.

Storage/Hobby
12' 0" x 17' 0"
8' 8" Clg.

1 Car Garage
17' 6" x 19' 4"
9' 0" Clg.

Entry Vestibule
16'-6" x 15'-0"

Elev.

Up

1 Car Garage
15' 8" x 21' 4"
9' 0" Clg.

Landing

A beautiful view of open spaces and indoor places make this house a dream come true.

rear elevation

main level

Dn.

© THE SATER DESIGN COLLECTION, INC.

Veranda
55'-4" x 5'-4"

Outdoor Kitchen

Great Room
25' 0" x 20' 4"
9' 0" Clg.

3-Sided Fireplace

Kitchen
12' 0" x 16' 6"
9' 0" Clg.

Dining
15' 0" x 15' 0"
9' 0" Clg.

Open to Above

Wetbar

Elev.

Closet

Walk-in Shower

Bath 2

W.I.C.

Linen

Bath 3

Foyer
8'-2" x 10'-2"

Up.

Dn.

Util.

Built-ins

Bedroom 2
12' 0" x 14' 6"
9' 0" Clg.

Closet

Bedroom 3
12' 0" x 14' 6"
9' 0" Clg.

Tub

Entry

Landing

© THE SATER DESIGN COLLECTION, INC.

Villa | 4139 SQ. FT.

© THE SATER DESIGN COLLECTION, INC.

Hyatt Park

This elegant Mediterranean design features square columns, balustrades and detailed radius windows. The stylish entryway opens to the interior gallery and great room, extending a sense of spaciousness to a wrap-around outdoor verandah. This main level of vast living space encompasses a two-sided fireplace, a pass-thru kitchen and three guest suites including ample baths. Further hosting a convenient powder room for visitors as well as a three-floor elevator, this home exudes luxury.

Double doors open to the custom master suite accented by a two-sided fireplace, tray ceiling, soothing whirlpool bath and a private deck for moonlit conversations. The upstairs catwalk views the great room below and leads to an additional bedchamber, which adds up to five beautiful bedrooms.

PLAN | *6818*

Bedroom: 5   Width: 62'0"
Bath: 4-1/2   Depth: 67'0"
Foundation: Island basement
Exterior Walls: 2x6

Main Level: 2,491 sq ft
Upper Level: 1,290 sq ft
Lower Level Entry: 358 sq ft
Living Area: 4,139 sq ft
Price Code: **L2**

1-800-718-PLAN

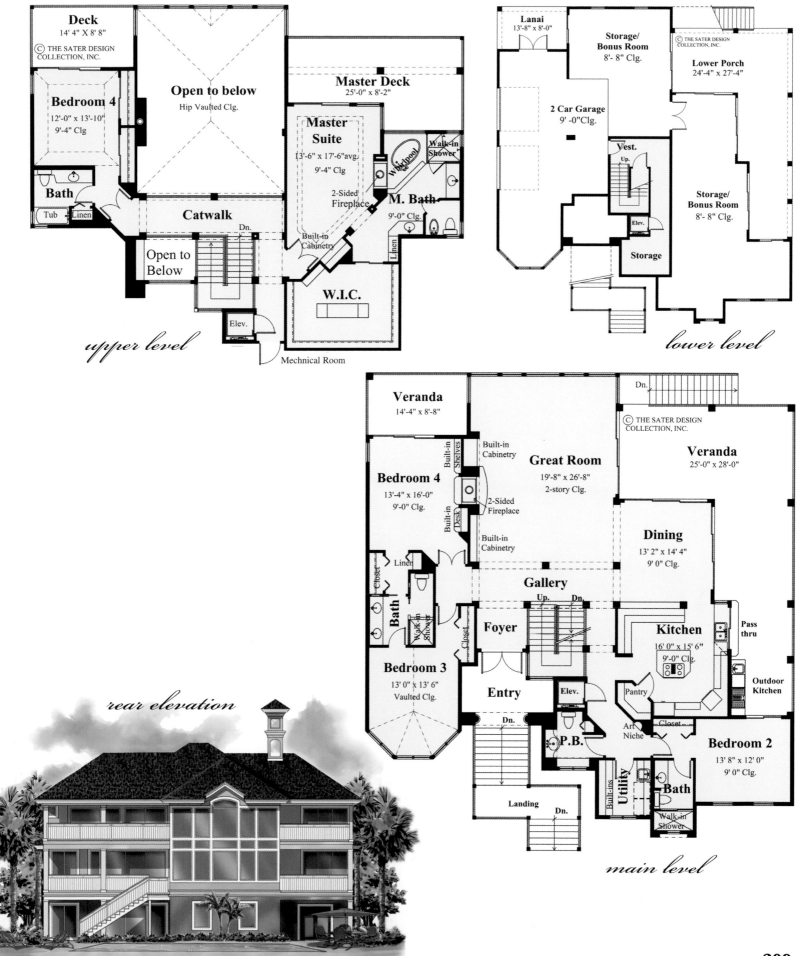

Deck
14' 4" X 8' 8"

© THE SATER DESIGN
COLLECTION, INC.

Bedroom 4
12'-0" x 13'-10"
9'-4" Clg

Bath

Tub Linen

Open to below
Hip Vaulted Clg.

Master Deck
25'-0" x 8'-2"

Master Suite
13'-6" x 17'-6"avg.
9'-4" Clg

2-Sided
Fireplace

Catwalk

Dn.

Built-in
Cabinetry

M. Bath
9'-0" Clg.

Whirlpool

Walk-in Shower

Linen

Open to Below

Elev.

W.I.C.

Mechnical Room

upper level

Lanai
13'-8" x 8'-0"

Storage/ Bonus Room
8'- 8" Clg.

© THE SATER DESIGN
COLLECTION, INC.

Lower Porch
24'-4" x 27'-4"

2 Car Garage
9' -0"Clg.

Vest.

Up.

Elev.

Storage

Storage/ Bonus Room
8'- 8" Clg.

lower level

Veranda
14'-4" x 8'-8"

Dn.

Built-in
Shelves

Built-in
Cabinetry

Great Room
19'-8" x 26'-8"
2-story Clg.

© THE SATER DESIGN
COLLECTION, INC.

Veranda
25'-0" x 28'-0"

Bedroom 4
13'-4" x 16'-0"
9'-0" Clg.

Built-in
Desk

2-Sided
Fireplace

Built-in
Cabinetry

Dining
13' 2" x 14' 4"
9' 0" Clg.

Linen

Bath

Closet

Walk-in
Shower

Gallery

Up. Dn.

Foyer

Closet

Kitchen
16' 0" x 15' 6"
9'-0" Clg.

Pass
thru

Outdoor
Kitchen

Bedroom 3
13' 0" x 13' 6"
Vaulted Clg.

Entry

Elev.

Dn.

P.B.

Pantry

Art
Niche

Closet

Bedroom 2
13' 8" x 12' 0"
9' 0" Clg.

Landing

Dn.

Built-ins

Utility

Bath

Walk-in
Shower

main level

rear elevation

© THE SATER DESIGN COLLECTION, INC.

Villa | 4359 SQ. FT.

© THE SATER DESIGN COLLECTION, INC.

Jupiter Bay

This European villa conveys open interior spaces that flow naturally into outdoor views through verandahs and covered lanais. A dazzling porte-cochere and a grand vaulted entry lead into the main house.

Walls of glass and nature flow into a lavish great room and open dining area. Perfect for entertaining, and within easy access to the gourmet kitchen, butler's pantry and wet bar, the formal dining room has a built-in server and expansive rear views.

On the upper level a gallery allows overlooks to the great room and foyer, and separates the master suite from a secondary bedroom or guest suite. Each suite is outfitted with a full bath and its own private verandah, a place to relax and enjoy the great outdoors.

PLAN | *6821*

Bedroom: 3	Width: 73'0"
Bath: 3-1/2	Depth: 70'0"

Foundation: Island basement
Exterior Walls: 8" CBS

Main Level: 2,391 sq ft
Upper Level: 1,539 sq ft
Lower Level Entry: 429 sq ft

Living Area: 4,359 sq ft

Price Code: **L2**

1 - 8 0 0 - 7 1 8 - PLAN

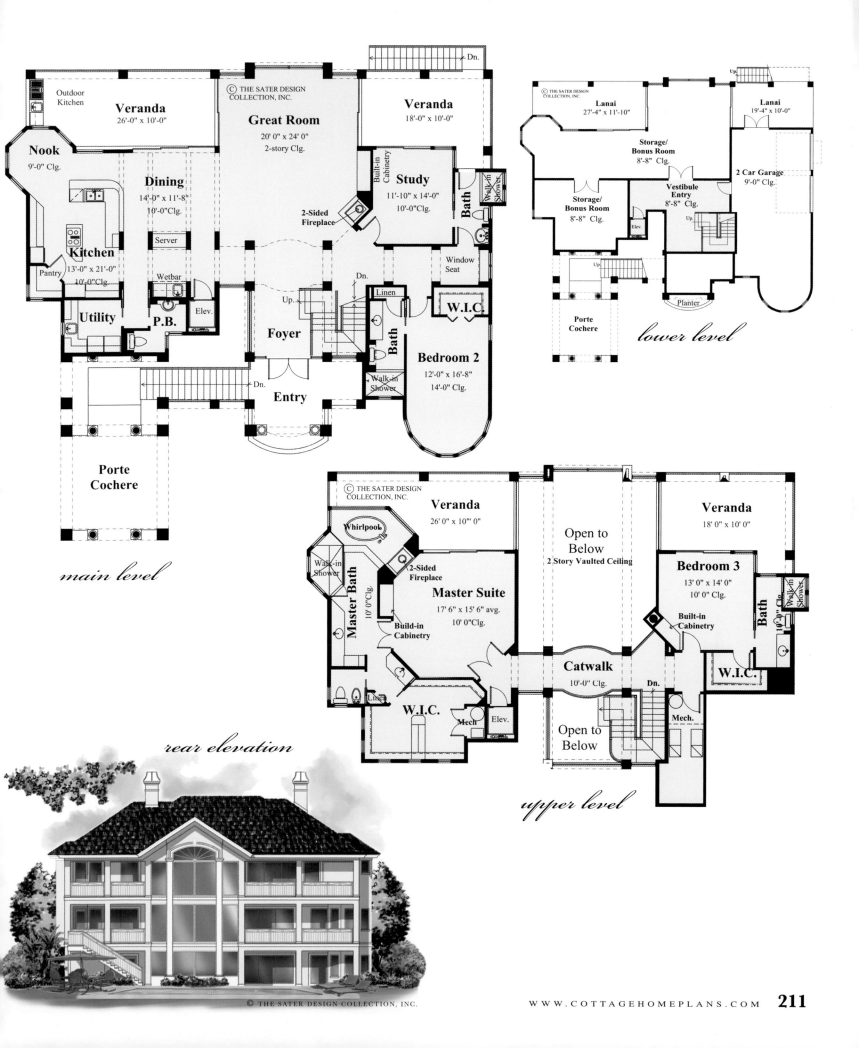

main level

Outdoor Kitchen

Veranda
26'-0" x 10'-0"

Nook
9'-0" Clg.

© THE SATER DESIGN
COLLECTION, INC.

Great Room
20' 0" x 24' 0"
2-story Clg.

Veranda
18'-0" x 10'-0"

Dining
14'-0" x 11'-8"
10'-0"Clg.

Built-in Cabinetry

Study
11'-10" x 14'-0"
10'-0"Clg.

Bath

Walk-in Shower

Server

Kitchen
13'-0" x 21'-0"
10'-0"Clg.

Pantry

2-Sided Fireplace

Wetbar

Utility

P.B.

Elev.

Up.

Dn.

Foyer

Linen

Bath

W.I.C.

Window Seat

Bedroom 2
12'-0" x 16'-8"
14'-0" Clg.

Dn.

Entry

Walk-in Shower

Porte Cochere

lower level

© THE SATER DESIGN
COLLECTION, INC.

Lanai
27'-4" x 11'-10"

Lanai
19'-4" x 10'-0"

Storage/ Bonus Room
8'-8" Clg.

2 Car Garage
9'-0" Clg.

Storage/ Bonus Room
8'-8" Clg.

Vestibule Entry
8'-8" Clg.

Elev.

Up.

Up.

Planter

Porte Cochere

upper level

© THE SATER DESIGN
COLLECTION, INC.

Veranda
26' 0" x 10'' 0"

Open to Below
2 Story Vaulted Ceiling

Veranda
18' 0" x 10' 0"

Whirlpool

Walk-in Shower

Master Bath
10' 0"Clg.

2-Sided Fireplace

Master Suite
17' 6" x 15' 6" avg.
10' 0"Clg.

Build-in Cabinetry

Bedroom 3
13' 0" x 14' 0"
10' 0" Clg.

Built-in Cabinetry

Bath

Walk-in Shower

Linen

W.I.C.

Mech.

Elev.

Catwalk
10'-0" Clg.

Dn.

Mech.

W.I.C.

Open to Below

rear elevation

© THE SATER DESIGN COLLECTION, INC.

Garages

More than safe harbor for the family fleet, detached garages add living space, storage and character to the property's edge. Although the architecture rarely competes with the design of the primary residence, the garage must take on the mood and era of the home and add its own inviting twist in order to maintain the disposition of the style. As important as its ability to provide a complement to the street presentation, an effective garage design contributes to the function and livability of the home. Flexible spaces above the garage floor easily convert to computer lofts, craft rooms and even home offices— or switch to guest quarters when needed. Sweetly casual or bold and formal, the garage enhances the entire design of the home

Garage | 484 SQ. FT.

© THE SATER DESIGN COLLECTION, INC.

© THE SATER DESIGN COLLECTION, INC.

garage
21'-0" x 21'-0"

Two-Car

Vented dormers and a high-pitched insulated metal roof dress up this two-car garage with quaint details that blend beautifully with any of the cottage homes. With three windows and a side entry, this garage is convenient and well lit.

PLAN | *6702*

Width: 22'0"   Depth: 22'0"

Total Area: 484 sq ft

Price Code: **G1**

1-800-718-PLAN

© THE SATER DESIGN COLLECTION, INC.

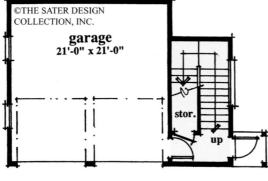

©THE SATER DESIGN COLLECTION, INC.

garage
21'-0" x 21'-0"

stor.

up

main level

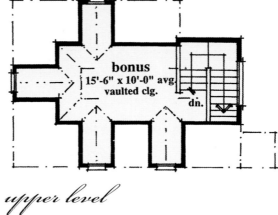

bonus
15'-6" x 10'-0" avg
vaulted clg.

dn.

upper level

Two-Car

A roomy vestibule offers additional storage space with this stylish two-car garage. Flexible space above may be developed into a hobby-craft area, a home office or even an extra bedroom. Charming dormer windows allow views and cool breezes to enhance the bonus level.

PLAN | *6703*

Width: 34'6"   Depth: 22'0"

Vestibule/Stairs: 137 sq ft
Upper Bonus Space: 264 sq ft
Total Area: 534 sq ft

Price Code: **G1**

1 - 8 0 0 - 7 1 8 - P L A N

Garage | 770 SQ. FT.

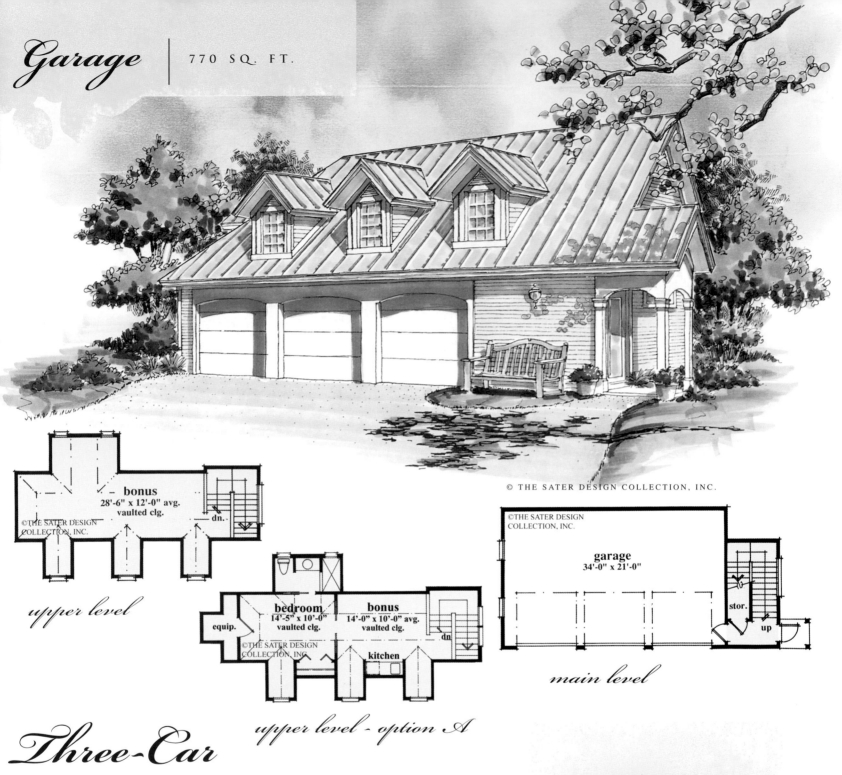

© THE SATER DESIGN COLLECTION, INC.

upper level

bonus
28'-6" x 12'-0" avg.
vaulted clg.

dn.

©THE SATER DESIGN
COLLECTION, INC.

upper level - option A

bedroom
14'-5" x 10'-0"
vaulted clg.

bonus
14'-0" x 10'-0" avg.
vaulted clg.

equip.

kitchen

dn

©THE SATER DESIGN
COLLECTION, INC.

©THE SATER DESIGN
COLLECTION, INC.

garage
34'-0" x 21'-0"

stor.

up

main level

Three-Car

A portico-style entry is a warm welcome to this detached three-car garage, styled to complement any of the cottage designs. Bonus space above offers an additional living area or a recreation room. With a morning kitchen, a full bath, a vaulted ceiling and three dormered windows, Option A may be developed as a comfortable guest suite or a charming artist's studio. The entry vestibule provides ample storage space as well as a wrapping stair to the bonus level.

PLAN | *6704*

Width: 47'6"   Depth: 22'0"
Vestibule/Stairs: 137 sq ft
Upper Bonus Space: 497 sq ft
Total Area: 770 sq ft

Price Code: **G1**

1-800-718-PLAN

Cottage Index

PLAN NAME	PLAN #	PRICE CODE	PAGE	SQ. FT.
Mallory Square	6691	A4	56	1,288
Church Street	6687	A4	58	1,470
Runaway Bay	6616	C1	60	1,690
Saddle River	6681	C1	62	1,706
Tradewind Court	6617	C2	64	1,764
Cayman Court	6694	C1	66	1,792
Plymouth Bay	6852	C1	68	1,794
Periwinkle Way	6683	C1	70	1,838
Nassau Cove	6654	C1	72	1,853
Jasmine Lane	6680	C1	74	1,876
Aruba Bay	6840	C1	76	1,886
Georgetown Cove	6690	C1	78	1,910
Santa Rosa	6808	C1	80	1,978
Charleston Hill	6855	C1	82	1,996
Duvall Street	6701	C2	84	2,123
Newport Cove	6843	C2	86	2,136
Abaco Bay	6655	C2	88	2,187
Admiralty Point	6622	C2	90	2,190
Tuckertown Way	6692	C2	92	2,190
Papillon	6813	C2	94	2,349
Linden Place	6805	C2	96	2,374
Spyglass Hill	6615	C2	98	2,376
Saint Martin	6846	C2	100	2,494
Carmel Bay	6810	C3	102	2,513
Bridgeport Harbor	6685	C3	104	2,520
Laguna Beach	6834	C3	106	2,555
Walker Way	6697	C3	108	2,569
Key Largo	6828	C3	110	2,650
Bridgehampton	6837	C3	112	2,657
Seagrove Beach	6682	C3	114	2,659

Villa Index

TO ORDER, SEE
PAGES 222 & 223

Garage Index

More Plan Books

FROM SATER DESIGN COLLECTION, INC.
1-800-718-7526

**EUROPEAN
LUXURY HOME PLAN BOOK**

EUROPEAN LUXURY HOME PLANS
65 elevations and floor plans

Italian, French, English and Spanish styles. Here are sixty-five truly innovative plans inspired by history-rich European styles as diverse as America's own culture. These coastal villas, romantic chateaux and rambling retreats reinterpret the past to create a new breed of authentic design, rich with links to the outdoors. With a host of amentities, such as courtyards, porticos, disappearing walls and richly detailed interiors, these designs are sure to be classics.

2,200 — 4,600 sq ft

$12.95 *160 full-color pages*

**COUNTRY COMFORT
FARMHOUSE BOOK**

COUNTRY COMFORT
75 elevations / 25 floor plans

Each with 3 styles: Classic, French Country & Victorian. These spectacular designs, styled from inviting floor plans, help fulfill even the most demanding version of the American Dream. Designs feature authentic recollections of the charm and comfort of country living with a sophisticated touch. These homes are beautifully rendered and provide the latest amenities and conveniences. You do not have to be confined to a rural setting to enjoy the comfort of the country.

1,800 — 2,400 sq ft

$12.95 *176 full-color pages*

**LUXURY—COASTAL
MEDITERRANEAN BOOK**

LUXURY — COASTAL/ MEDITERRANEAN STYLE HOMES
49 view-oriented luxury home plans

Take a photo tour of 21 stunning homes. Luxurious photography provides an inside look at unique plans with gracious master suites, pampering baths and spacious patios complete with fireplaces and built-in kitchens.

2,500 — 6,800 sq ft

$12.95 *112 full-color pages*

Blueprints | WHAT'S IN A SET

Each set of plans is a collection of drawings that show exactly how your house is to be built. Actual number of pages may vary, but most plan packages include the following:

A-1 COVER SHEET/INDEX & SITE PLAN

An Artist's Rendering of the exterior of the house shows you approximately how the house will look when built and landscaped. The Index is a list of the sheets included and page numbers for easy reference. The Site Plan is a scaled drawing of the house to help determine the placement of the home on a building site.

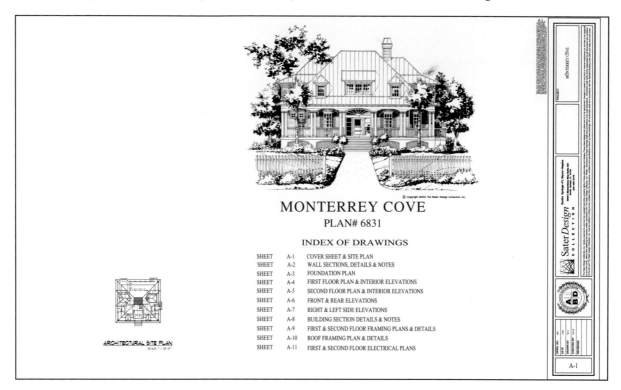

MONTERREY COVE
PLAN# 6831

INDEX OF DRAWINGS

SHEET	A-1	COVER SHEET & SITE PLAN
SHEET	A-2	WALL SECTIONS, DETAILS & NOTES
SHEET	A-3	FOUNDATION PLAN
SHEET	A-4	FIRST FLOOR PLAN & INTERIOR ELEVATIONS
SHEET	A-5	SECOND FLOOR PLAN & INTERIOR ELEVATIONS
SHEET	A-6	FRONT & REAR ELEVATIONS
SHEET	A-7	RIGHT & LEFT SIDE ELEVATIONS
SHEET	A-8	BUILDING SECTION DETAILS & NOTES
SHEET	A-9	FIRST & SECOND FLOOR FRAMING PLANS & DETAILS
SHEET	A-10	ROOF FRAMING PLAN & DETAILS
SHEET	A-11	FIRST & SECOND FLOOR ELECTRICAL PLANS

ARCHITECTURAL SITE PLAN

A-2 WALL SECTION / NOTES

This sheet shows details of the house from the roof to the foundation. This section specifies the home's construction, insulation, flooring and roofing details.

A-3 FOUNDATION PLAN

This sheet gives the foundation layout, including support walls, excavated and unexcavated areas, if any, and foundation notes. If the foundation is monolithic slab rather than basement, the plan shows footing and details.

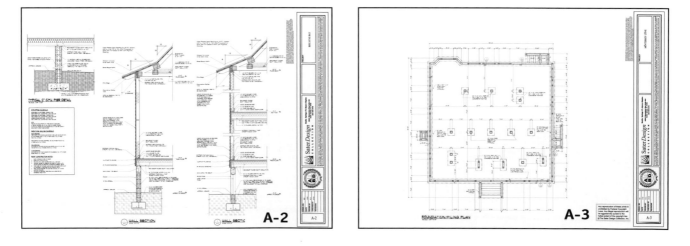

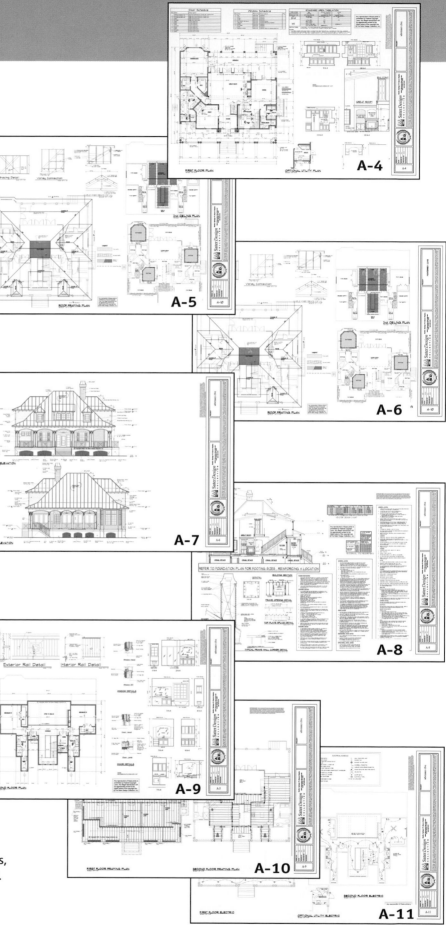

A-4 DETAILED FLOOR PLANS

These plans show the layout of each floor of the house. Rooms and interior spaces are carefully dimensioned and keys are given for cross-section details provided later in the plans, as well as window and door size callouts. These plans also show the location of kitchen appliances and bathroom fixtures, etc.

A-5 CEILING PLAN

Sater ceiling treatments are typically very detailed. This plan shows ceiling layout and extensive details.

A-6 ROOF PLAN

Overall layout and necessary details for roof construction are provided. If trusses are used, we suggest using a local truss manufacturer to design your trusses to comply with your local codes and regulations.

A-7 EXTERIOR ELEVATIONS

Included are front, rear, left and right sides of the house. Exterior materials, details and measurements are also given.

A-8 CROSS SECTION & DETAILS

Important changes in floor, ceiling and roof heights or the relationship of one level to another are called out. Also shown, when applicable, are exterior details such as railing and banding.

A-9 INTERIOR ELEVATIONS

These plans show the specific details and design of cabinets, utility rooms, fireplaces, bookcases, built-in units and other special interior features, depending on the nature and complexity of the item.

A-10 SECOND FLOOR FRAMING

This sheet shows directional spacing for floor trusses, beam locations and load-bearing conditions, if any.

A-11 ELECTRICAL PLAN

This sheet shows wiring and the suggested locations for switches, fixtures and outlets.

QUICK TURNAROUND

Because you are placing your order directly, we can ship plans to you quickly. If your order is placed before noon EST, we can usually have your plans to you the next business day. Some restrictions may apply. We cannot ship to a post office box; please provide a physical street address.

OUR EXCHANGE POLICY

Since our blueprints are printed especially for you at the time you place your order, we cannot accept any returns. If, for some reason, you find that the plan that you purchased does not meet your needs, then you may exchange that plan for another plan in our collection. We allow you sixty days from the time of purchase to make an exchange. At the time of the exchange, you will be charged a processing fee of 20% of the total amount of the original order, plus the difference in price between the plans (if applicable) and the cost to ship the new plans to you. Vellums cannot be exchanged. All sets must be approved and authorization given before the exchange can take place. Please call our customer service department if you have any questions.

LOCAL BUILDING CODES AND ZONING REQUIREMENTS

Our plans are designed to meet or exceed national building standards. Because of the great differences in geography and climate, each state, county and municipality has its own building codes and zoning requirements. Your plan may need to be modified to comply with local requirements regarding snow loads, energy codes, soil and seismic conditions and a wide range of other matters. Prior to using plans ordered from us, we strongly advise that you consult a local building official.

ARCHITECTURE AND ENGINEERING SEALS

Some cities and states are now requiring that a licensed architect or engineer review and approve any set of building documents prior to construction. This is due to concerns over energy costs, safety, structural integrity and other factors. Prior to applying for a building permit or the start of actual construction, we strongly advise that you consult your local building official who can tell you if such a review is required.

DISCLAIMER

We have put substantial care and effort into the creation of our blueprints. We authorize the use of our blueprints on the express condition that you strictly comply with all local building codes, zoning requirements and other applicable laws, regulations and ordinances. However, because we cannot provide on-site consultation, supervision or control over actual construction, and because of the great variance in local building requirements, building practices and soil, seismic, weather and other conditions, WE CANNOT MAKE ANY WARRANTY, EXPRESS OR IMPLIED, WITH RESPECT TO THE CONTENT OR USE OF OUR BLUEPRINTS OR VELLUMS, INCLUDING BUT NOT LIMITED TO ANY WARRANTY OF MERCHANTABILITY OR OF FITNESS FOR A PARTICULAR PURPOSE. Please Note: Floor plans in this book are not construction documents and are subject to change. Renderings are artist's concept only.

HOW MANY SETS OF PRINTS WILL YOU NEED?

We offer a single set of prints so that you can study and plan your dream home in detail. However, you cannot build from this package. One set of blueprints is marked "NOT FOR CONSTRUCTION." If you are planning to obtain estimates from a contractor or subcontractor, or if you are planning to build immediately, you will need more sets. Because additional sets are less expensive, make sure you order enough to satisfy all your requirements. Sometimes changes are needed to a plan; in that case, we offer vellums that are reproducible and erasable so changes can be made directly to the plans. Vellums are the only set that can be reproduced; it is illegal to copy blueprints. The checklist below will help you determine how many sets are needed.

Plan checklist

_____ **Owner** (one for notes, one for file)

_____ **Builder** (generally requires at least three sets; one as a legal document, one for inspections and at least one to give subcontractors)

_____ **Local Building Department** (often requires two sets)

_____ **Mortgage Lender** (usually one set for a conventional loan; three sets for FHA or VA loans)

_____ **Total Number of Sets**

IGNORING COPYRIGHT LAWS CAN BE A $1,000,000 *mistake!*

Recent changes in the US copyright laws allow for statutory penalties of up to $150,000 per incident for copyright infringement involving any of the copyrighted plans found in this publication. The law can be confusing. So, for your own protection, take the time to understand what you cannot do when it comes to home plans.

WHAT YOU CAN'T DO!

YOU CANNOT DUPLICATE HOME PLANS

YOU CANNOT COPY ANY PART OF A HOME PLAN TO CREATE ANOTHER

YOU CANNOT BUILD A HOME WITHOUT BUYING A BLUEPRINT OR LICENSE

SATER DESIGN COLLECTION, INC.

25241 Elementary Way, Suite 201
Bonita Springs, FL 34135

1-800-718-7526

www.saterdesign.com

sales@saterdesign.com

ADDITIONAL ITEMS

11x17 Color Rendering Front Perspective $100.00
Additional Blueprints (per set) $65.00
Reverse Mirror-Image Blueprints $50.00
Basement Plans* $275.00
Pool Plans* $250.00
Landscape Plans* $225.00
Pool/Landscape Plans* $425.00

*Call for availability. Special orders may require additional fees.

POSTAGE AND HANDLING

Overnight $45.00
2nd Day $35.00
Ground $25.00
Saturday $65.00

For shipping international, please call for a quote.

BLUEPRINT PRICE SCHEDULE*

	5 SETS	8 SETS	VELLUM
A2	$515	$560	$700
A3	$570	$630	$775
A4	$625	$685	$855
C1	$675	$730	$910
C2	$720	$775	$970
C3	$765	$830	$1045
C4	$815	$850	$1115
L1	$935	$1020	$1260
L2	$1010	$1090	$1380
L3	$1115	$1200	$1530
L4	$1220	$1315	$1685
G1	$150	$180	$210

* Prices subject to change without notice

Order form _____

PLAN NUMBER _____

☐ 5-set building package . . . . $_____
☐ 8-set building package . . . . $_____
☐ 1-set of reproducible vellums . . . . $_____

____ Additional Identical Blueprints @ $65 each $_____
____ Reverse Mirror-Image Blueprints @ $50 fee $_____

Sub-Total $_____
Shipping and Handling $_____
Sales Tax (FL Res.) 6% $_____

TOTAL $_____

Check one: ☐ Visa ☐ MasterCard ☐ AmEx

Credit Card Number _____

Expiration Date _____

Signature _____

Name _____

Company _____

Street _____

City _____ State_____ Zip_____

Daytime Telephone Number (_____)_____

Check one:

☐ Consumer ☐ Builder ☐ Developer

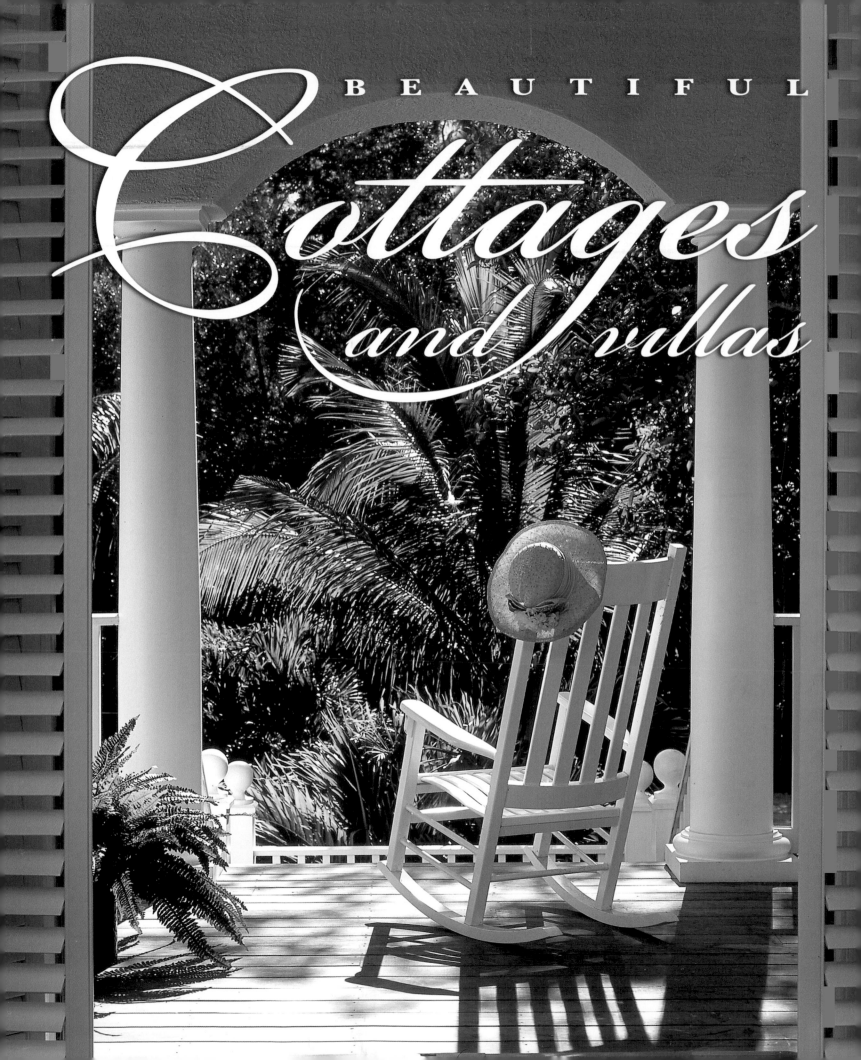

BEAUTIFUL
Cottages
and villas